DA CAPO PRESS SERIES IN
ARCHITECTURE AND DECORATIVE ART
General Editor: ADOLF K. PLACZEK
Avery Librarian, Columbia University

Volume 37

FOUR GREAT MAKERS OF
MODERN ARCHITECTURE

FOUR GREAT MAKERS OF MODERN ARCHITECTURE

Gropius

Le Corbusier

Mies van der Rohe

Wright

*The Verbatim Record of a Symposium Held at the
School of Architecture, Columbia University, March-May, 1961*

DA CAPO PRESS • NEW YORK • 1970

A Da Capo Press Reprint Edition

This Da Capo Press edition of *Four Great Makers of Modern Architecture* is an unabridged republication of the first edition published in New York in 1963. It is reprinted by special arrangement with the Trustees of Columbia University.

Library of Congress Catalog Card Number 78-130312

SBN 306-70065-4

© Trustees of Columbia University—1963

Published by Da Capo Press
A Division of Plenum Publishing Corporation
227 West 17th Street, New York, N.Y. 10011

FOUR GREAT MAKERS OF MODERN ARCHITECTURE

Gropius   Le Corbusier   Mies van der Rohe   Wright

A verbatim record of a symposium held at the
School of Architecture from March to May 1961

Columbia University in the City of New York

Grayson Kirk, Ph. D. , LL. D.   President of the University
Lawrence H. Chamberlain, Ph. D. , LL. D.   Vice President of the University
Jacques Barzun, Ph. D.   Dean of Faculties and Provost of the University
Kenneth A. Smith, S. B.   Acting Dean of the Faculty of Architecture

PREFACE

The Four Great Makers program, perhaps the most ambitious symposium on modern architecture ever held, was designed as "a program in celebration of the great founders of contemporary architecture; a call for critical re-examination of the central issues facing us today; a plea for a new formulation of principles and perspectives for the future." The edited papers in this volume reveal that the first part of the design was admiraably fulfilled, while the second and third parts were not. Only occasionally was there suggestion that central issues existed which needed to be faced, and only incidentally was there any glimpse of future perspectives.

But if the program was primarily retrospective, it was merely symptomatic of the time. Architects, in the spring of 1961, seemed in full flight from the principles of the contemporary tradition, and the fundamental issues of man and civilization had only slight impact on the form and nature of the most-noticed architecture.

It seemed thus most logical to reorganize the papers around the four great makers themselves: Frank Lloyd Wright, Mies van der Rohe, Walter Gropius, and Le Corbusier. In this form, it is hoped, they will serve the purposes of history. Not history themselves, the papers are, at the least, footnotes to history. Not always accurate, they are personal testaments to achievements and times of greatness. Sometimes nostalgic, occasionally resentful, the papers contribute a mosaic surrounding an already thoroughly documented history.

In a sense, then, the papers are a re-examination of the beginnings of contemporary architecture by its founders, and by their second- and third generation offspring.

Eight programs, called "Cycles," took place from March through May, 1961, during the first year of Charles R. Colbert's tenure as Dean of the Faculty of Architecture at Columbia. Three special convocations were assembled in the Low Rotunda of Columbia University. At two of the convocations, the degree of Doctor of Humane Letters honoris causa was conferred upon Walter Gropius and upon Charles-Edouard Jeanneret (Le Corbusier). The papers presented by the recipients on these occasions are central features of the collection. At the third convocation, Mies van der Rohe, who could not make the trip, was represented by a taped interview. The fourth of the great makers, Frank Lloyd Wright, who died in 1959, is not represented in this collection by an original paper.

It would be impossible to single out all the people who contributed, both financially and with prodigious expenditure of time, to the program. However, Professor James Marston Fitch, who was the primary organizer of the program, should be mentioned. His contribution continued in the assemblage and editing of the papers themselves. The preparation of the papers would have been an impossible task without the encouragement and assistance of Linn Cowles, and the careful typing and proofreading of the finished text by Sally Hill and Miriam Trushin contributed greatly to the final result, as did Katharine Kosmak's invaluable editorial advice.

Richard A. Miller
School of Architecture
Columbia University
June, 1963

CONTENTS

v

CONFORMITY, CHAOS, AND CONTINUITY

Charles R. Colbert

To these meetings we attach the utmost importance and the highest hopes. Our purposes are several: to honor four pioneers of our profession to whom we owe an immeasurable debt and in the spirit of these men to honor the profession itself, to reaffirm our faith in its controlling and its ordering power without which our threatened civilization could indeed succumb to waste, confusion, ugliness, and violence. And lastly we assemble, humbly and proudly aware of our powers and responsibilities, for an even greater purpose: to call for a critical re-examination of the central issues facing us today and to plead for a new formulation of principles and perspective for the future.

I am aware that this can be no easy undertaking and one that can never be fully complete. But we are convinced that there is a constant need for such re-examination, and, indeed, that the times demand it.

I am not an historian, but a practicing architect and teacher, and I am thus directly and doubly caught up in the uncertainties, the dilemmas, and the challenge of the architectural movement. The general situation of architecture today is a serious one. Our cities and all our human establishments have become so disordered and squalid that most of the visual beauty we find in our human environment is accidental. Certainly, factors have entered over which the architect has no control, if we define architect in the broadest possible sense: not only as the designer of structures, but also as the planner of communities; not only as the draftsman of projects, but also as the realizer, the builder, the entrepreneur; not only as the imaginative artist, but also as the engineer.

1

Architects all know these factors, although we have not yet found ways to cope with them. There is the vast increase of population, whole cities doubling and tripling within a few years without adequate plans to shape their outward growth or to prevent their central deterioration. There is the invasion of all human settlements, large and small, by unending streams of automobiles, the invasion of the townscape as well as of the landscape. There is the inevitable and universal loss of privacy and dignity, the escape into identical patterns, television without inner vision. There is the mass production of carelessly designed and cheaply manufactured objects in a competitive consumer society. There are the rapid and fundamental social changes accompanied by inadequate psychological, moral, and educational adjustments. There is, most of all, the ever-present threat of total destruction, the atmosphere of collective fear and individual helplessness.

Yet we also know that these factors have by no means been all negative; they have raised the living standards of our people, made machines, tools, and shelter available to them as never before, protected the weak and helpless, conquered ancient diseases, and banished much of the pain and physical drudgery attendant on our daily lives. In this the architect has had a hand.

Now we are on the threshold of a next phase, a phase which may mean total annihilation of life on earth, or an unimaginable expansion of our physical powers. We may be able to reach into outer space, but we also may be able to destroy one another across the sea. We are thus faced with many paradoxes: we are in the midst of sprawling chaos, but also in the midst of a mass-born, mass-produced, standardized and streamlined conformity. It is an inescapable fact that conformity and chaos seem to feed on each other, that external conformity is often the result of internal chaos. External chaos would not be possible were it not for an internal conformity which cravenly or lazily accepts it, a spurious continuity which clings to outworn habits, tastes, traditions, and ornaments; to historical clichés and eclectic compromises. In other words, these three aspects of our present condition -- conformity, chaos, and continuity -- are by no means successive. They can very well be simultaneous or overlapping.

Many definitions have been given for each of the three words. Conformity is togetherness of shape, a state of having been shaped together. Chaos is a very old Greek word and refers, according to the Oxford English Dictionary, to the first state of the universe. Continuity comes from continere, which means hanging together, being held together. Aristotle in his Metaphysics, defines contiguous as "that which is successive and in contact." The continuous is a species of the contiguous. I call two things continuous when the boundaries which keep them in contact become one and the same. In other words, it is not by mechanical repetitions that we can lay claim to the spirit of the past, but by our inner contact, our sameness and our oneness. We are not only formed by our history; we are history. To quote Henri Bergson, a more contemporary philosopher: "There is beneath these sharply cut crystals in this frozen circus, a continuous flux which is not comparable to any flux I have ever seen. There is a succession of states, each of which announces that which follows and contains that which precedes it."

It is evident, then, that conformity, continuity, and chaos, all three, are positive as well as negative forces. It depends on us, on how we are affected by them, and even on the meanings we attach to the words. Men, again in Bergson's words, "have the choice." Conformity can either be a "being shaped together," a forming of the bedrock of our social experience and self-actualization, or it can be a mere succumbing to pressure. Chaos, the seed of things, can either grow into an unmanageable jungle or into a flowering garden. And continuity can be an unbroken contact, a one and the same between the past and the adventure of the future, or it can be a clinging and an imitating.

It is only our own qualitative determination which can decide all this. For the very essence of change is value judgment. In the case of the architect, it is based on the conviction that the material things are the expression of general values, be they social, esthetic, or moral, and a belief that change in material form can create change in these values. This was the conviction

3

of the four great makers, and it is that same conviction which we have to re-create out of that discordant seed of things we call chaos.

What can the architect do? When I said that the forces which endanger not only architecture but human society as a whole are beyond his control and not of his making, I certainly did not mean that he should abdicate. On the contrary, never was there greater need for leadership by architects, leadership not only in social planning and esthetic education, but also leadership in the design of objects in our daily life and in the never-ending battle against shoddy design, shoddy production, and misleading promotion. If we believe that architecture is really the central art, the "mother" art as it has been called, if we believe that it is the activity which creates order out of space and matter, then that order must animate the small and the large, the seemingly unimportant as well as the decisive.

The architect must live with a concept of order. He may begin with it and move toward idea and emotion; he may begin with idea or with emotion and move towards order. But he can never function without any order at all.

This means that the architect's interest is in the total problem. He must weigh the social context, the individual purpose, the material means as well as the three dimensions. He may start with conformity, but as he charts his way he may suddenly find himself surrounded by chaos, and his sense of continuity will help him overcome it. Or he may start out with chaos and arrive through continuity to a hard won conformity. There are various ways in which to arrive at the next phase. Individually, the architect may stand against, ahead of, or with his time and his group. But never can he be behind it. And always a concept of order must be his guiding star.

The architect will, if he can attain that leadership which we demand from him, be a jack of many trades. He will be a Pied Piper and a high priest, a judge, an analyst, a salesman.

4

But whatever he does, he will stand for the qualitative principle and the whole problem, not merely the easy, normative answer. He will not want to sell products, but counsel; he will not process, but create; he will not succumb to his client's demands and to his society, but will reasonably conform with them. He will speak to his client and to society with the voice of logic: the logic of concrete, steel, and glass, the logic of material in a structure, and, particularly, the logic of spirit. This, indeed, is a sort of conformity -- a conformity with the nature of things as they are. But it is also a continuity, a remaining in contact successively and contiguously.

But the more we become masters of matter and masters of space, we will, as we enter the next phase, need a sense of utopia. This ineradicable, perennial belief in utopia remains one of our continuities throughout the centuries of unceasing upheaval. It means simply a conviction that we can do better, that, indeed, we may do perfectly. It is a conviction that links the builders of the Parthenon and the builders of the New Towns -- not always successfully, because utopias remain utopias. But even a failure is preferable to the almost total lack of basic concepts from which we seem to be suffering today. It may be that we are suffering from false utopias, masked as affluence or as easy solutions. But the belief in the true utopia and the possibility of the perfect will remain indespensable to our renewal.

So what, then, did we hope for from these meetings? Not for a spelling out of utopias, but for a reaffirmation of the need of them; not for a literal definition of order, but for a restatement of our faith in it; and certainly not for specific agreement, but for an agreement on principles, or even better, on intentions and needs. We assembled to honor, to listen, to talk, to disagree, and to unite. And it is my personal belief that we left with a keener sense of order -- social as well as individual, environmental as well as domestic, visual as well as psychological. As architects,

5

we simply cannot afford to fail. The most deadening
conformity with the lowest of standards, the most
unbridled chaos, and the most spurious continuity
would be the result.

Mr. Colbert, a graduate of the School of Architecture
at Columbia and a Fellow of the American Institute of
Architects, is now a practicing architect in New Orleans.
It was during his term as dean of the School from 1960
to 1963 that this symposium was organized.

THE ARCHITECT AND THE ASPIRATIONS OF HIS DAY

Jacques Barzun

It is an axiom of modern art history that an art and its times
are related, each acting as a formative condition of the other.
This relation seems especially evident in architecture, since most
of its products answer a temporal demand. But do the times give
rise to anything we may call aspirations? The term is vague and
somewhat effeminate. Aspirations suggest wishing and sighing in
the comfortable assurance that nothing can be done. This is not
the mood in which great artistic movements begin. A new art means
only new forms, and new forms arise from one or both of two
causes: new needs and new possibilities. The two often overlap,
and they are brought to the conscious mind by the sudden discovery
of new attractive sensations, of unfamiliar realities, of striking,
paradoxical connections in daily experience.

These facts and relations are first felt by the men whose special
sensibility and energy singles them out to be the creators of new art
and new thought. It is only in retrospect, when we look at the new
art or new ideas, that we begin to see a pattern in the perceptions
which roused the makers to do their work. The historian then puts
convenient labels on groups of similar events and declares in a
self-assured voice that all the while "the age" was aspiring to do
what it succeeded in doing. This is altogether right and proper: the
historian's duty is to organize the past so that we may understand it.

Granted these premises, we conclude that the aspirations of
the twentieth century that molded modern architecture grew
out of the needs and possibilities, the perceptions and sudden
visions, which distinguish our century from its predecessor.
What is new about our age? First, perhaps, the New Look
of industry. In the nineteenth century the advent of the railroad

and the factory meant the uglification of life. The factory was the enemy of art, and, as such, was fought by the best minds for eighty years. But by the turn of the century, a glimmer of light shone through the smoke and filth. It was seen that electricity and the new materials -- steel and concrete -- would permit industry to symbolize just the opposite of darkness. The modern factory or power plant would be shining white, clean, orderly, and even quiet. Like the machines within, it would become a model of the new beauty.

At the same time, the internal combustion engine (prerequisite to aviation), the motion picture, and the wireless telegraph were changing men's age-old perceptions of space and time. Looking at the earth from above while traveling at 100 miles per hour and hearing disembodied words from a loud speaker liberated man from his semi-vegetable condition as an earth-bound being, unable to move faster than a few miles an hour, unless he doubled his legs by climbing a horse. In 1900 the poet and sportsman, Wilfred Scawen Blunt, took his first automobile ride, attaining a speed of fifteen miles an hour. He exclaims in his diary, "Certainly an exhilarating experience!" The more recent exhilaration of Major Gagarin is but a trifling intensification of Blunt's feelings and powers. The significant change came when the Wright brothers got off the ground, and speed began to affect our senses, including our sense of what is most real: it is no longer stability and weight; it is motion and weightlessness.

The new mobility had, of course, begun earlier with the railroad, but it was only in the early 1900's that artists and thinkers became fully aware, first of the psychological result, and next of the social. Out of single, knowable individuals, the ever-increasing ease and frequency of motion made a generalized anonymous mass. Though population had been multiplying for a century, it was not numbers alone that turned men into the abstraction we call the mass society. It was the stripping away of differences through the practical need to

8

treat everyone alike -- and en masse -- for the purpose of
transportation.

The large railway terminals of the nineteenth century
must be thought of as the harbingers of modern architecture,
if only because of their size and function. The twentieth century, seeing their reason for existence, conceived a new desire: to express the function in new and unique forms. And
this function of handling large crowds of anonymous beings
was no longer limited to the occasions of travel by rail. It
extended to all the necessities of the city -- office buildings,
department stores, apartment houses -- the block and the
super block.

Let me digress a moment here in case the words "anonymous" and "mass" suggest ideas of contempt or imputations of
inferiority. None is implied. For the word "mass" one could
say "very large numbers having identical requirements at the
same time." For the word "anonymous" one could say
"uninvited, unpredictable as to age, sex, name, or private
purpose." For these are the characteristics of daily urban
activity which the twentieth-century architect could not help
pondering when he framed his new ideals of design. The practical need generated a social and psychological conception, and
this in turn led to certain expressive choices in architecture.
Thus, wide-open space, long vistas, unbroken and reflecting
surfaces became esthetic elements, that is, sights pleasing in
themselves as well as adapted to mass use and mass production.

These choices were reinforced by that other new fact I
spoke of a moment ago, the presence of new materials. For
the new art, iron (and soon its derivative, steel) was the great
new acquisition, and the love of it first inflamed the engineers.
It was a bridgebuilder, Gustave Eiffel, who first imagined the
delight of building a great openwork tower of metal, for the
first Paris World's Fair of 1889. It is noteworthy that the French
mills at that date were unable to turn out the quantity of wrought
iron needed for the construction. And equally indicative is the

9

public response to the masterpiece. During the Fair it was admired and gaped at as an outsize toy, but afterwards everybody supposed that the curiosity would be taken down. When this did not happen, the most eminent guardians of good taste -- artists and men of letters -- signed a petition pleading for immediate dismantling. But for the fact that governments always dislike petitions, the first great monument of metal-frame construction would no longer exist.

It was left to an American, Louis Sullivan, to achieve expressiveness through buildings hung upon such a frame. Characteristically, it was the Transportation Building at the Chicago World's Fair of 1893 that signalized the innovation. Thereafter, technology and transportation turned from being destroyers of art and artists to being sources of inspiration and possibility. Sullivan's metal-frame skeleton supplied the modern parallel of a Gothic architecture for a new, "medieval" mass society. Modern and Gothic agree that walls do not support or constitute the edifice; they merely fill in the blanks between columns whose interlocking is the new form. To put it differently, walls are simple partitions between the client and the weather; they could be omitted were he not so fussy about his health and comfort.

Since buildings are for shelter, however, walls are usual, and the new architects found another new and endlessly adaptable material with which to make them esthetically interesting. That material was reinforced concrete, and its use by Auguste Perret early in the century is the second great innovation of the new age, affecting form and texture as well as answering aspiration. For in twentieth-century Gothic, other needs than religious instruction, entertainment, and worship determine architectural design.

The violent changes I mentioned in the perception of time and space, coupled with the spiritual effect of anonymity, induced in the sensitive artist a relentless tendency toward abstraction. I mean by this, the urge to bring out the geometry

10

of things, the love of fleshlessness characteristic of all the
twentieth-century arts. One may wonder how airplane speed,
or motion pictures, or anonymous crowds lead the sensuous
artist to such a mental ideal as abstraction. The connection
is quite simple. Abstraction is the natural result of distance
and motion. Let the observer move -- at once detail is lost,
contours flatten out, softness turns rigid; what is left is the
framework. Look at the loveliest landscape from above, at
a fast clip, and you see an abstract, geometrical pattern in
which the shadows lose their earthly function of giving round-
ness and become like everything else, angular patches. Use
the motion picture camera for special effects of speed or angle, and you abstract out of faces and objects their lifelike-
ness, leaving an equivalent pattern like some unusual map
projection.

As for the human mass, it is abstract by sheer statistical richness and the impossibility of focusing on any one individual. Perhaps the famous "Nude Descending the Staircase,"
by Marcel Duchamp, is the best demonstration of the new visual truth. The figure in the picture is not at any one step on
the staircase; it has no recognizable face, age, sex, or iden-
tifying feature: is it grave or gay, beautiful or ugly, rich or
poor? We do not know and do not care: it is representative;
it is abstract man in motion, seen by the light of a new consciousness.

How does the modern architect abstract? For the most
part quite naturally. Unlike the painter, he does not have to
discover his framework by the X-ray of imagination; he starts
with a ribcage, and it is, of course, fleshless. Since he believes in showing underlying forms without disguise, his outer
covering will be flat, with strong edges reproducing the original simplicity of his skeleton. The repetition of simple forms,
chiefly right angles, will give any beholder, from any stand-
point, a geometrical design in which straight lines and intersecting planes predominate -- a cubist painting against the sky,
or the patchy earth seen from the air.

11

Nor is it only for convenience that the modern architect chooses to leave surfaces bare, or at most, tolerates a semi-traditional low-relief sculpture over his doorway. Unbroken flatness has the double intention of increasing the apparent scale and preventing the eye of anonymous man from dwelling on the particular. Within bare walls of some size, even a large crowd will be dwarfed. In this regard, modern monuments achieve not a Gothic but an Egyptian impressiveness. And in the absence of rich and varied decoration, indeed, in the absence of any decoration, the mind is filled only by the single idea of space, conveyed simply by light or color. Nothing else is provided as a visual resting place, no carved trefoil or gilded molding, no cherub's face or leafy vegetation to entice the senses and suggest to the beholder that only particular objects exist and that abstraction is an empty dream.

If I am right so far, the aspirations of the twentieth century have concentrated on giving form to the strange sensations born of speed, the conquest of empty space, and the pressure of men taken in the mass. To the obvious industrial and technological sources of these new feelings, science and philosophy added the new conceptions of relativity, radiation, and simultaneity, which also have visual embodiments. Just as the people of our century were the first to find beauty in a machine -- even in a well-polished piece of a machine -- so the new physics was the first science to provide spectrographs and tracks of particles which can be hung on the wall like pictures.

It could be said that the creator of the cosmos was a modern artist. All the arts of our age have returned the compliment by reflecting these remote experiences. And no art, perhaps, has been so fully responsive as architecture. Certainly, it began the revolution in the common mind. It was the first to be "modern" by breaking away from the intense individualism of the symbolist period of art for art's sake, the first to acknowledge the claims of collective life, and, by its public monuments, to democratize the new taste. One is not surprised that this was so, for architecture is by its nature an art for men in groups.

12

But modern architecture was first also by virtue of its awareness that the life of the city would have to be planned. The previous century had developed industry haphazardly, as chance and competition dictated. To repair the damage and make use of new knowledge, industrial democracy must apply to its evolution the techniques of the engineer and the architect: full specifications, detailed plans, and coordination with existing and future artifacts. From the days of Patrick Geddes, the ultimate aspiration of the modern architect has been to design, not merely a building or a cluster of buildings, but the shelter of a whole civilization.

It will not have escaped notice that in sketching the cultural environment of the modern architect, I have repeatedly gone back to origins and found them in the first decade of this century. I have done this for what I consider good reasons, of which one is the very source of my interest in the subject. I mean that I and the art whose half century we are celebrating were infants together, and rather intimate. Almost my earliest memories are of architectural discussions among my elders, at the house of one of the founders of modern architecture, August Perret. That house, which he built for himself at 25 <u>bis</u> rue Franklin, was the first modern apartment house in Paris. Going into it with my parents, I would often see, to my continued surprise, little knots of sightseers outside; snickering and pontificating and occasionally struck dumb by its height, its multiple exposure to light and air, its concrete and ceramic façade. I remember also, in the ground-floor offices of the Perret brothers, the drawings of their modern dock constructions in Morocco and the Theatre des Champs Elysées in Paris. And it was in another house built by Perret, not far from the first, that I saw him for the last time, a few years before his death in 1954.

If I evoke his memory here, it is not solely out of personal and historical piety, nor as an indication of the ease with which the amateur, if caught young enough, accepts a new style without a murmur. My chief reason for venturing to

13

mention these biographical details is to suggest that when we look for the aspirations of our age and their strongest expression in art, we must turn to the decade when Perret and his peers first set their hands to lasting work, the decade before the first world war, the decade which posterity is beginning to call "The Cubist Decade."

I know that in common opinion modernism dated from the 1920's. This is the effect of the cultural hiatus produced by the four devouring years 1914-1918. It was before 1914 that all the new and living ideas of our age were stated and embodied. After the war, some of those ideas were forgotten, others rediscovered as if new, still others carried forward in the full knowledge of their ancestry. Thanks to these last, a kind of dammed-up pressure finally broke through the crust of public indifference. To speak of architecture alone, the International Style came into its own in the mid-twenties, concurrently with the superb flowering of the decorative arts, which in the thirties gave us mass-produced modern furniture and the first infiltration of suburban modern -- a third of a century after the creation of the parent genre.

Meanwhile the great disciples, the prolific geniuses of the second generation, those who had studied with Sullivan or Perret or Behrens or had seen their works, were establishing the individual styles which will give them and our age enduring renown. It would be presumption to try to add by words to the fame that such men as Wright, van der Rohe, Gropius, and Le Corbusier have won with their own hands. It is more fitting, as well as more profitable, to ask what, if any, new aspirations disclose themselves in the present confusion which the works of these men so easily dominate. In other words, if the first half of our century has magnificently worked out the theorems proposed in the very first decade of the age, do we now simply refine and repeat the solutions, or are there new needs and possibilities leading to new fulfillments?

I think the question can be answered without having recourse to prophecy. For one clear tendency of the latest architecture implies the existence of a desire as yet unsatisfied. I have in mind the various attempts to break the regularity of the geometrical with rounded or asymmetric shapes. One thinks of country churches shaped like a whale or the extended wings of a bat, one thinks of private houses reared on the principle of the bivalve or modeled after the double boiler, one thinks of the convoluted helix of Wright's last work, the Guggenheim Museum, which seems so pleasing an approximation to the geography of Dante's Hell.

The aspiration to which these are answers might be put in the form of a problem: how to reconcile the spacious, smooth bareness which dwarfs mankind, the practical and functional which rebukes the fancy, the control of every medium which leaves no sense of difficulty overcome; how to reconcile all these virtues with the passion of the human soul for the wayward, the irregular, the unexpected, the miraculous.

I say the reconciliation, not the substitution of one set of virtues for the other. Only by the strong combination of opposites will the sense of freedom and miracle be aroused. When we have functionalism and fancy, easy mastery and the sublimity of a tour de force, magnitude and no loss of human dignity, we may have what the contemporary mind and the genius of architecture are uneasily groping for.

This is not the place, nor have I the competence, to brandish a T-square and issue a call to arms. But a caution about movements and aspirations is perhaps in order. The caution is: let the artist aspire freely, on any basis of thought and feeling and in any direction, but let him beware of "ideas." I mean by "ideas" in quotation marks something for which there is as yet no recognized term, but which is a common danger for the artist. The evil of the so-called "idea" lies in its rigidity and remoteness from life. Even if born of a true observation, it is unmodified by reflection or by a second observation. It soon becomes a pure formula, a pseudo-principle, the parallel in art to ideology in

15

politics. The result for the mind is a progressive distortion
of experience, the exclusion of true ideas, and ultimately the
paralysis of intuition and invention.

To make this difficult contrast clear, one might say that
the great expressive artist is and remains a man of thought,
not of "ideas." He is not an obsessive verbalizer who tightly
grips a set of merely plausible notions. On the contrary, the
man able to perceive and fulfill contemporary aspirations
ought to cultivate a calm indifference to systems, and especially
to the fragments of systems which form the staple of intellectual
talk. He will, let us say, build arcades around an office building
because he knows their use, likes their appearance, and feels
their attraction for the passerby. But he will not do so merely
because he has read a sociological work that says the modern
world lacks "community" and arcades will correct the deficiency.

The modern artist is peculiarly vulnerable to the error of
intellectualism because there are so many books lying about, and
he has learned to read -- in fact to read and write. It is deplor-
able for art that modern artists have been put by the public under
the necessity of defending or expounding their works. Few can
do it and not succumb sooner or later to an "idea," in the sense
I mean, of a bare and unexamined proposition. For whatever may
be the case in philosophy, in art truth does not reside in propositions. It resides in objects and those objects must, like a living
being, be the fruit of desire as much as forethought; of brooding
care as well as clear intelligence.

Mr. Barzun, Provost and Dean of Faculties, and Seth Low
Professor of History, Columbia University, is the author
of Berlioz and the Romantic Century (1950), The House of
Intellect (1959) and many other books of cultural history.

16

ARCHITECTURE AND THE AVANT GARDE

James Marston Fitch

One of the most striking features of the world of contemporary art is the unprecedented prestige which surrounds the new, the novel, the advanced. There has always been change in art, and it has always been welcomed by certain sectors of society. But, until recently, the new and novel had always to meet and win over to its side a conservative majority. This process of conversion took time. Thus, at any given moment, the old form had always the support of the majority. By the time the new art had won predominance, it had ceased to be new.

Things are quite otherwise today. A new stylistic movement needs only to be hailed as avant-garde, by some critic or curator, in order to be at once accorded the status of the significant, demanding our most serious attention and prompt approbation. Any reservations we might express about the basic validity of the art form itself are dismissed by the avant-garde establishment as reactionary.

If we persist in airing our misgivings, this verdict is screwed shut (like the lid of an old-fashioned coffin) by a most persuasive historical analogy: all the great intellectual and artistic innovators of the past, we are told, were always denounced by the reactionaries of their period. We are sharply reminded that the impressionists were barred from decent museums and post-impressionists called wild beasts; that Seurat was denounced as a charlatan, Picasso as a madman; that Bruno was burned at the stake and Galileo threatened with it for advancing innovations in celestial mechanics. Wrapped in this borrowed mantle of martyrdom, the newest artistic tyro wins an asylum from critical assessment as secure as any offered by the medieval church.

17

Of course, it is true that social or artistic invention usually provokes a counteraction -- the more profound the one, the more violent the other. Historically, the avant garde is attacked as being either mad or subversive. This has certainly been the case with the great creators of modern architecture -- Wright, Gropius, Mies, and LeCorbusier. It took them decades of resolute struggle to win a decisive audience to their point of view, to tip the scales of public opinion in their favor.

But the current theory of the infallibility of the avant garde is based not so much upon these noble precedents as upon a hidden corollary -- namely, that all self-styled avant gardes have proved to be of equal worth and durability; hence that all artistic dissenters merit the same respect as Picasso and Wright.

History does not support this corollary so tidily. On the contrary, the record is full of movements hailed by their protagonists as the road of true advance, the unique and inevitable route to the future. But many of them subsequently turned out to lead into cul-de-sacs, dead ends, wrong turnings going nowhere. And many an artistic innovator described by his contemporaries as being crackpot, poseur, or madman turned out to have been precisely that. It is, in short, a clinical possibility for the artist to be mad, mistaken, or mediocre.

The whole argument turns upon what we mean when we use the term "avant garde." It derives, of course, from French military practice, in the days when an army sent out scouts ahead of the main column, to locate water and forage for horses and men; to spy out the disposition of the enemy; to sample the temper of the local population. From this practice derives the more poetic use of the word to describe one who explores and then describes for us the intellectual or artistic terrain of the future. But the favorable connotation of the term depends upon the accuracy of his reports.

We award this title to the great prophets and innovators of past times, but we should remember that their own audiences

18

felt compelled to wait for confirmation or disproof of their reports. Because of this inevitable time lag, the innovator himself was often dead of starvation or neglect before his audience could give him his just rewards. But, we must be careful with the historic record, for sheer survival is, by itself, no absolute index of artistic validity. It would be nonsense to argue that all artistic movements which died a-borning died because they were "bad," just as it would be foolish to assume that all those which enjoyed a normal span of popularity thereby established their validity. Nevertheless it is still demonstrably true that those artistic movements which responded to the broad social and cultural necessities of their time are the ones which proved most viable. The avant-garde establishment of today will be apt to deny that any such correlation is possible (it is the first in history to feel it necessary to do so), but the proposition is quite readily demonstrated in architecture.

Today's avant-garde establishment has still another polemical weapon with which to beat back any objective evaluation of its activities. This is the accusation that the hostile critic, in denigrating a specific work of art, is secretly striking at the artist behind it. What is actually in jeopardy, so this argument goes, is not the artistic statement but actually the artist's right to make it. The avant garde points out that artistic freedom in the modern world is closely tied to political freedom generally. Where one is infringed, the other is surely threatened. American artists have had vivid proof of this during the recent McCarthy period, and they are understandably sensitive on this point. But here, too, there is an important corollary which is often overlooked. If we are to protect the artist's right to create and speak as his conscience dictates; if he be free to engage us, his audience, in a dialogue whose terms he sets; then, at this same level of civil liberties, his audience has the right of response, of query, even of rejection.

The artist's right to speak to me should not rob me of my right of reply. Yet it is precisely this right which the avant garde does not always recognize. Indeed, it often responds to

19

any dissent quite as imperiously as ever did any old-fashioned academy or salon. And this suggests that, beneath a fancy dress of artistic nonconformism, there is already concealed a new apparatus of vested interest: not an advanced guard at all but a rear guard, an old guard.

The critic who accepts the self-proclaimed pretensions of the avant gardists to infallibility, inevitability, and untouchability is trapped in a prison house of cliché. To escape, he need only apply a simple test: does the future, as it unwinds, confirm their reports of it? The four great makers of modern architecture -- Wright, Gropius, Mies, and Corbusier -- have long ago established their right to the title; the idioms they invented half a century ago are the basic grammar of the style today.

But a second, and indeed a third, generation is now in the field, jousting for the right of succession. To whom should we listen? A review of two centuries' experience with other avant gardes should help us in evaluating those clamoring for our support today.

The avant garde architecture of Europe and America was almost always utopian in content, the direct outgrowth of political or literary movements. The utopian buildings were usually more weatherproof than the novels or paintings -- but they promised the same escape from mundane reality. Whether they looked forward (like the Phalansteries of St.-Simon or the ideal industrial communities of LeDoux) or backward (like DeMonville's truncated column) or merely sidewise (like the Hameau of Marie Antoinette) -- this depended upon the social perspectives of the client. But the stylistic idiom in which they are developed often seems capricious.

Thus, to house his beehive democracy, St.-Simon chose the Baroque style of absolute monarchy. To escape the boredom of that same monarchy, Marie chose the archaistic mode of a peasant village; while to facilitate the state-owned armament industry of her royal protector, LeDoux proposed to employ a

20

greatly simplified version of the Classic. This, too, was the
idiom of the revolutionary painter, David, and the revolutionary
architect, Boullée, whose noble forms for the new institutions of
the Revolution were distilled from the classic to a pure geometry
of cube, sphere, and pyramid.

Each of these idioms was hailed in its day, by some circle
of society, as "advanced," "radical," "dernier cri" -- i. e.,
avant-garde. But history has modified these estimates. The
more frivolous the needs of the patron, the more trivial
the scale of the architect's conception, the more idiosyncratic
his idiom -- and the more certain his quick fall into oblivion.

Queen Victoria's century produced many utopian schemes --
public and private, secular and religious -- and a corresponding
spectrum of avant-garde modes of expression. Those which
dealt with the external world of new social institutions tended,
in general, toward a rational, nonallusory expression of structural
and volumetric fact. Those for private persons tended to be
idiosyncratic, replete with romantic allusions to the long ago and
far away. Monumental and religious architecture, rejecting the
rationality and materialistic scientism of the period, resurrected
the Gothic idiom of medieval feudalism.

This division was never absolute, since Victorian architects
crossed from one mode of expression to another as their clients
changed. Burton worked in the classic style, Paxton in the
"Elizabethan" and Dobson tried apologetically to hide his wonderful
glass-and-metal train sheds behind a Georgian street front. Time
has nonetheless proved that the Palm House, the Newcastle Station,
and the Crystal Palace did, in fact, mark the road to true advance
while eclecticism led into a cul-de-sac. Those other gifted men:
Wyatt with his preposterous lath-and-plaster "abbey" for a homo-
sexual arriviste; neurotic Pugin with his plausible rationale of
functionalism for an historically impossible revival; tormented
Ruskin with his ethical-esthetic analogues, so pat and so misleading; and William Morris, socially radical and technologically
retrograde -- these eloquent Englishmen convinced Victorians that

21

the true road to the future lay through the land behind. The result was one of the biggest detours in artistic history. It would require decades for Louis Sullivan to rediscover what Burton, Dobson, and Paxton had clearly stated: e. g. that viable architectural form can derive only from function correctly served.

The avant-garde architects of our century have been serious, socially-oriented men who responded to the needs of the new industrialism and were stimulated by its architectural possibilities. Their attitudes were generally evangelical, their work polemical in nature. But in the manner of their expression, two divergent tendencies are apparent. One sought to extract from the impersonal, rationalized, and repetitive nature of industrialism a pure, abstract, and suprapersonal style, independent of historically-derived motifs or private, capricious judgments. Gropius and his Bauhaus gave us the clearest theoretical formulation of this proposition, while the utopian cities of Garnier, Sant'Elia, and Le Corbusier afforded dazzling images of its application to urban design.

Other men like Gaudi and Horta, using the same new materials to construct a new idiom, regarded the resulting architectural tissue as, fundamentally, a plastic medium for expressing an inner poetic vision. They could, when required, produce perfectly rational designs for an apartment house or a trade union center. But their most complete and eloquent work was done for private persons who could sympathize with their taste and subsidize its three-dimensional realization. Gaudi's fabulous masonry or Horta's spidery glass-and-metal dome depended on their actual presence. It was handcrafted, expensive, and -- above all -- unique. The idiom was too personal for transmission, the artifact itself too special for mass production. Like Morris before them, they were doomed along with their work and would become mere historic curiosities.

The two other giants of the period, Wright and Mies van der Rohe, oscillated between these two extremes. Wright had two basic modes of expression: a cubist one of space enclosed by

22

folded and intersecting planes; and a plastic one whose inner volumes are sculptured by the container itself. Mies, on the other hand, defined space by an elegant, linear diagram of steel and glass. Their positions, formulated many decades ago, are basic to our vocabulary today, proof enough of how well they comprehended the terrain of the future.

Mr. Fitch is an art historian, and former editor of the Architectural Record, the Architectural Forum, and House Beautiful. He has published, among other critical works, American Building (1948) and Architecture and the Esthetics of Plenty (1961). He is at present teaching courses in history and theory as professor of architecture, the School of Architecture, Columbia University.

to date, 1943; The Disappearing City, 1932; Architecture and Modern Life (with Baker Brownell); Frank Lloyd Wright on Architecture, 1894-1940 (edited by Frederick Gutheim); In the Nature of Materials (edited by Henry-Russell Hitchcock), 1941; When Democracy Builds, 1946; Genius and the Mobocracy, 1949. The founder and the conductor of the "The Taliesin Fellowship," a cultural experiment in the arts, by way of a non-profit organization entitled The Frank Lloyd Wright Foundation situated at "Taliesin" in Wisc. (Apr.-Nov.) and Ariz. (Dec.-Mar.), about 40 apprentices participating. Editor of "Taliesin" Fellowship magazine, pub. 6 times a year; and The Taliesin Square Papers pub. from time to time at Taliesin. Home "Taliesin," Spring Green, Wis.; and "Taliesin West," Paradise Valley, Phoenix, Ariz. Died Apr. 9, 1959.

-- from Who Was Who in America, Volume 3. Chicago: A. N. Marquis, 1960. (Used with permission of the publishers.)

Now, how should a space end? How should a line end? Sullivan said: "Take care of the extremities and the rest will take care of itself," and gave us an example: He said a man dressed in an old suit, wearing new gloves, a new hat, and shined shoes appeared to be very well dressed. Now this is very true. Find a distinctive end or a distinctive way to end a play and you will have a Broadway hit. Indeed, in any activity or design, find a way to end or begin and you are pretty sure to be on the right track. An exclamation mark is far more intriguing than a minus sign simply because of that little dot. The rule is: distinguish the ends from the whole.

I think this point of taking care of the extremities had a great effect on Mr. Wright. He didn't talk very much about this, but I've noticed in his planning and, in fact, in whatever he did, he always takes care of the end. This is almost a distinguishing mark of the students from Taliesin. Unconsciously this has become important: take care of the end and the beginning; do something special with each of them.

Finally we come to what I think was Mr. Wright's greatest discovery: designing with a grid system. Some call it modular planning. He said this idea came from the building blocks his mother gave him as a child. I believe it also came from his desire to master the machine. The machine is a great duplicator, so why not have a design system composed of duplicates? The grid system is the answer. You design duplicates. He chose sides for the design grid which were scaled to the human being -- 3x3, 4x4, or 5x5, based on the floor area that will comfortably accommodate a single person. This automatically gave his buildings a sense of human scale.

I've found it interesting to work with different grid systems, different sizes. A 3x3 or a 5x5 module makes a great difference in the resulting plan. The building blocks should be a division of the grid system. Such divisions greatly enhance the design possibilities. First of all, the fundamental sides might be the smallest square, perhaps a foot square.

The next fundamental unit is twice this size or a rectangle one by two. With those two elements you can play and develop some wonderfully rich forms. The next step, of course, is to go into a 16x16, or a 4x4, and so on.

Now in judging quality, we need to break it down into smaller parts. To say a thing is good or bad is not enough. You must be able to say this much is good, this is bad, and this is weak. A thing can never be totally good or totally bad. I would like to offer a test that I use to judge whatever we do in the office; it even applies to our meals at home; it's become part of our family life and work. This system of judgment first of all involves honesty. It can't be a copy in any way; it can't be preconceived; it cannot be anything but an original. Then it must have what I call humility. I stretch Webster's meaning of this word just a little. Humility is the ability to give or take gracefully. When a thing has humility, it contributes. When a building has humility, it contributes to its site and the site in turn contributes to it. A bouquet sitting on a table, if it has humility, adds tremendously to the beauty of that table, and the table in turn adds to the bouquet. Finally it must have enthusiasm. A building must not be just a box with a plant on the lawn and a sign over the entrance. It must be all kinds of architectural developments that indicate without question that this is the entrance and that this room is a certain kind of a room and that this space inside is a particular and distinct space.

Mr. Dow, a practicing architect in Midland, Michigan, was a Taliesin Fellow and a graduate of the School of Architecture, Columbia University.

THE FINE ARTS AND FRANK LLOYD WRIGHT

Edgar Kaufmann, Jr.

Frank Lloyd Wright spent the last decade of his life blasting away at (among other things) modern art; at the same time, he was engaged in a long and eventually successful campaign to build the Solomon Guggenheim Museum for modern art. On these grounds he is accused of designing the museum to show the superiority of his own art -- architecture -- over the arts of painting and sculpture. Now Wright dearly loved a fight and even more a paradox, but it would never have occurred to him to betray a professional trust. When he accepted any commission, it was not as a self-monumentalizer; else he would have aimed his whole career differently. His original museum clients, Solomon Guggenheim and Hilla Rebay, had a specialized, didactic, and developmental program which offered him a chance to build for what Wright thought were the hopeful aspects of modern art. With a change of clients after Solomon Guggenheim's death, came the clash of purposes which transformed the Guggenheim museum into a half-thing. Even as a half-thing, it has proved astonishingly vital.

Did Wright really hate the fine arts generally, as competitors with architecture? A simple survey of his long practice, in contrast to his many words, shows that Frank Lloyd Wright was in love with fine arts, that life without them was inconceivable to him. His was an astonishingly old-fashioned love, however, with manifestations that require some effort before they can be comprehended today. In fact, to understand them at all, some thought must needs be given to the ideas of art that were current when Wright was young, particularly among people like his pious, well-read, and progressive family.

27

Wright's heritage in the arts was centered on ideas and ideals common to liberal British intellectuals of the mid-nineteenth century, when many able men and women, like Wright's forebears, found it necessary to leave the overpopulated homeland of the Industrial Revolution. This specific heritage has been encapsuled by one of Wright's favorite authors, Emerson, in his essay, "Art," published in 1841. Emerson thought that rather than being imitative, "the painter should give...only...the spirit...the gloom of gloom and the sunshine of sunshine"; he should "convey a larger sense by simpler symbols." Yet the writer continued, "The office of painting and sculpture seems to be merely initial. The best pictures can easily tell us their last secret.... Painting and sculpture are gymnastics of the eye, its training.... Away with your nonsense of oils and easels, of marble and chisels; except to open your eyes.... Under an oak-tree loaded with leaves and nuts, under a sky full of eternal eyes, I stand in a thoroughfare, but in the works of our plastic arts and especially of sculpture, creation is driven into a corner. And the individual in whom simple tastes and susceptibility to all the great human influences overpower the accidents of a local and special culture, is the best critic of art.... Art has not yet come into its maturity if it does not put itself abreast with the most potent influences in the world, if it is not practical and moral.... But the artist and the connoisseur now seek in art the exhibition of their talent, or an asylum from the evils of life.... Art makes the same effort which a sensual prosperity makes: namely to detach the beautiful from the useful, to do up the work as unavoidable, and hating it, pass on to enjoyment. These solaces and compensations, this division of beauty from use, the laws of nature do not permit.... Now men do not see Nature to be beautiful.... They reject life as prosaic, and create a death which they call poetic.... Beauty must come back to the useful arts, and the distinction between the fine and the useful arts be forgotten...." He concludes the essay, "Find holiness and beauty in new and necessary facts, in the field and roadside, in the shop and mill.... When science is learned in love, and its powers are wielded by love, they will appear the supplements and continuations of the material creation." His last point was polemically elaborated years later

28

by William Morris, who said, "It is allowing the machines to be our masters and not our servants that so injures life nowadays."

Wright followed these thoughts and developed them; all his reactions to modern art are inherent in Emerson's formulation. To understand Wright's hopes and fears for art, one should keep in mind the Emersonian text. Emerson represented a synthesis of attitudes that had been built up by men like Cobbett and Coleridge, Southey and Owen. They were followed by Carlyle, John Stuart Mill, Pugin, Ruskin, and Morris. Many of these men's works were actually read by Wright as a youngster, along with those of Victor Hugo, penny dreadfuls, the poetry of Blake, and the essays of Viollet-le-Duc.

It will suffice merely to mention Wright's early fascination with Froebel's educational toys and the music of Beethoven and Bach, for these are well-investigated aspects of his education. Less notice has been taken of his childhood recreations: painting, drawing, piano playing, singing, and reading aloud. To these add decorating crockery and confecting trifles to be sold before Christmas for pocket money, and you have the very image of a progressive, provincial upbringing in the era of the esthetic movement. After all, it was just as Frank Lloyd Wright was being trained in physical and moral fortitude on his uncle's farm that Oscar Wilde lectured in America on the beauty of the machine, and Patience opened in London. A few years later, when Wright determined to seek his fortune in Chicago, his cultural equipment was pretty much that sketched here; he had acquired a knowledge of engineering, to be sure, and an enduring enthusiasm for Maya, Aztec, and Inca ruins.

When he arrived in Chicago, Wright, still in his teens, found his place at Louis Sullivan's elbow in the Adler and Sullivan office. The great Auditorium Building was the center of activity. It was designed to be the most superb home for grand occasions -- opera, concerts, and political rallies -- in the New World. It was abundantly ornamented within; numerous oil paintings were commissioned as murals. The concept of architecture and fine arts working together was never questioned, despite the results!

About this time, too, the Art Institute of Chicago began to form its collections. The heroic El Greco, the lovely set of Hubert Roberts, and many Dutch seventeenth-century paintings were on view, along with the contemporary Salon art of France. (Chicago's great impressionist paintings were just entering private collections.) The Art Institute held numerous passing shows of contemporary American painting, sculpture, and artistic crafts in those years, and a large collection of casts, some architectural, were also seen.

All this was grist to Wright's mill, but perhaps even more important to him were the opportunities Chicago provided to enjoy full-scale professional performing arts. Sullivan and his friends were alert to these influences. Wright eagerly went along. Hard after the successful opening of the Auditorium, came preparations for the World's Columbian Exposition; Chicago filled with aspiring artist-decorators. In 1892, while this was going on, Sullivan's firm opened the Schiller theater building, where, not for the first time, they employed a sculptor to complete the decorations. Then, if not earlier, Wright met this sculptor, Richard Bock, who later worked closely with him over many years.

Probably in the same year, Wright and his friends learned to admire another young sculptor, fresh from the Indian Southwest and, earlier, a student in the Paris academies, Hermon Atkins MacNeil. In 1895 or 1896, MacNeil left his brief but successful Chicago career for the American Academy at Rome. His works may be seen in photographs of Wright's own home, in the company of oriental painting and assorted bric-a-brac, and deliberately featured in the entrance hall of Wright's first independent house of great quality, the Winslow. Wright's statuette, a Hopi runner, was reputedly modeled at the Villa Aurelia, where it must have looked extra exotic; it probably should be dated 1895 or later. In that same year, the sculptor Bock helped Wright complete the entrance to a studio annexed to the architect's home. Flanking the entry, two cowering muscle men on plinths seem pure Bock; the four pilaster caps, however, were sketched and programmed by Wright. Some similar collaboration, with Wright

30

guiding a painter, would account for a mural in a new children's playroom added to the residence about then; the correctly drawn figures seem outside Wright's skills. Within the studio annex, other photos show a landscape in oils and numerous, rather lively, naturalistic statuettes.

There can be no question that at this point Wright was absorbed in an attempt to mix architecture, painting, and sculpture, as he had learned to do with Sullivan. To compare Wright's use of painting and sculpture with examples from Sullivan's works in the years around 1890, is to see progress on the side of the younger man. Not all of it was due to cumulative experience; Wright had a more acute sense than his erstwhile master of scale, composition, and rhythm. In 1897, when Sullivan's only New York building was going up with vaguely classical winged figures modeled in the topmost spandrels, Bock executed very similar but freer figures for a roof loggia on Wright's Heller house. Such ladies, no doubt inspired by figure 4 of Viollet's essay on Roman architecture, appeared in flat paint only on the Transportation Building, Sullivan's masterpiece at the Fair; but fortunately for American art, after 1897 they never winged their way to the top of another Sullivan or Wright building. Russell Lynes has reminded us that in 1898 Wright gave one of his popular talks at the annual meeting of the Central Art Association on "Art in the Home." He lived with what he talked about; Bock even modeled Wright's young son life-size in bronze, adding wings. Seemingly, it was a volatile period in American sculpture.

At the turn of the century, C. R. Ashbee, a leading light of the English Arts and Crafts movement, spent some time in Chicago; we know he and Wright became friendly. Wright agreed to head a committee for the preservation of historic buildings which Ashbee wanted set up in connection with the English equivalent. Ten years later, when Wright's executed buildings were published in a German volume, Ashbee wrote an enthusiastic introduction. Likely enough it was Ashbee who provoked Wright's famous Hull House lecture on "The Art and Craft of the Machine" in 1901. This aired views contrary to Ashbee's, but by 1911, the year of his

introduction to Wright's book, Ashbee announced himself ready
to work with, rather than against, the current of the times, as
Wright had done at Hull House.

The original contact with Ashbee around 1900 may have spur-
red Wright to consider how far he had drifted from the ideals of
his youth, from the concepts of Emerson's essay. Over the next
ten years, Wright made extraordinary and remarkably successful
efforts to integrate the fine arts and the applied with his architecture. Three great houses testify to this: the Dana, 1902-04; the
Martin, 1904; and the Coonley, 1908; to these should be added
the famous and unique Larkin office building, 1904; Browne's Book-
store, 1908; and the Thurber Art Gallery, 1909; commissions
offering special but smaller opportunities. Even a mid-decade
vacation in Japan, the first visit to a land Wright admired and
learned to love, exerted no perceptible effect on his work (though
his ten- or twelve-year-old passion for Japanese prints increased).
One great building of the period, Unity Temple, 1906, was barren
of fine arts no doubt because funds and interest were equally absent among the clients. When one considers how St. Bartholo-
mew's in New York had just been artistically enriched, it is clear
how much Wright was able to achieve in the Midwest in the 1900's,
with artists considerably inferior to those that architects in the
East or in Europe could call on.

Wright's extra-legal nuptial flight to Europe in 1910 was spent
largely in Florence working on drawings for a luxurious publication
of his works which was issued in Berlin just prior to the more modest volume of photographs that Ashbee introduced. Projects for
himself, a studio in Florence and a city house in Chicago, show
Wright more ready than ever to make a feature of exterior sculpture. The first country home that Wright built for himself, called,
like its sequels, Taliesin, after the Welsh bard, was also fully,
but less formally, embellished. Few records of it survived the
fire that destroyed it in 1914.

This disaster occurred just as Midway Gardens, a complex
of restaurants and clubs complete with large garden and music

shell, opened in Chicago. Wright had designed it with wonderful boldness. Sculpture and painting played important roles, upholding a festive, exhilarating mood. Here, significantly enough, Wright seized the initiative, designing murals (and, in part, the sculptures) in an abstract idiom all his own, one as fully abstract and asymmetric as any avant-garde European art of the moment. Midway Gardens was executed in a rush, and this may well have forced Wright to impose, rather than to elicit, the artistic qualities needed to complete the architecture and furnishings. Whatever the cause, Midway Gardens marked an epoch in Wright's reactions to fine arts. He was forced to see that the painters and sculptors around him felt an intrinsic affinity to his work. The teamwork of the arts that Ruskin and Morris predicated, that Wright had witnessed in Japan and in Europe's monuments, was broken; art was intent on making "the effort...to detach the beautiful from the useful" that Emerson had observed three quarters of a century earlier.

Wright's new-found skill to design his own fine arts for his buildings can be traced back to humble beginnings in colored window compositions, abstract and derived from his Froebel training, that he used in his own house as early as 1895. The earliest of Wright's fully elaborated, asymmetric abstractions for glass seems to have been made in 1911 or 1912 for the Coonley playhouse. These are exactly contemporary with the first documented European abstractions, by Kupka, Larionov, and Delaunay. Wright designed a timidly asymmetric and very nearly abstract relief for a house in Milwaukee, 1916. Nothing prior in modern art is recalled, but a similar spirit is seen in an entirely abstract ornamental relief of 1902 by Josef Hoffmann. Wright was well aware of the Sezession and its works, thanks to his admiration for Hoffmann's teacher, Otto Wagner.

After Midway Gardens, Japan called Wright, and the next years were largely devoted to the complicated commission of the Imperial Hotel. Its rich ornamentation reached a peak in the ballroom. Neither Japanese influence nor the taste of the White Russian refugees with whom Wright then associated can be traced

in this work. It is tempting to attribute its rather overcharged
air to psychological pressures exerted on Wright by his extremely
erratic, bohemian mistress. However that may be, Wright's
next expansive client belonged to a similar, if less hectic, world
and over the fireplace in the livingroom of Olive Hill in Hollywood,
1920, the architect presented himself more effectively as a sculptor than, perhaps, anywhere else in his career. Here, his stone
abstraction is as free of symmetry as his murals and glass had
been long since.

Here also, oriental art is used -- in the form of Japanese
screens built into the room. Here Wright found an art that had the
quality of repose that he sought and that -- more than his own
and more than any modern art he could commission -- seemed
to have been created according to the Emersonian recipe "only the
spirit..."; able to "convey a larger sense by simpler symbols."
The more Wright understood Far Eastern art, the less tempted
he was by the introspective trend of some Western art or by its
unsophisticated abstractions, laboring under the weight of inap-
propriate techniques and caught in the tangle of European ideology. The characteristics he could admire in Western art were
better deployed in Eastern.

Wright then designed in California several houses for owners
devoted to visual arts. I remember visiting Mrs. Millard and
her Renaissance antiques: they looked charmingly at home. Taliesin in Wisconsin was again rebuilt after a second fire in 1925,
again replete with oriental art of every kind and of various qualities. A Gustav Klimt, donated by the decorator Paul Frankl,
represented modern art in a notably insufficient way; later, a
handsome O'Keeffe, a gift of the artist, was in evidence.

About this time Wright began publically to sing the praise
of the Japanese tokonoma niche. The reserved place, a chance
to group painting, sculpture, and flowers (or other fragments of
nature) appropriately to a season or an event, seemed an ideal
way to acclimatize the very personal quality of much modern art.
Painting and sculpture, thus temporarily exposed and treated

34

preciously, were closer to the performing arts of music, theatre, dance, and recitation, which Wright had always loved. In these arts, he had never shied away from strongly personal effects, since they could be displayed or set aside as seemed fitting. What seemed wrong to the architect was a permanent display of such effects in a home or public building (other than an art gallery). The tokonoma was a cogent solution to these problems, but, even in Wright's own surroundings, it had limited application. The major works of art in both Taliesins tended to remain in place for long periods of time.

With the resurgence of interest in Frank Lloyd Wright in the 1930's (due to his remarkably winning autobiography and to better times), opportunities returned for the association of the arts in his work. Abstract pattern, like that he formerly used in ornamental glass, now was allocated graphic duties: as part-titles in An Autobiography and on the cover of the January, 1938 Architectural Forum.

But in his seventh decade the architect increasingly looked toward broader horizons: he developed ideas of area planning and of type-homes for modest living. He surrounded himself with young people, forming a community to evolve a way of life that he believed the necessary pre-condition to learning any of the arts: performing arts and tokonoma-like arrangements were both features of this life. In 1938, the community built Taliesin West, designed by Wright, as its winter home, and art, mostly oriental, was introduced as part of the ensemble.

One of Wright's last architecturally sculptured walls was designed for my father's office. In plywood, it was more delicate than the stone abstractions of fifteen years earlier. Fallingwater, the country house for the same client, was conspicuously free of Wrightian ornament. As the years went on, Wright used to come to visit at Fallingwater, and he was always very aware of the modern sculpture that accrued around it. He was, of course, as outspoken in our house as everywhere else, but curiously he never made a sarcastic remark about these works to us, nor

attempted to persuade us to other tastes. However, he would
invariably ask to have new statues relocated, often only a few
feet from where they were. Then he would settle back to enjoy
the new piece, directing the sculpture into a telling position
where it accentuated a feature of the architecture, and in turn
gained the support of its setting. From this experience, I feel
sure that Frank Lloyd Wright retained his early enthusiasm for
and sensitivity to the fine arts.

He found the artists near him during his life working on
problems of their own rather than on mutual ones. When he
built a museum for them, it was with equal amounts of questioning
and hope, but not with disrespect. It wouldn't occur to him to
demean his own architecture by assigning to it the task of demeaning
another's work. He was too proud and strong an artist himself
for that.

In looking back over Wright's long career, then, we see a
series of episodes in his relations to the fine arts. First, there
are the home-taught attitudes, typical of the Arts and Crafts era
and admirably summarized forty years before in Emerson's
essay, "Art." These attitudes remained influential, though not
decisive, throughout Wright's development. Then came a period
of experimentation with the works of artists around him, modeled
on Sullivan's usage, which was no more than a measured application of Beaux-Arts conventions. About 1900 (perhaps stimulated
by discussions with the Arts-and-Craftser Ashbee), Wright assayed
an integration of the arts, using mediocre sculptors and painters
to extraordinary effect. Then came the adventure of Midway Gardens, 1914, and the start of Wright's experiments with his own
painted and carved architectural embellishments. The years in
Japan confirmed his ready affinity with certain aspects of oriental arts, though, encouraged by artistic and bohemian associates
in Japan and in California, Wright continued to develop his own
expressions for some time. Eventually, oriental arts proved
more apt to his sense of architecture as space for living than
either his own works or any Western painting and sculpture available to him. By the 1930's, Wright's attitudes towards the arts

36

had jelled, and the full flowering of his architecture at the end
of his life had little or no effect on this aspect of his practice.
Assuming the role of senior prophet, which in some degree he
had earned, Wright castigated modern art for its failure to conform to the image of arts integrated with life, found in the Emerson essay. Yet, faced with particular instances of the power of
modern art and its exploratory courage, Wright responded to its
value. He willingly worked with modern art despite instinctive
reservations expressed in verbal denunciations; he hoped to
see it round the corner into a fertile relationship with architecture, which to him remained the key art in human cultural expression.

Mr. Kaufmann, adjunct professor of architecture at the School
of Architecture, Columbia University, and a former Taliesin
Fellow, owned until recently the famous Fallingwater house
designed by Frank Lloyd Wright. His latest book is Frank Lloyd
Wright: Writings and Buildings. He has been chairman of the
design Committee of the Institute of International Education and,
in 1962-1963, a visiting professor in the Department of Art History
and Archaeology at Columbia.

FRANK LLOYD WRIGHT AND THE TALL BUILDING

Grant Manson

The skyscraper and the tall building did not loom very large in Frank Lloyd Wright's life. In fact, he built only two buildings which we can conceivably call "tall buildings," and neither of them were "skyscrapers." But he constantly thought about tall buildings; indeed, they were almost a fixation in the back of Wright's mind. From the time he was first independent in the eighteen nineties until he died, he was continually toying with ideas for tall buildings.

There's one rather human and fascinating story about Frank Lloyd Wright that is often heard. Although he lived to see his work praised and to realize that he was one of the first geniuses of world art, he was bitter about the fact that he had never been asked by the Federal Government to build a building for our country, neither an embassy nor a building for Washington. Nor did his own State of Wisconsin ask him to build a building. There were constant projects for a great civic center in Madison, Wisconsin, but nothing ever came of it, and this was a source of frustration for Wright.

Another thing that annoyed him was that he almost died without having built a building in New York City. He did, fortunately for us, leave us the Guggenheim Museum, but this annoyance was unusual in a man who, all his life long, publicly disparaged New York City. In fact, there was in him a tremendous bitterness towards New York City, even though at the end of his life he was living as much in the Plaza Hotel as he lived in either of the two Taliesins. I think that if Wright had died without getting at least one building up in Manhattan, he would have died embittered and frustrated.

38

Another thing that he regretted was that he had never built a true skyscraper, and after all, the skyscraper is the American building. At least, it is certainly the one building that everyone thinks about as the American contribution to building. It's the kind of architecture we do supremely well; it's not the building that counts; it's the act of building it. I often think of skyscrapers as being an example of "action architecture": the result doesn't matter so much, but putting it up is terrific. This act appeals to American ingenuity, American know-how, and American love of doing things, all qualities very deeply ingrained in Wright.

This romantic Americanism of Wright is one reason why I would like to write an article on him that would, perhaps, cause a little fluttering in the dovecotes. I would call it: "Frank Lloyd Wright, the Last Great Architect of the Victorian Age." There is something in Wright that harks back to the nineteenth century, perhaps only naturally because he was born in the last half of that century, but there was in Wright, as there was in Sullivan, a romantic urge to build a tall building.

Oddly enough, when we look back into Wright's career, we find that he did start early with a building that was a skyscraper: the San Francisco Call Building (or the San Francisco Press Building), the design of which dates roughly from 1912. The building never got built, but he loved to have a large plaster model of it around him, as part of his milieu. In fact, there were two pieces of plaster that Wright never was happy without. One was a model of the San Francisco Call Building, and the other was a replica of the Winged Victory of Samothrace.

An even earlier design that Wright did build was very close to his heart: the windmill, Romeo and Juliet, which he built on his aunts' property at the Hillside Home School in Spring Green, Wisconsin in 1893-1894. This structure is a skyscraper in spirit, the kind of skyscraper that Wright conceived in the back of his mind very early in his career.

It was called Romeo and Juliet, because Romeo was the great, stalwart, lozenge-shaped spine and Juliet the circular element

39

that clings to him for strength and support. Although the windmill is no skyscraper, there is a very pertinent illustration of
Wright's idea of a skyscraper in Romeo and Juliet. In this windmill, you see at once Wright's basic feeling about the construction
of a tall building: it should have a single, powerful, central
spine, triangular or lozenge-shaped in plan, and around it should
be a secondary space that laps or hangs on. Interestingly enough,
from this time on, Wright's ideas about tall buildings hardly
changed.

Even in the case of a great genius like Frank Lloyd Wright,
out of whose mind there seemed to spill an endless range of
ideas, the basic concepts are relatively few. But with these
concepts, he managed to invent a new architecture out of his own
mind. Unlike many other great architects who came along and
projected what other people dream and conceive through centuries
and generations, Wright simply gave birth by parthenogenesis,
out of his own mind, to a whole new attitude toward architecture.
Now I know that architecture is a continuum, and I also know
that "there is nothing new under the sun, " but, nevertheless, insofar as it is possible, Wright was a spontaneous genius. If you
look back to Wright's early work, you will find, in fact, the genes
and chromosomes of all the things that came out of his mind in
the last two-thirds of his career.

In the windmill, you have the genes and chromosomes of
Wright's inmost ideal of what a tall building should be. It should
be a building arranged, as we observed before, on a spine, with
useful spaces arranged around it; it should have interpenetrating
and intricately interrelated spaces; it should be deeply planted
down in the ground like a great fencepost, if you will; and the
principal spaces of the building should cantilever out from that.
Wright stuck to these ideas all the way through, so that when he
actually began coping with the problem of the multi-layer
building or the skyscraper, in the tall buildings he designed over
a twenty-year period -- from St. Mark's-in-the-Bouwerie in 1928
to the tower for Johnson Wax in Racine in 1949 -- he used the same idea.
He varied it, of course, when he actually built the two tall
buildings which were the only ones executed, the Price Tower
at Bartlesville, Oklahoma and the Johnson's Wax Tower at Racine,
Wisconsin.

There's an extraordinary difference between these two buildings, so extraordinary that I can't quite understand how Wright, using the same principle, could arrive at two buildings so utterly different in appearance.

What accounts for the tremendous difference between these two buildings? There is not very much difference in time between them. The building in Racine was built between 1947 and 1949; the building at Bartlesville during 1953-1954. Here, of course, we commit heresy, but could there conceivably have been any influence brought to bear upon Wright from the International School? I think there was undoubtedly a period in the thirties and forties when Wright felt the influence of Le Corbusier and Mies and Gropius. He did forget for a little while the wonderful complexity of form and the wonderful richness of materials for materials' own sake which was a sort of nineteenth-century quality. This makes me think of Wright as a man who straddles two centuries. In only two outstanding designs did Wright abandon to a large extent the tremendous richness of detail and surface that characterizes most of his work: the building at Racine for Johnson Wax and Fallingwater, the Kaufmann house at Bear Run, Pennsylvania. These represent moments in his career when he definitely responded to influences from the unwelcome contemporaries from Europe.

In this appraisal of Wright's playing and toying with the tall building, there is, finally, the Mile-High skyscraper. Did Wright ever intend it to be built? This building, designed in 1950, was to be built somewhere around Grant Park on the lakefront in Chicago. Wright called it the "Illinois Building," but it was promptly dubbed the Mile-High skyscraper. With 528 stories (whether that would quite amount to a mile or not I don't know), it would have pierced the clouds, gone above weather.

I never know what to say to students when they ask me about the Mile-High building; they ask with a wicked gleam in their eyes, because they want to see how I'll fall all over myself trying to give them an answer. But there is no answer. Nobody knows;

41

the master himself never gave the word on the Mile-High
building. I've talked casually to engineers about the building --
they always say that you could build it. It probably is erectible
if you plunged the steel spine thousands of feet down in the
ground below. You probably could get a building 528 stories
high. It would, of course, be an economic catastrophe. And
one can imagine what life would be like with the wind howling
around it and the oscillation of the building on the 479th floor
being, maybe, ten feet.

I'm told that tall buildings cease to produce any kind of reve-
nue beyond the fortieth floor; that beyond that they are simply
monuments to somebody's ego. The Mile-High would have been
the most monumental monument to anybody's ego that the world
had ever seen.

Aside from the cold facts of the Mile-High building, what
does it mean? I think it is a kind of final explosion in Wright's
mind of the romanticism of the nineteenth century. It was the
last statement of how the Tower of Babel could actually be
built in the United States of America, where we were capable
of building things endlessly tall. Even more important, it is
the final statement of frustration, of envy on Wright's part that
he didn't build skyscrapers. Now, whether or not you agree that
this is an intelligent explanation, or agree that it was worth-while
for Wright to waste anger or frustration upon the skyscraper
(which in a way is a dying form of architecture except in cities
like Manhattan), it points to the fact that Wright was a man who
practiced sixty years without getting the big opportunities. That's
about as long a career as we'll find in any architectural record.
He was an American architect, and in any ordinary long American
architectural career, we're going to find a lot of tall buildings,
a lot of skyscrapers. It was one of those strange sorrows in
Wright's life, that he had no such chances. No matter how successful we become, there is always something that robs us of a
true sense of our own success. And in Wright's case, it was
those three things -- nothing for the government, nothing for the
state of Wisconsin, and no record of large skyscrapers, tall
buildings.

42

There was, at the end, another thing which influenced Wright, and that was the inheritance from Sullivan, the lieber Meister, the one man whom Wright persistently and openly admired. And since Sullivan had built skyscrapers, I think Wright felt that he should have built skyscrapers, too.

Just for the record, the one other kind of tall building which Wright occasionally considered is represented by the so-called Luxfer Prism Building designed for Michigan Boulevard in Chicago in 1895. The interesting thing about this building is that it showed Wright thinking of the tall building as a glass-fronted slab. But, nevertheless, the important notion in Wright's mind was always the idea that came from Romeo and Juliet and finally, at the end of his life, reached its rather ridiculous, but nevertheless touching climax, in the Mile-High building in Chicago.

Grant Manson is author of Frank Lloyd Wright to 1910: the First Golden Age. He teaches at the School of Architecture, University of Southern California.

THE SOCIAL IMPLICATIONS OF THE SKYSCRAPER

Henry S. Churchill

It is not possible to consider the tall buildings of the four architects, or of those of any architects, without giving at least passing consideration to the social implications of tall buildings. Such consideration could occupy the time of a full consistory of city planners, sociologists, economists, demographers, and other necromancers. I think we can, nevertheless, come quickly and without too much doubt to the same conclusion they would reach after the usual research: that regardless of whether the super-elevated structural shelter is good or bad, it is here to stay. Indeed, this conclusion has already been concurred in by such high authority as Sir Hugh Casson, a sort of primate of British architecture, who in a recent interview in the London Times stated, "I think you've got to face the fact that you have got to build high these days. When and where is the problem."

I have no intention of reciting here the city-planning problems which are involved, as I am sure you are all well aware of them. I would only have you bear in mind that it is still possible to build low, and that in the background lurks the ghost of that enormous catalyst, Ebenezer Howard. Howard was not an architect; he was not aware of skyscrapers, but he remains a potent ghost for all that. It was his disciple, Sir Raymond Unwin, who said there was nothing gained by overcrowding. If they and our own Clarence Stein are not included in our galaxy, it is because the tall building had so little impact on them. Yet, they materialize every time the word "social" creeps into an architectural discussion, and it is as impossible to keep it out today as it was to keep out the word "function" only yesterday.

44

There is one point that should be borne in mind. It is that the tall building is an American economic invention. It was developed here almost entirely as a by-product of speculation in land. Until quite recently it was regarded as the inevitable economic solution to the economic scarcity of land. Its esthetic aspects then were the concern of only a few; its social implications were the concern of none; while to the many it was the epitome of American architecture and the salient symbol of our culture.

Yet, Le Corbusier notes in When the Cathedrals Were White how disappointed he was in the skyscrapers of New York. They seemed to be built of massive masonry with holes cut in for windows. They rose in cluttered array from the sidewalk, shutting out each other's light and air and view. They were dingy and tiresome. Only at night did they come alive, incredibly alive and vigorous, particularly in Times Square, which he loved. But the city was choking itself to death, and, in 1936, New York was a nightmare to the creator of La Ville Radieuse. It still is.

Le Corbusier, more than any other of his time, had explored the possibilities of the tall building as an instrument of city rebuilding, as a means of providing a new way of urban living, not just a new esthetic. Gropius was aware of the changes it made in urban land use. He made studies of residential groupings and densities, but he did not reach the extreme and iconoclastic position that Le Corbusier took, first in La Ville Radieuse and later in the Voisin plan. It has always been his gift to be able to state the most doubtful hypotheses as axioms. His papal infallibility has been matched only by Wright's Pauline dogmatism.

This is not beside the point. Clarity is necessarily incorrigible. In Corbu's scheme of things, tall buildings were inseparable from his vision of a new way of building cities. His vision was social and reformist. Carthage must be destroyed, the old city torn down and replaced. The skyscraper was to be the means of turning the rotten and chaotic ancient inheritance into the ordered, clean, and enlightened city of his future.

La Ville Radieuse was the first clear architectural statement of such an attitude, an attitude diametrically opposed to the purely sociological reforms of the Garden City. It is French rationale against Anglo-Saxon sentimentality. The Voisin plan was the first urban renewal plan since Haussmann, the first resolutely clear call for urban destruction and replacement as opposed to the idea of emigration to a New Town and laissez-faire renewal for the city that was left behind.

The idea of urban renewal has taken hold here, but hardly in the spirit of Le Corbusier. It has taken hold here because it provides a mechanism by which people without power or money can be dispossessed by people having money and power, under the guise of social purpose. Any resemblances, so far, to Corbu's vision are merely accidental. This vision has gone around the world, from the failure of his own scheme for St. Dié to the quasi-successes of Rotterdam and Stockholm and the ultimate paraphrase of Brazilia. The force of his influence on the form of these urban designs is evidence of the interplay of architectural forms and social forces.

In his design of Broadacre City, an idea in every way the opposite of La Ville Radieuse, Frank Lloyd Wright has made as clear an architectural statement for the horizontal expansion of life as Le Corbusier made for the vertical concentration of life. It is a beautifully articulated and very intricate pattern; it has none of the casualness of the Garden City or New Town. But because it offers neither pseudo-social theory nor opportunities for fancy speculation in land (nor even for spectacular architecture), it has been generally ignored.

Neither Wright nor Corbu have been able to see their urban theories developed into actuality from their own designs. (Chandigarh is obviously not a western city nor an automotive one.) Corbu, however, has been able to build the Unité d'Habitation at Marseille, which embodies many of his social ideas. The Unité is not, of course, La Ville Radieuse, but it could very well pass for a neighborhood in that city, a neighborhood stood on end, or perhaps more correctly, a vertical village. As such it presents a curious effort at social isolation, like our own early public housing projects, but these were purposefully isolated in order to quarantine, as it were, the deserving upper-class poor from those remaining unfortunates who were not yet tainted by public assistance.

Le Corbusier, it is superfluous to say, certainly had no such intention. He was, however, obsessed by the notion that confused and illiterate social ideas could be enclosed in a clear and literate architectural form. He was, I think, mistaken. People cannot be cast into an arbitrary architectural mold. The architecture must fit the social requirements, and, at most, perhaps -- and only perhaps -- good architecture will help clarify social customs.

In creating a neighborhood or a Unité, present habits must be considered. Many habits are age-old, so old in fact that impatient reformers often look upon them as senile, fit for euthanasia. Among such habits are the desire for gregariousness and the desire for privacy, or the need of shop-keepers to make money. To put a shopping street in the middle of a tall building is to go counter to ancient custom. No one from the outside will come to it. And since the fun of shopping is gone, no one from the inside will come either. The purpose of shopping is not just to buy something, but to see new people, to gossip with old friends, to get away from the house, to walk to the next block, to have a choice of merchandise, to see the sky, and to curse the mistral.

So, too, the roof garden of the Unité for all its famous sculptural forms, is not a satisfactory substitute for a playground in which children can run, nor is its artificiality, no matter how artful, a substitute for the use of the extended available ground that is the principal excuse for building high. One cannot play boules on a roof. One could perhaps bowl on a roof; it is a channeled and directed game. But boules is unorganized and simple -- though difficult -- and needs lots of cheering and vociferous criticism and confusion from the side lines. This is not possible on

47

a roof. Even the view from the roof of the Unité is cut off by the parapet, a confinement that is inexcusable except that it unifies an arbitrary architectural conceit.

Wright never worked out any such complete system of urban design as did Le Corbusier, nor any such unified single statement of the tall building as was made by van der Rohe in that famous first sketch. Wright basically was without social purpose; indeed his whole character ran counter to participation in group effort, and in spite of his genuine devotion to Jeffersonian democracy, he had as little use for the common people as did Jefferson himself. Nor was he, despite the continuous preaching of an "organic architecture," a great theorist after the manner of Le Corbusier and Gropius, or a profound searcher after an unique truth like Mies. Like Picasso, who resembles him in so many ways, Wright was a vastly prolific producer and an endless experimenter, continuously inventive. He was not interested in making abstract sketches of ideas; he preferred to develop his ideas as sketches for a specific job that he hoped to build. The only exceptions I can recall are Broadacre City and the Mile-High Tower.

The first of Wright's tall building projects was the design for the Press Building in San Francisco, done in 1912. It derives directly from Sullivan in its articulation, with important modifications at the top and a balancing of the main masses of the building that is suggestive of his future treatment of horizontal and vertical elements. Although it is an elegant and strong design, it is of little significance compared with his next major effort, a proposed building for the National Life Insurance Company in Chicago. He started work on this in 1920, the year Mies van der Rohe published his famous sketch for an all-glass tower. For National Life, Wright worked out, here for the first time in thorough detail for construction, almost all the basic elements characteristic of his tall buildings: the central spine and cantilevered floors of reinforced concrete, the copper and glass sheathing with "vertical blades of copper acting in the sun like the shades of a blind," the elaborate counter-point of vertical and horizontal, the rich interplay of form and surface, the exuberance that is beauty. It is in striking and

48

significant contrast to the already absolute starkness of Mies's concept. Each was to grow in his own way: Mies ever probing and refining, Wright ever elaborating and expanding.

Wright's next design was a small tower apartment house for St. Mark's-in-the-Bouwerie in New York. Here, in 1929, are the ideas of the tap root and the angular design, the duplex floor plan, the partly two-storied living room, the private balcony. He later expanded this scheme into a set of connected structures which can be compared, at least for living quality, to the apartment layout of the Unité. Wright's plans are shallow, and consequently the second floor bedrooms, which, like those of the Unité, are set back from the front wall to allow double height to part of the living room, are well lighted and pleasant. There are no inside or badly-shaped rooms, and advantage is taken of utility equipment, as well as of the heavy structural components, to obtain privacy between dwelling units. Otherwise the living concept is entirely conventional; there is no effort to provide community services. The client would probably have been revolted at the mere thought of them, and Wright was not the man to push for social innovations if he could have his way with the architecture.

Wright had no use for the city and was willing to leave it to its own devices. The skyscraper, he proclaimed, belonged in the country. He did not see in it an instrument for urban regeneration; it had only esthetic value, and it had that only if he designed it. Slums and congestion did not concern him except as he considered the whole city a vast slum. His ideal of Broadacre City was a bourgeois concept of spacious and pleasant living. He had neither Corbu's vision nor courage to propose a plan based on the destruction of a large part of the city. If, as Wright once said, there is nothing more timid than a million dollars, he in turn had great respect for those same millions. He devoted two of the Princeton lectures to the Skyscraper and the City, and they pretty well sum up what he had to say about them as theory. (When Democracy Builds is expansion and amplification.) They are mostly diatribes and ranting against real estators and landlords

49

whose greed is responsible for the ugliness and congestion of cities. The root of all evil, Wright did not propose to wipe them out; he had, to put it pleasantly, too great a sense of the reality of realty.

Thus we have the paradox of Le Corbusier, who loves the city, proposing to tear it apart and replace it with an ideal pattern of tall buildings and a road network based on fast transportation, while Wright, hating the city and trying his best to ignore it, is proposing an ideal pattern of a semi-rural community with a few tall buildings for variety in both living and looking. This ran counter to the current thinking, and Broadacre City was even less regarded in practical circles than were the Garden Cities or the New Towns. Corbu's ideas, on the other hand, were guidance to wishfulness and so took hold.

In 1940, Wright designed his most spectacular multi-residential building. This was the Crystal Heights Hotel which was to have occupied the splendid triangular site at the intersection of Connecticut and Florida Avenues in Washington. This, too, was a series of centrally-supported cantilever towers, of varying heights. They were set far back from the avenues, with stores, movies, and a three-level parking garage on Connecticut Avenue integrated with a series of terraced gardens entered from Florida Avenue. Besides its architectural brilliance, it was, as a solution to the design for urban living and for the use of open space and parking, far ahead of anything that had been proposed for Washington up to that time. But it was not compatible with the local zoning, nor was the timing right, and it was never built.

Finally and at last in 1955, he built the Price Tower. Except that this is a combined office and apartment building, it is almost exactly the design of St. Mark's. It is, as Wright rejoicingly proclaims, the Tower in the Park. He has overlooked the Alden Park Manor Apartments, five towers in a park in Philadelphia, built about 1923. They are hideous, it is true, but they are towers-in-a-park just the same, and they still have a long waiting list. I mention this only to observe how meaningless is the clamor for priority. Who does it, and how it is done, are more important than when.

50

The Price Tower is the place where Le Corbusier and Wright could at last have met for a semantic duel, T-squares in hand and seconded by students bearing pamphlets and aphorisms. But Corbu, by now, was far off on other things and thoughts, and the issue was never joined; indeed it was perhaps no longer an issue.

The Price Tower was Wright's last tall building to be erected, but his final say on the subject was the proposal for the Mile-High Tower. This, because of its impudent mockery of much current city-planning patter, must have given him great joy. Here is the utmost concentration of people to provide the utmost in non-usable empty space around it. It is the last hurrah for mechanical transportation, vertical as well as horizontal, a cynical and sardonic use of every fad and cliché expounded by the urban theorists. Whether so intended or not, it was also a last slap at his old adversary, the reductio ad absurdum, by a great humanist, of the machine for working.

Walter Gropius and Mies van der Rohe have approached the problem of the tall building somewhat more pragmatically. Gropius, in particular, has contented himself with working out the customary formulae for the ratios of height to open land as a problem of residential densities without evidencing much interest in the more general problem of the effect of high-rise structures on the pattern of cities. The great contributions of his genius have been in other fields.

Mies has never been a great propagandist, and I suspect social theory bores him, as well it might. Since the war he has built numerous tall buildings for understanding clients who gave him his own way in design. Unlike Wright and Le Corbusier, Mies has not ventured into the realms of experimental or expressionist construction. He adopted, with his adoption of the United States, our most usual form of construction, the steel skeleton frame. It is this that he has ever sought to perfect, within the limits of his own experience, much in the spirit of the French poet who said, "La nuance, seulement la nuance, et tout le reste est littérature."

51

Much has been made of the notion that Corbu's use of massive concrete is an affirmation of belief in the Future of Man and the permanence and dignity of Architecture. (This, of course, is in contrast to the transitory and fragile nature of steel.) But, it may be that the future is fragile too, the present little worthy, and that the curiosities of our economy and the obsolescence of our urbanity may make it desirable to have buildings that can easily be torn down and replaced.

Whatever the uncertain future, Mies has presently achieved the mastery of the steel skeleton, which he has clothed in the purest and most elegant garments imaginable. The Seagram Building is indeed one of the "topless towers of Ilium," subject as they were, to betrayal by the Trojan Horse of mediocrity. For it is in this that there lies the peculiar social impact of his work: that by his persuasive perfection of our customary building methods, he has been able to set a style which is as much the hallmark of our time as the limestone monotony of the Paris Boulevards are of theirs.

Perhaps, since this is a pseudo-sociological discourse, I should say a word about the alleged unlivability of some of Mies's apartment buildings. The various allegations must have some foundation in fact, at least for some people. However there seem to be plenty of others who find no difficulty in living with these errors. In any case, in due time, economic retaliation will take its toll of esthetic perfection. I do not see such things as being of much social consequence, as some do, for I believe, rather that esthetic values given us forever are more important than the temporary discomfort of a few tenants. Eventually and finally, esthetics triumph over economics. The Parthenon, after all, had no public toilets.

The tall structures of neither Wright nor Corbu have been so successful as prototypes as have those of Mies. The impact of Mies has been almost entirely in the field of esthetics, largely because he has not complicated his esthetics by structural innovation or social implication. Hence, any architect who has a good structural engineer thinks that without thought he can do as well as Mies.

52

The work of Le Corbusier, and to a lesser extent that of
Wright, has been much affected by the various other aspects
of their purpose, both structural and social; and as a result,
the world is not full of mediocre Wright or Corbu skyscrapers,
but only of bad and dilapidated echoes of their eccentricities --
while on the other hand it is full of second-rate Mies done by
men who turn "less is more" into less than nothing.

We are too close to these men properly to assess their
influence. That their influence is great and widespread
is evident enough, modified though it necessarily has been
by arbitrary forces of economics, custom, and inconsequence.
Reconstruction in Europe and urban renewal here are witness
to the penetration of their dogma. These have, of course,
lost their pure form, just as the doctrines of Ebenezer Howard
have lost theirs. This may be for better or for worse in the
social scene, but the perversion of doctrines is the way of
change if not always of progress. In any case, one cannot blame
Le Corbusier for the frightful evisceration of our cities by
the Highwaymen, nor can Wright be held responsible for urban
sprawl, nor Mies for the perpetration of such monstrosities
as the Grand Central City building or the proposed horror that
Malraux wishes to see rise at Montparnasse. All these architects have had their vision of more ordered physical setting,
in which living would be easier and beauty would be paramount.
This has been, always, the vision and hope and dedication of
great architects.

It is perhaps worth noting that since the great active
era of Wright and Le Corbusier, and in justice one must
here again add the name of Clarence Stein, there has been
no advance at all in the concepts of physical city planning.
Granted that the administration of cities is deeply and
necessarily concerned with statistical interpretation, economic
analysis, and sociological semantics, nevertheless the city

is and must be a physical entity or it ceases to exist.
Here is the opportunity for our contemporaries and heirs
to fill in the desert void of the planners, to conceive of
more noble cities in which architecture can rise to
greater heights.

Mr. Churchill practiced as an architect and planner with
the firms of Thompson and Churchill, and Churchill, Fulmer
Associates in New York. As a critic, his principal work was
The City is the People (1945). He died in 1963.

BROADACRE CITY: WRIGHT'S UTOPIA RECONSIDERED

George R. Collins

Broadacres, the Wrightian substitute for the city, is well
known to us all, but a schematic presentation of some of its major
principles and elements might be in order.

Wright's four square-mile model was divided into mile-square
sections A, B, C, and D, and was to accommodate approximately
1,400 families (Figure 1.). Its basic elements were to be arranged
loosely, subject in part to accidents of the terrain. The major
determinant of his planning appears to be the arterial highway of up
to twelve truck and car lanes (railways have been eliminated),
beside which were situated supermarkets, heavier industry, and
decentralized hotels (motels). Then came little factories (with
dwellings upstairs), workers' homes, and orchards. The central
zone was comprised of small dwellings clustered about schools.
The county seat overlooked the lake, and recreational facilities
were scattered along the creek or constructed on the hill to the
northeast along with wealthier homes, community church, the
university, and zoological gardens. On the fringes of the area were
small farms and small industry, and high on the northeastern hill
an automobile objective for drivers. Scattered here and there are
gas stations -- which were also to serve as community centers --
and landing fields for his aerotors (vertically-ascending airplanes).

More important, perhaps, than the individual components and
their specific placement are the theoretical principles and social
motivations by means of which Wright himself explained his plan.
First of all, Wright believed in decentralization: as he commented
to an interviewer in 1957, "You come to see me, I suppose, as an
individualist and a decentralist." He believed that modern technological

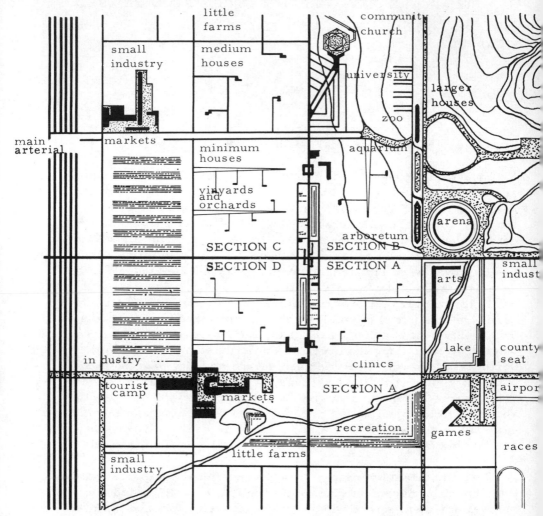

Figure 1. Plan of Broadacre City. From Wright, Frank Lloyd, <u>When Democracy Builds</u>, Chicago: University of Chicago Press, 1945, plan facing page 54.

progress and distributive methods make possible a radical
dispersal of industry, commerce, and administration, saying:
"It is in the nature of universal electrification that the city should
not exist. " Secondly, Wright considered that man's salvation lies
in the ground , as worked by his own hands; an acre to a person,
hence the name of his plan: "...., when every man, woman and
child may put foot on their own acre and every unborn child finds
his acre waiting for him when he is born, then does an Organic
Architecture become the greatest servant of Man. " Or again,
"In the city of yesterday, ground space was reckoned by the square
foot. In the City of Tomorrow ground space will be reckoned by
the acre: an acre to the family. " (A numerical discrepancy here,
but the meaning is clear.)

He declared the three "inherent rights of man" to be: (1) the
social right to a direct medium of exchange -- some form of social
credit (he was an admirer of the system of the Scot C. H. Douglas.);
(2) the social right to his place on the ground -- land to be held only
if used and improved (Henry George); (3) man's social right to
ideas by which and for which he lives -- the public ownership of
inventions and discoveries (I presume this to be from Edward Bellamy).

Others of his basic principles were that goods distribution would
be direct, from producer to consumer without middlemen; and that
coal, similarly, would be burned at the mine to produce electricity
for high tension lines. In both these respects he calls to mind his
contemporary Henry Ford, who shook the Midwestern retailing system
to its roots when he opened his company supermarkets in the nineteen-
twenties and who remarked that through the transmission of electrical
power the necessity for industrial centralization had been eliminated
(1929). To Wright, the resources that would make his Broadacre City
possible were electrification, automation, mobilization, and modern
architecture (!). On another occasion he listed these resources as:
(1) the motor car, (2) the radio, telephone, and telegraph; and (3)
standardized machine-shop production. As for the citizen of Broadacre
City, he wrote, "Birds sing, the grass grows for him, rain falls on
his growing garden while the wheels of standardization and invention

turn for him, not against him . . ." As Henry Ford said, "With the advent of the airplane, the radio, and the motor car, people are no longer compelled to stay in the house, but may travel about, economically, and see things." Wright assumed that the automobile service station would become the shopping center and the community center of the future.

But most of all, Wright liked to describe his plan in terms of slogans, for example:

No Institutes

No Petty officialdom

No Landlord . . .   No Tenant

No Politicians . . .   No Academicians

No Traffic Problem

No Back and Forth Haul

No Poles . . .   No Wires in sight

No ditches alongside the roads

No headlights   No visible lamps

No Policemen

No Minor Axis   No Major Axis

No Yards for Raw Materials

No Smoke

No Radio or Billboard Advertising

58

No slum	No scum
No Railroads	No street cars
No Public ownership of private needs	No private ownership of public needs

Etc.

As for how this revolution would be brought about -- it was an architectural problem, he insisted. "From the roads that are its veins and arteries, to the buildings that are its cellular tissue, to the parks and gardens that are its ' epidermis ' and 'hirsute' ornament, the new city will be architecture." Or: "All Broadacre City needs to come into existence is the application of the principles of an organic architecture to the life of the people, and the interpretation of that life in terms of architecture."

One is puzzled as to how to categorize the Broadacre plan formally. Morphologically it is unique; as a regional planning form it seems to have no specific prototype. Insofar as Wright's model "lieth four-square, and the length is as large as the breadth," it recalls the Mormons' plat of the City of Zion which had been employed frequently in our Western expansion during the nineteenth century and, we are told, owed its shape in part to the Congressional mile-square rectangular survey of 1785. However, that was a centralized city form with blocks laid out in a rectangular grid and thus was unlike Broadacres which employed the grid only as an underlying module.

The origins of the Broadacre form would seem to lie rather in the vocabulary of Wright's own architecture and site-planning.

59

Although he derided the use of axes, Broadacres is clearly in
the cross-axial or four-sectioned tradition of his earliest group
planning and of his later duplex housing. We illustrate his
"Residential Land Development" for the Chicago City Club of 1913
(Figure 2.) and his Usonian housing of 1939 in Ardmore (Figure 3.).
Also comparable would be his Ladies Home Journal plot of February
1901 and his St. Marks apartment layout of 1929. He said in
exhibiting his model, "In Broadacres all is symmetrical but is
seldom obviously and never academically so." The cross-axes
observable in the Broadacres model are admittedly the sections
of his model and not necessarily land subdivisions, but they seem
to underlie what is generally a De Stijl composition. That Wright
himself visualized his plan as a picture is evidenced by the fact
that it was sometimes displayed, in Milwaukee for instance,
standing on its side against the wall. So although it was in theory
schematic and formless, Broadacres seems to have actually been
laid out according to one of Wright's favored plan types and
subdivided by his rectangular modular system.

I have felt that there is some justification in classifying this
scheme as a linear plan. Wright spoke of the splendid highways
and their gaiety of movement, saying, "The stems for the flowering
of the new City . . . will be the great topographical road systems . . . .
These great roads unite and separate -- separate and unite in endless
series of diversified units passing by farm units, roadside markets,
garden schools, dwelling places, each on its acres of individually
adorned and cultivated ground and developed homes, all places for
pleasure in work or leisure." Or again, "If you can see the extended
highway as the horizontal line of Usonian freedom, then you will see
the modern Usonian city approaching."

Such a fascination with highway travel and automobile traffic
was characteristic of the period in which Wright evolved his scheme.
America's vast national highway system was then under construction,
as he himself mentioned constantly. In 1923 Arthur Comey of Harvard
had suggested that the entire country be redesigned in conformity with
an arterial network of highways (Figure 4.). About 1930 in his Porte

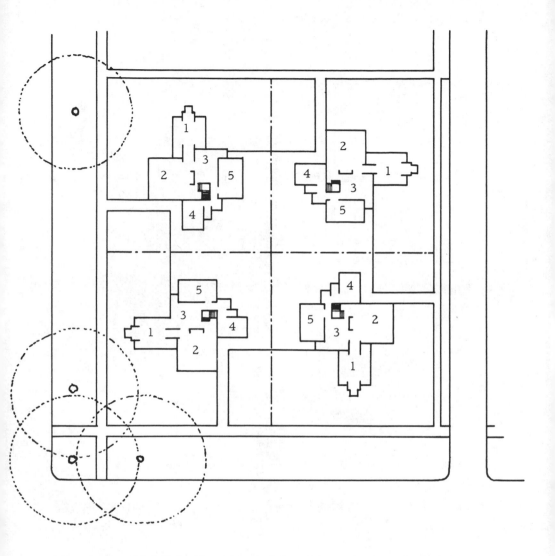

Figure 2. Wright's Residential Land Development Plan for
the Chicago City Club Competition of 1913. From de Fries, H.,
Frank Lloyd Wright: Aus dem Lebenswerke eines Architekten,
Berlin: Ernst Pollak, 1926. 1, porch; 2, living room; 3, dining
room; 4, informal dining room; 5, kitchen.

61

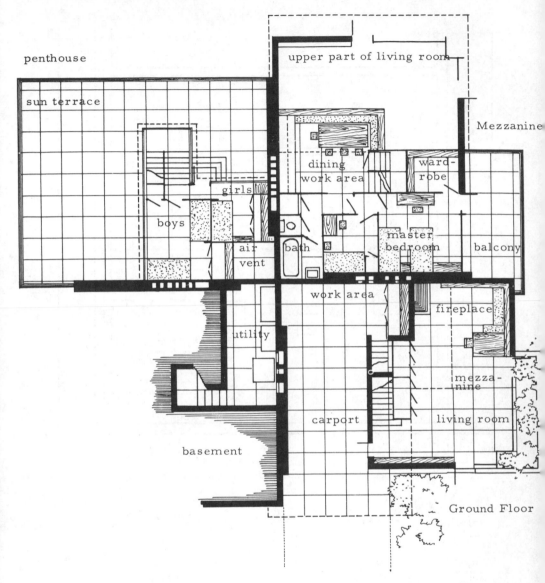

penthouse

sun terrace

upper part of living room

Mezzanine

dining work area

wardrobe

girls

boys

master bedroom

balcony

air vent

bath

work area

utility

fireplace

mezza-nine

carport

living room

basement

Ground Floor

Figure 3. Suntop Homes, Ardmore, Pennsylvania. Quadruple-dwelling unit. From Wright, Frank Lloyd, The Natural House. New York, Horizon Press, 1954.

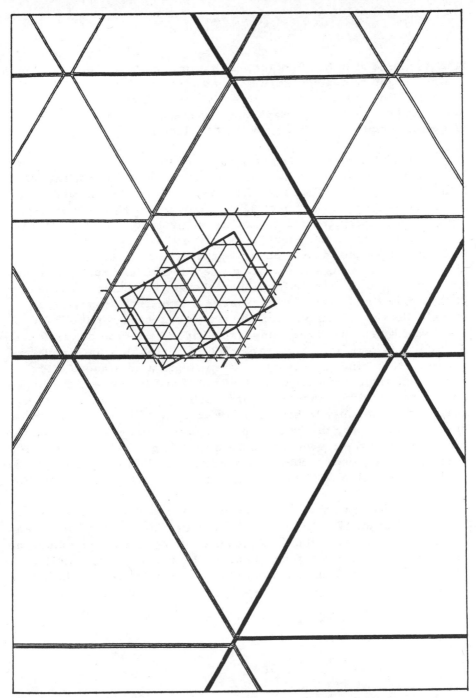

Figure 4.   Diagram of Cardinal Arterial System of a Nation.
From Comey, Arthur C. , Regional Planning Theory: A Reply
to the British Challenge.   1923

Maillot plan and in his Radiant City theory, Le Corbusier's designs began to depend more on roadways, and in the same years the Russian linear plan was invented. Over-passes for the efficient and speedy interchange of traffic became the subject of special scrutiny by many, Wright included.

It may also be that Wright's brand of linear planning derived from Henry Ford, whom he admired and resembled in many ways. In his first presentation of the Broadacres idea Wright cited Ford's Muscle Shoals project, a fact that is enlightening as regards both Wright's plan and his gullibility in general. In 1921, in what might have become the greatest "steal" in history, Ford had offered to take the Muscle Shoals electric and nitrate resources off the government's hands. As a presidential aspirant at the time, Ford proposed the electrification of the entire country, harnessing "every creek and brook" that crossed a farmer's property. At Muscle Shoals, which Senator Norris was to save for the TVA, Ford would have used the Tennessee River dams for power to manufacture fertilizer and tractors in a series of small industrial centers stretching for seventy-five miles in a continuous city. Giant industry could thus decentralize, Ford theorized, the broken-down city would be abandoned, and each family would have its own acre in a community of houses and gardens. The small industrial units would employ the winter time of farm workers, who could in turn construct their own homes bit by bit from the most modern materials produced by the Ford quantity production lines. Modern industry replenishing the country: Broadacre City in a nutshell.

Some writers have classified Broadacres not as linear but as "a-focal," since Wright said, "Broadacre City is everywhere and nowhere." However, the 1935 model of it (apparently the only one prepared) represents a focal point -- the county seat -- in the infinite extension of his plan along the artery of transportation.

It is of interest to trace the development of Wright's planning concepts. Broadacres emerged only in the last half of his life, and in the last third of his career, and was, in fact, not published until he was in his sixties. That progressive tradition in American architecture to which Wright owed his descent -- Richardson, Sullivan, and the early Chicagoans -- had demonstrated little interest in matters of city planning; such concerns had figured larger among conservatives like Olmsted, Burnham, or Griffin. Wright's early ideas about subdivisions (Como Orchards of 1910, Chicago City Club plan of 1913) were up to date, communal in character, and were given privacy by use of greenery; they lead directly to his later Usonian settlements of the nineteen-thirties and forties, but do not really foreshadow Broadacres in other than the strictly formal aspects already mentioned. He himself dated the beginnings of his "Broadacre Studies" variously, tending to push their origins back as he aged. His earliest suggestion was 1921, for which no evidence exists; then in 1923 he is supposed to have prepared a pamphlet on the urban crisis in Los Angeles; at another time he suggested 1929, the year of the crash. It is clear that the matter arose during the interval 1922-1931, that great interregnum in his life when Wright was at first languishing unemployed in the midst of the American building boom and then was sharing the general chaos that invaded his profession after 1929. The bitterness engendered by that period and the idle reading that he was apparently engaged in at the time were woven tightly into the fabric of Broadacre City when it emerged.

The first phase of Wright's concern with city planning might be called "Away with the City" and is marked by his diatribes against metropolises, traffic congestion, skyscrapers, unearned increment, and other manifestations of the vested interests. He described the city variously as a fibrous tumor and as a whirling vortex. This appeared with the Princeton Lectures of 1930, was expanded and illustrated in The Disappearing City of 1932, and became a permanent part of his autobiographies. Although Broadacres and a variety of Usonian elements were described in The Disappearing City, no plan was drawn, the only pictures being of the congestion of the city and of a Whitmanesque country path. "The City," Wright remarked, "is as troublesome to life as static

65

is to radio." It was running a fever! "We must choose between the automobile and the vertical city. . ." "The unnatural structures of verticality cannot stand against natural horizontality." He had not always been of this opinion; at the beginning of the century in his Hull House address he had rhapsodized about the beauties of the great machine that metropolitan Chicago represented. But, characteristically, he now spoke of The City and New York City interchangeably, venting his spleen on the moneyed interests of the East, as had Sullivan and as did the Agrarians with whom Wright was associated in the nineteen-thirties. We note that in 1932 there hardly existed a Wright building east of Buffalo; "America begins West of Buffalo," Wright remarked.

The Broadacre City plan as we have described it was illustrated only in 1935 when the model, having been constructed by his new Taliesin Fellowship in Arizona, formed part of the Industrial Arts Exposition at Rockefeller Center and was published in the American Architect and in the Architectural Record of that year. Many things came together at this moment which may explain the unique form of this model. There are a number of aspects of his layout -- the landscaping, the somewhat irrational juxtaposition of its elements, the distinct categories of building types, the emphasis on recreationa and educational facilities -- that cause the Broadacre model to look like a fair grounds. We know that from 1931 on Wright had resented his exclusion (in part his own doing) from the planning of Chicago's Century of Progress Fair, and that he prepared a number of alternative fair projects, all of which were dramatic and some self-advertising. The landscaping of the Broadacre model recalls Olmsted's work at the 1893 Fair, and the only excuse I can find for the "automobile objective" built on the hill is that it was to be an earthbound successor to 1893's famous Ferris Wheel.

It may also be noteworthy that the Broadacre plan included at least a dozen of Wright's unsold building projects of the nineteen-twenties. In fact, the Broadacre model presents an architectural repertoire that can probably be equalled only in the city plans of Tony Garnier and Claude-Nicolas Ledoux. Ledoux's book is, I think the more apt comparison here -- a somewhat self-righteous

advertisement of a career's designs, many unbuilt. If
Broadacre City was, then, a gimmick, a three-dimensional
advertisement of Wright's wares, it also served as a sort
of WPA project to tide over one of the first winter seasons
of the Taliesin Fellowship before there were many commissions.
The Fellowship, founded at about this time, appeared in Broadacre City as the Design School, and its members were presumed
to practice the Broadacres life in fact.

The model, which had been made possible by a subsidy from
Mr. Kaufmann, went on a tour of exhibitions (that in Washington
being financed by Mrs. Avery Coonley) and then was prinked up
for the big Wright show at the Museum of Modern Art in 1940.
A special issue of the magazine Taliesin, prepared for this last
occasion, is perhaps our most compact and informative publication about Broadacres. The model also figured in later exhibitions,
particularly the European ones of the early nineteen-fifties, but
was apparently unchanged in form.

Other major publications by Wright in which Broadacres
came under discussion include his dialogue with Baker Brownell
in 1937, his London lectures of 1939, and an annoying sociopolitical
screed -- a pamphlet which purports to be Book VI of the 1943
edition of his autobiography but gives one the impression that it
might have been edited out of that volume by the publisher. The
book The Disappearing City was republished in 1945 as When
Democracy Builds and in 1958 as The Living City; there occur
certain changes in punctuation and connectives, perhaps to avoid
copyright infringement, and a variety of acrid remarks about
Le Corbusier and others drift in and out of the successive editions.
A couple of new science-fiction illustrations added to the 1958
volume testify to Wright's professed early fascination with Jules
Verne. But the major change observable between the first
announcements of Broadacres in the early thirties and the later
publications of the forties is the insertion of more and more
social and economic theory and the citing of additional authorities
whom Wright knew or had read in the New Deal days; to this we
must now turn.

A study of the sources of Wright's ideas for Broadacre City is an education in itself. In the course of lecturing and writing about his plan, Wright openly and generously acknowledged his debt to more than thirty individuals. To list some whom he mentioned: The Arabian Nights, The Bahaist writings, Edward Bellamy, William Blake, Ralph Borsodi, John Brown, Samuel Butler, Thomas Carlyle, C. H. Douglas, Ralph Waldo Emerson, Henry Ford, William Lloyd Garrison, Buddha, Henry George, Silvio Gesell, Johann Wolfgang von Goethe, Heraclitus, Thomas Jefferson, Jesus Christ, Lao-tse, Abraham Lincoln, Giuseppe Mazzini, George Meredith, Thomas Paine, Paracelsus, John Ruskin, Percy Bysshe Shelley, Louis Sullivan, Henry David Thoreau, Leo Tolstoi, Jules Verne, Victor Hugo, George Washington, Walt Whitman. They are all, indeed, present· (and more besides) in an orgy of literary eclectism, in fact a creaky eclecticism which Wright would never have countenanced in his architectural designs. Obviously I cannot touch upon the contribution of each on this occasion but can only discuss a few obvious sources, some not acknowledged, and I must assume on your part a certain familiarity with the general content of Wright's utterances.

First it might be remarked that not one of the names I mentioned is ordinarily associated with modern town planning either as a practicioner or as a critic; Wright's scheme came into being outside the mainstream of the modern planning tradition. There are no allusions to or resemblances to either garden-city planning or neighborhood planning, both of which were current in the United States at that time. Although he was enthusiastic about assembly-line mass production, he never likened his arterial layout to the efficiency of such line production as did the Russians and other linear planners of the period; characteristically, he said " [its] connections [are] planned as a bunch of grapes on a stem. . . . " Nor did he think in terms of a schematic layout of the different functions of his plan in overlays as Le Corbusier and the CIAM were doing. Instead he plunged directly into an analysis of the habits and foibles of Man as a social being, and, in a somewhat Ruskinian manner, set about to reshape Man by manipulating the architectural elements of his environment: "It is desirable to repeat that architecture again must be the logical background and framework of modern civilization. . . The medieval spirit was the nearest to the communal, democratic spirit of anything we know."

A feature of modern society with which Wright became increasingly concerned in his "Broadacre Studies" was rent, known as "interest," "surplus value," or "unearned increment." The word "rent" starts out in lower case, later becomes capitalized, and eventually serves as a chapter heading in his books. His usual authority in these matters is Henry George, whose preface to Progress and Poverty Wright recommended heartily to his readers. On the occasion of an early exhibit of the Broadacre model Wright passed out copies of a classic parody on interest, "The Parable of the Water Tank" from Edward Bellamy's Equality, a book, by the way, that also deals with urban decentralization. Wright also recommended the preface to Silvio Gesell's Natural Economic Order. Gesell, in order to eliminate interest, devised a money that shrank when hoarded so that it had to be spent quickly and could not be capitalized. This idea suited Wright's personal tastes as we know them, and was more up to date than Henry George and Edward Bellamy, having exerted considerable influence in America during the depression when his stamp-scrip or Free Money was adopted in many areas and nearly became official governmental policy. To illustrate Gesell's thinking about more general matters than money: "A man must be something, not appear something; he must be able to stride through life with head erect -- to speak the truth without incurring the risk of hardship or injury . . . An economic order . . . founded upon egoism is in no way opposed to the higher impulses which preserve the species . . . The Natural Economic Order stands by itself and requires no legal enactments; it makes officials, the State itself, and all other tutelage superfluous . . ." This sounds like Wright himself speaking!

Wright also stands firmly in the tradition of Fourier -- seeking a device to make work a joy. To him this becomes joined with a love of nature, perhaps through Emerson, whom Wright quoted as follows: "The glory of the farmer is that, in the division of labors, it is his part to create . . . The first farmer was the first man, and all historic nobility rests on the possession and use of land. Men do not like hard work, but every man has an exceptional respect for tillage . . ." Again, from Emerson: "The city is always recruited from the country. The men in the cities who are the centers of energy, the driving-wheels of trade, politics, or practical arts, and the women of beauty and genius, are the children or grandchildren of farmers, and are spending the energies which their fathers' hardy, silent life accumulated in frosty furrows, in poverty, in necessity, and darkness. Whitman, Wright's poet, wrote:

"Now I see the secret of the making of the best persons,

It is to grow in the open and to eat and to sleep

with the earth." (Song of the Open Road)

As we have seen, Wright came to side with Emerson in this typically American sport of belaboring the city for its sins, but Wright's idea of tillage was one of a scientific sort, close by small industry, much as the gentle anarchist Kropotkin had described in his Fields Factories and Workshops of 1898, or William Morris in A Factory as It Might Be, and, of course, Ebenezer Howard. In this connection, Wright also admired Ralph Borsodi's experiments with home industry in Suffern, N. Y., and may have been tutored in these matters by his co-author Baker Brownell, who did much to disseminate the ideas of Chesterton and Belloc in America through his "Conference on Distributive Society and Integral Life." Wright is sometimes overgenerous in his acknowledgement of influences. For instance, he had great respect for Samuel Butler and attributed to him the famous "Usonia" (as having come specifically from Erewhon); but actually Wright must have invented the term himself, as it is not to be found in any of Butler's works. (The expression very probably lodged in Wright's mind during his first European

70

trip in 1910 at which time there was considerable talk about
addressing the States as U-S-O-N-A in order to avoid confusion
with the new Union of South Africa; Wright appears to have
first used "Usonia" in 1928.)

Intellectually, then, Wright drew on two traditions: first,
on that of the late nineteenth century, obsessed as it was with
the evil dynamics of rent and the love of nature; then later on the
agrarian tinkering of the nineteen-thirties. There is always an
element of faddism, too. For instance, he responded enthusiastically to the American motorcar craze of the thirties.
Along with its acre, each family would have a car, at least a
secondhand Ford -- in fact, house sizes in Broadacres are
designated by the terms "one-car," "two-car," etc. "Let the
auto take the city to the country," he said; the new scale of
space measurement was to be established by the man seated in
his motorcar. As one of his critics put it, "A house to Frank
Lloyd Wright is a place where a man puts his car in the garage
and is king of all he surveys." Wright's own taste ran more to
Packards, Auburn Cords, and Lincoln Continentals than to
flivvers, and we know from his son John that he was fascinated
with getting places at high speed on four wheels: "Papa was a
handsome figure in the driver's seat with linen duster, goggles,
and his wavy hair dancing in the breeze . . ."

One would expect that such a rich, heady, and synthetic
mixture of ideas might have fallen easy prey to critics, but
the majority of reviews of Wright's publications on Broadacres
have been either perfunctory notices or eulogies, taking
exception occasionally to his writing style. The literature of
planning has paid surprisingly little attention to his scheme;
penetrating critiques have usually appeared in publications
outside the professions of architecture and planning. Reviewers
of his Princeton lectures of 1930 took little account of the part
about the City, in which he made his first statement of Broadacres -- apparently not yet taking Wright seriously on civic

71

matters. Nor was there much reaction when the same
material appeared in the first edition of his autobiography
in 1932. However, after he fell into the hands of the
agrarians (Architecture and Modern Life, 1937), he began
to invite criticism of his social and economic theorizing.
In 1938 in the Partisan Review Meyer Schapiro demolished
Wright's plan and Brownell's theories so devastatingly as a
social, economic, or political blueprint that little more need
be said on that count: "A shabby streamlined Utopia, " he
called the scheme. When Wright carried the battle to London
with his famous Watson lectures of 1939 (An Organic Architecture) he was sharply questioned from the floor by earnest
young architects and did not come off too well according to
Patrick Abercrombie, who wryly observed that "his system
was . . . only suitable for the vast open spaces of Arizona."
It was two years later that the News Chronicle cabled Wright
asking how he would rebuild bombed-out London; his recipe
for a decentralized, motorcar, aeroplane London was not
well received.

Then in 1942 the value of Broadacres both as architecture and as community planning was seriously questioned by
Paul and Percival Goodman in the Kenyon Review. Since
Wright's life was a never-ending struggle against the forces
of darkness and evil, we are not surprised to find that his
later publications on Broadacres contain parenthetical asides
aimed at the critics of his earlier efforts - - although as far
as I know he never tilted with any of the gentlemen just
mentioned.

By way of conclusion, there remains the question:
Should Wright's Broadacre City be taken seriously as
planning?

To begin with, much that he has written on this subject,
especially the social doctrine, will do his reputation no good

in the eyes of future historians. Cliche'd, repetitive,
inconsistent. For example, he extolled Henry George --
but no Single Tax! He said, don't worry, this is Capitalism,
"Organic Capitalism" -- but prohibited interest on money.
"Democracy, " he proclaimed, "is the highest form of
Aristocracy." "Broadacre City, " he told the English, is
not a back-to-the-land movement;" but to the American
steelmakers he said, "We once had a gift of agronomy
that made industrialization unnecessary. "

Wright had no more use for the planning profession
than for the architectural. "I am suspicious of all planners, "
he told Robert Moses -- "anyone can make a plan." And
as for the people: "let them suffer in hell and all, " he said,
"until they know why they suffer. " He addressed Moses as
"the Mole" (because he worked in five boroughs), and
accused him (rightly) of overemphasizing matters of traffic.
Yet the traffic problem began and remained one of Wright's
principal concerns about the modern city; his Broadacre
studies show him to be literally obsessed with the design of
overpasses for traffic flow, although he gives us no details
about the movement of traffic or goods amongst the various
units that make up his plan. We are forced to conclude that
the spatial and circulatory problems of such a split-level
construction as an overpass held a fascination for him like
the laying out of the Coonley House , but the matter of getting
Mr. Usonia to work daily was of little consequence. As a
national highway system, Broadacres is primitive when
compared with Comey's triangulation system, of which we
have illustrated the regional framework in Figure 4. It
seems never to have occurred to Wright that his own
triangular module would have been more suitable for country-
wide transportation planning than his rectangular one.

But ultimately, practical or impractical as it may appear
to be, any ideal plan will stand or fall on its popular appeal.
Although ostensibly populist in character, Broadacre City was
a very personal ideal, unresponsive to the "group conceptions"

73

that Mr. Churchill mentioned the other evening. The world
was not electrified by Wright's agrarianism in the nineteen-
thirties the way it had been by Le Corbusier's Futurism in
the nineteen-twenties. Le Corbusier has, as a planner, responded
to the times. Since the beginning Le Corbusier's planning has
shown a steady evolution in response to historical changes.
Wright intensified and fortified his arguments, but never revised
his plan.

        It has not been my primary intention to pass professional
judgment on Wright's scheme, but rather to try to describe how
and why it arose and flourished in the mind of the artistic genius
who conceived it. I have found that Broadacre City serves as an
excellent pilot study of the historical development of Wright's
concepts -- the way that an idea grew with him, attached itself
to other schemes and images -- the way in which his architectural thinking got tied up with his prejudices about politics and
economics and with his paternalistic image of his own family and
apprentices -- the way in which he created by borrowing, fighting,
polemicizing, interweaving essential ideas with a richly expressionistic verbiage and ornament. Key historical figures of his
acquaintance pass through its pages. He provoked uncritical
adulation, party-line condemnation, professional jealousies --
but through it all he remained unperturbed. To the very end he
fended off his critics, commenting, ". . . as for the clichés, . . .
I made the original of every cliché myself."

        His Broadacre City is not a usable enough scheme to be
palatable to the professional planner, and it is too private a
dream to satisfy our definition of Utopia. As a receptacle for a
society it seems incomplete in many respects. On the other
hand it exudes the desperate hopes of the depression-wracked
nineteen-thirties, when Wright was designing it. And irritating
as his manner of presentation may be, there were truly prophetic
words to be found therein -- his irritation with the state of the
City is shared by many of us who are most attached to that
institution.

As Ray Stannard Baker (Wright's exact contemporary) wrote in his Adventures in Contentment which so many of us were required to read in school: "It was good to escape that place of hurrying strangers. It was good to get one's feet down into the soil. It was good to be in a place where things are because they grow, and politics not less than corn! Oh, my friend, say what you please, argue how you like, this crowding together of men and women in unnatural surroundings, this haste to be rich in material things, this attempt to enjoy without production, this removal from first-hand life, is irrational, and the end of it is ruin. If our cities were not recruited constantly with the fresh, clean blood of the country, with boys who still retain some of the power and the vision drawn from the soil, where would they be!"

Thus spoke Frank Lloyd Wright, too.

"Looking backward," then, Broadacre City as an idea has much in common with the Model "A" Ford in whose image it was, in part, conceived by Wright: chugging down the "centerline" of a vast highway system, noisy and repetitive, ungainly and unbeloved, dripping oil, belching smoke, scattering its nuts and bolts far and wide, but going on and on through edition after edition by virtue of some inexplicable miracle of its tenacious, even if phony, Americanism.

George R. Collins is Professor of Art History at Columbia University. One of his special fields is the development of modern city planning. He is writing a book on linear planning theory, parts of which have appeared in the Architectural Review (November, 1960) and elsewhere. In press (Phaidon/Random House) is a new English translation and analytical study of Camillo Sitte's Der Städtebau, prepared by Professor Collins and his wife.

THE DOMESTIC ARCHITECTURE OF FRANK LLOYD WRIGHT

Norris Smith

It has become customary nowadays to praise Wright for such things as his "use of space", his development of the free or open house plan, his organic adaptation of the house to its natural site, and his ingenious exploitation of the nature of his materials. Whether or not Wright was in fact solely responsible for these innovations in house design, his name has come to be associated with them, and they are generally thought to embody his chief contributions to modern domestic architecture. Well before his death they had all been so widely accepted as to have become the clichés of contemporary style -- yet he himself was disappointed in the results of that conquest and felt that the point he had tried to make had largely been missed.

One can thumb through any publication of recent houses and find innumerable examples of the tree-shrouded or cliff-hung dwelling, with its wide-open plan and its striking structural novelties, but one does not readily mistake such buildings for Wright's work; they are not specimens of what he called "the natural house." Wherein does the difference lie? We cannot find out, I believe, by refining our methods of esthetic and structural analysis so as to better describe the differences between Wright's and other houses. His own were too various to be dealt with in terms of a manageable typology. We would do better, instead, to consider his commitments and his convictions, which were not those of the conventional modern architect.

I should like to submit that Wright's distinction as a domestic architect stemmed not so much from his inventive originality as a designer, or from his use of space or materials or structures, as from his profoundly ethical concern for the institutions of the state, the city, and the family, and for the relation of the free man to those institutions. I would celebrate, therefore, not so much Wright's modernity as what he himself recognized from the very beginning to be his conservatism.

Wright understood, as most modern architects apparently have not, that the great buildings of our past have served as structural metaphors, declaring in their own ordering something about the power of institutions to give order; affirming in their structural patterns something about those patterns of relatedness among men which make possible the existence of that more or less precarious fabric of institutionalized relationships which constitutes the state. As early as 1900, Wright wrote that civilization must take the natural man to fit him for his place in this great piece of architecture we call the social state. Later, in his Autobiography, he declared that "since all form is a matter of structure, it is a matter of government as well as a matter of architecture; a matter of the framework of a society." It was this relationship between buildings and institutions, as Wright saw it, which had made architecture the very embodiment of the "spirit of law and order."

During the nineteenth century, however, architecture had come to be put to a novel and quite different use: namely, that of conjuring up, in the single observer, emotionally charged associations with one or another of the great ages of the historical world-drama -- Roman, Gothic, Renaissance, and so on. It was presumed that each of those ages had possessed a unique spirit or rhythm or tonality of its own; that the architect's function had always been to express the spirit of his age in visible forms; and, furthermore, that a great building in a given style could somehow arouse or inculcate a corresponding spiritual attitude in a modern individual -- whence the enthusiasm for building Gothic churches in the days of Ruskin and Carlyle. In all this, the structure-giving role of the institution was made secondary to, or eliminated in favor of, the emotional experience of the private person.

77

It seems generally to be taken for granted today that the distinctively modern architecture of the twentieth century had its origins in a drastic reaction against this historicistic aberration. I would argue, on the contrary, that our mechanistic contemporary style is based on precisely those Victorian presuppositions about architecture which undergirded the Gothic revival a century ago: it results, that is, from a self-conscious attempt on the part of the architect to invent a style that will express what he presumes to be the scientific and technological spirit of our age and that will at the same time propagate and inculcate that spirit in a recalcitrant populace which inclines all too readily toward a thoroughly nonscientific emotionality, irrationality, and even violence. His concern for institutional metaphor, however, is no greater than was his eclectic predecessor.

Taking the broadest view of the matter, then, I would celebrate Wright's memory because he brought back to life a conception of architecture as an art of eloquent affirmation concerning those institutions upon which rest the integrity and stability of the social order. The cause, as he himself avowed, was conservative, but has not architecture always been devoted to the maintenance of tradition and to the preservation of the establishment? One might well argue that a nonconservative architecture would be in its very nature an anomaly -- suitable at best only for housing such institutions as Trans-World Airlines and the House of Seagram, institutions toward which we are not invited to feel loyalty and in the existence and survival of which we have no emotional stake whatever. Perhaps it has been the greatest of disasters for modern architecture that such institutions are very numerous and very rich in this day and age, and that their managerial directors have come to look upon expensive new buildings as prime status symbols and good advertising.

The greatness of Wright's architecture, on the other hand, is bound up with his profoundly conservative commitment to an institution and to a tradition. The institution, of course, was the middle class private family. From first to last he was a domestic architect, the greatest house-builder of his century -- and for the very

78

reason that his own relationship to the institution of the family was so charged with emotion and so ambivalent. By his earliest childhood experiences he was made aware of the trying aspects of marriage, as well as to the blessings of family solidarity, while his own much-publicized difficulties with the institution of matrimony are common knowledge. It was the strength of his architectural imagination that he found the essence of the problem of human relatedness to reside in the structure of the private family. At the very end of his life he could still write, "The true center (the only centralization allowable) in Usonian democracy is the individual in his Usonian family home. In that we have the nuclear building we will learn how to build." His concern scarcely extended beyond its limits. He was relatively indifferent to both the constitutional theory and the political realities of the United States government; and while he loved Chicago, his interest in the structure and planning of cities, as they presently exist, was confined to the residential suburb.

The tradition Wright defended was that of romanticism -- specifically, that strain of romanticism which descends from Rousseau by way of Goethe, Carlyle, Emerson, Thoreau, and Whitman. Now one of the distinctive characteristics of romantic thought is its attraction toward opposite and extreme positions -- in contrast to the classicist's preoccupation with the median and the norm. Wright's life and outlook were filled with apparently irreconcilable contrasts. In his very nature he was a radical and rebellious conservative, an ostentatious defender of unpretentious simplicity, a champion of machine-age modernity whose highest admiration was reserved for the culture of feudal Japan. He could advocate, in Broadacres, a program of decentralization so thoroughgoing as to eradicate the city from the landscape; but at the same time he could design the Mile-High building, which would have brought about the greatest concentration of humanity ever envisioned in the history of architecture. He was an anarchist, intransigent in his opposition to the claims of governmental authority, and simultaneously a pan-archist, capable of conceiving a society in which virtually every aspect of life would be brought under the supervision of the state. All this is part and parcel of

79

a tradition which can be traced back at least as far as Rousseau, between whose books, _Emile_ and _The Social Contract,_ one finds this kind of polar opposition to exist; and beyond Rousseau there lies a venerable religious tradition in which paradise is envisioned at one and the same time as an open garden and as a fortress city.

The ethical tradition is a very old one. However, the art of architecture has generally done service in defense of its collective and institutional aspect rather than, and even at the expense of, its personal and individualizing one. The art of building has all too often been the monopoly of a ruling aristocracy, serving the special interests of that class. Today it is no longer the instrument of that class; institutions claim less for themselves, individuals claim more. Yet it does not follow that the values of personal freedom are all-sufficient -- that the values of loyalty and commitment need no longer be matters of concern to us -- that we have no desire to experience a meaningful and responsible participation in the body politic, no anxiety about the possibility of doing so. Not at all. There is much in modern life that diminishes the ethical stature of man -- much that suggests it is possibly the case that when the traditions and institutions of our society become meaningless, our personal freedom becomes meaningless, also. Such was Wright's conviction, at least, and he was concerned throughout his life to defend and to reinterpret that polaristic tradition of high spiritual tension to which Bellini and Rousseau and Whitman, in their different ways, had been devoted, and to reassess the institution of the family in the light of that tradition.

In Oak Park Wright tried to create a new image of the free man's family home within the context of the gridiron pattern of the American city, and tried at the same time to establish for himself a new and different kind of family within the context of the prevailing conventions of the American suburb. In neither effort was he successful. He and his wife brought into being a large and lively family of six children, in a household which, we are told, had the perpetual air of a jolly carnival; yet the very closeness of the relationship apparently caused Wright to feel

80

trapped and possessed, stifled by suburban domesticity -- so
that in the end, and in defiance of every law and convention, he
abandoned his home and fled.

In architecture, during that same period, he oscillated
continuously between two poles: on the one hand, that of a formal
regularity that bespoke the sheltering unity and structural integrity of the family; on the other, that of a rambling irregula-
rity which affirmed the relative independence of the component
members from one another and from a single all-governing principle of order. One finds a similar contrast frequently between
his dining rooms and his living rooms. The former are like state-
ly council chambers, emphasizing the family's containment within
a single pattern, its oneness of purpose at the dinner table; while
the latter are composed of what Wright himself called an architecture of disarray, a casual assembly of varied and loosely joined
members, affirming the value of what is spontaneous, personal,
informal, and diversified in domestic life.

While Wright found it difficult to reconcile these opposing
principles within a single house, he found it still harder to set his
houses into the framework of the larger community. He liked them
to look novel and distinctive -- different from one another and different from the works of other architects; yet at the same time he was
very much committed to an idea of social and cultural unity and
looked forward to the day when his kind of architecture would be uni-
versally adopted (though nothing was more offensive to him than for
someone else to build a house that resembled one of his own). He
would have liked to see, he said, as many styles of house as there
are styles of person and argued that every house should express the
unique personality of its owner; yet he repeatedly returned to his
Quadruple Block proposal, which would have put an indefinitely
large number of identical houses, in groups of four, on a series of
identical city blocks -- not for the sake of economy but rather for
the sake of a unified image of the city.

81

Already as early as 1902 another possibility occurred to Wright, which was to abandon the city's grid altogether and to root his rambling houses directly in the irregularities of the natural landscape. Eventually he himself found it necessary to escape the trap of suburban conventionality by fleeing to the country, there to begin again with a new kind of a marriage and a new kind of house, but he did not by that act resolve the problem of the proper expression of the values of membership, collectivity, and agreement -- the problem of the city. In purely theoretical terms he resolved that dichotomy, that horned dilemma that was inherent in his polaristic romanticism, in his vision of Broadacre City; but he recognized clearly enough, even though he did not often admit it, that Broadacres could not possibly be built under the conditions of our corrupt and mortal existence. For Broadacres is an earthly paradise into which we are not eligible to enter.

Let me conclude with a quotation from the late Albert Camus. "As a result of rejecting everything, even the traditions of his art, the contemporary artist gets the illusion that he is creating his own rule and eventually takes himself for God. At the same time he thinks he can create his reality himself. But cut off from his society, he will create nothing but formal or abstract works, thrilling as experiences but devoid of the fecundity we associate with true art, which is called upon to unite." While many an architect today would readily acknowledge the applicability of Camus' criticism to recent painting, there appears to be a strong inclination in the profession to believe, as I have already suggested, that the modern architect is doing what architects have always done -- that is, to meet his society's needs by exploiting its technological potentialities, and in so doing to express the spirit or character of his age. But all of that has nothing to do with the ethical and spiritual traditions of our society, nor with the traditional concern of the architect to interpret, through structural metaphors, the patterns of relatedness that make it possible for a society to endure. Wright's architecture, I believe, possessed the fecundity of true art precisely for the reason that he was not cut off from such traditions but recognized, instead,

that what the artists of all ages have been called upon to do is
to reassess, in the light of a changing situation, that body of
meaning and of civilizing truth which has been received.   And
in an age that values originality and inventiveness, he demonstrated that that can be done without adopting the architectural
vocabulary of an earlier period.

I do not mean to say that Wright's buildings should serve
as models for a new generation of architects, or that the traditions of Rousseauistic romanticism are preeminently worthy
of our regard.   My contention is only that great architecture
arises, not out of technological achievement but out of a warm
and sympathetic commitment to the institutions and the traditions
of a civilization.

Dr. Smith is a graduate of Columbia University and, at present,
professor of art and archaeology, and an architectural critic,
at Washington University in St. Louis.

WRIGHT AND THE SPIRIT OF DEMOCRACY

James Marston Fitch

Frank Lloyd Wright did his most prescient work at what was really the very dawn of our present era, but in his approach to the problem of industrialization and modern technology, he established certain criteria in design which are still extremely viable. When Wright first appeared on the scene, science, technology, and industry were highly advanced, placing in solution all the old verities of Jefferson's republic. A new world was waiting to be born, and with it, a new architecture.

To its creation, Wright contributed as much as any man alive. He has been called the inventor of the modern American house. And, certainly, during a long and fruitful life, he brought to it a level of comfort and amenity which, before him, could have been found only in Newport or Fifth Avenue, and a kind of domestic beauty which was entirely new. His houses have made available to the ordinary middle class American family an environment of spacious ease and luminous urbanity such as only the rich could have afforded before him. Like Jefferson, whom he admired immensely, albeit in a quite different context and on a much higher level, he took the burgeoning material accomplishments of his world and put them to work for the enrichment of our people generally.

When Wright began his architectural practice in Chicago in the early 1890's, a basic change had already occurred in American life. The old self-sufficient family of Jefferson's republic which produced most of the food it ate, the clothes it wore, the furniture it lived with, the very house that sheltered it -- this family and this way of life were already declining. In that family's place was appearing a new kind of family -- a family of

84

consumers, which, instead of producing what it ate and wore, bought it with earned wages from the stores. Today, beset with contemporary problems, we may tend to regret this change when we look back at this pre-industrial way of life with a nostalgia not always very firmly bedded in fact. Today, the very word homemade and handmade are terms of praise, trademarks of chic. But, fifty or seventy-five years ago, these same words were terms of disparagement, reproach, and contempt. Now, there are doubtless real merits to homemade, home-baked bread, home-cured meats, and home-woven cloth. But the hard, often noisome labor connected with their preparation was not one of them. Here we must take the word of our own grandmothers who had to do this work and only too gladly gave it up. For them, housework meant the stupefying heat of the kitchen on a July day, the squalid labor of the washtub, the stench and flies from the pigpen. The fact was that most homes were little factories, and most wives were slaves to a sweatshop schedule.

Under such conditions, most houses were uncomfortable to live in and unbeautiful to look at. Here again, we must take the testimony of the women. Why did they labor so hard to create front yards, front doors, front rooms, if not to conceal the ugliness of the rear? Why this effort to create little islands of peace and beauty? Why, if not for occasional escape from the grinding routine of the pre-industrial household?

For these women, cleanliness meant a constant struggle. Comfort was sometimes won, beauty almost never. No wonder they were turning with such enthusiasm to the labor-saving, comfort-making devices which American factories were turning out in the decade that Wright began to work. Thanks to industrialization, the never-ending drudgery of housekeeping was being lifted from the housewife's shoulders. The most degrading and stultifying processes of family sustenance were being removed from the home. The ordinary housewife was becoming able to join the human race, to enjoy the comfort, leisure, and self respect which had hitherto been the prerogative of rich, slave or servant attended women.

85

But there was another, and for architects an even more important side to this phenomenon: the same process which had been removing from the house the causes of most of its hard labor, inconvenience, and discomfort, was also removing the cause of most of its ugliness. For the first time in history, the home of the average family could be a thing of beauty; not just the front parlor, or the front yard, but all of it, inside and out, could be an object of pleasure and delight. We can say -- I think without fear of contradiction -- that Wright was the first American architect fully to understand this new fact, fully to explore its possibilities. It would be nonsense, of course, to claim that Wright, in those early days of the new American house, was the only, or even the first, architect to use central heating, plumbing, electricity, or all the host of new structural materials. His contemporaries used all these things enthusiastically. But they forced them into old, conventional designs. They employed steam radiators, but they meshed them behind Renaissance grilles; steel columns and beams, but they sheathed them to look like wood and marble; modern plumbing fixtures, but they patterned them to look like bishop's chairs.

Wright's role was of quite another order. He saw that all these developments taken together demanded nothing less than a totally new system of architectural expression. The old traditional forms simply could not contain the new order -- a new kind of beauty was called for.

The technology which had wrought such profound changes in family life had also given the architect a whole new palette of building materials: steel, reinforced concrete, plywood, huge sheets of rolled plate glass. And Frank Lloyd Wright, almost alone in those early days, argued that these should be employed boldly and honestly in new forms and not tortured into traditional ones. As a result of his independent approach, Wright was able to make very important architectural contributions to design -- contributions which became standard elements in the modern house. Only consider: by 1900 everybody who could afford it demanded central heating, either hot-air furnaces or steam heat. All the architects were including these in their new houses, but only Wright understood their ultimate implications, for they made obsolete the old honeycomb plan of boxy, airtight rooms strung like beads on a string. This had been a logical arrangement in cold climates so long as fireplaces and stoves were the only ways of heating rooms. But Wright was quick to see that, if all rooms could be kept equally comfortable with almost invisible heat sources, rooms could flow freely one into the other. Doors and whole walls could be eliminated. Rooms could dissolve into one another. The open plan was the result, the instrument which enabled Wright to create those splendid interior vistas for which his houses are justly famous.

Or again, by 1900 everyone was aware of the therapeutic value of sunshine, and was demanding more of it in his houses. Plate and rolled glass made possible windows of unprecedented size. But while other architects used more glass, they used it in conventional patterns, cutting up their sash into little Colonial rectangles, Elizabethan diamonds, or leaded Medieval bulls-eyes. Only Wright saw the dramatic possibilities of these huge transparent sheets. He saw that with them he could destroy the iron boundary between indoors and out. Here was another instrument of great power and beauty at his disposal. With it he could extend the living area to include not merely the enclosed space, but the terraces, porches, and gardens beyond. He thereby brought his interior space into a new and exciting proximity with nature.

Or, finally, by 1900, everyone was demanding electric lighting in his house. Its advantages over oil lamps and gas were obvious and immense. But electricity was not merely a substitute for coal gas and kerosene: it made possible a totally new concept of illumination. Instead of the niggardly pin-points of earlier light sources, electricity made it possible to flood whole areas with light. Spaces could be modeled, forms dramatized, textures enhanced. Who besides Wright, in those early days, understood this? While the rest of the profession continued to mask their Mazda bulbs in fixtures of conventional form -- candelabra, chandelier, and sconce -- Wright went boldly ahead building the anatorg bulb into the very fabric of the house. Light itself, and not just the fixture, became the source of pleasure and delight.

Wright always insisted upon his absolute independence from the esthetic forces of his time. He seemed to consider it an affront to his integrity as an artist to suggest that he might be influenced by his contemporaries. Influence was, for him, synonymous with plagiarism. He had spent so many arduous years fashioning his own idiom of expression, years in which his contemporaries were the most shameless eclectics, that he could not tolerate the suggestion of a connection, no matter how remote or indirect, with the men around him. He denied all such connections, and this sometimes led him into absurd semantic difficulties as when he called Sullivan "lieber Meister" and simultaneously asserted that he owed nothing to the older man. The fact is that Wright, like all truly great artists, was extremely sensitive to the world around him. Verbally he might deny the influence of Sullivan, of Japanese art and art nouveau, of cubism, of the North American Indian, and pre-Columbian art; artistically his buildings contradict him. They show beyond a shadow of a doubt how responsive he was. Like a seismograph, his work registers every insignificant tremor in the world of art. But unlike a seismograph, his great creative talent always transformed these external stimuli into forms inescapably his own.

It is sad to think that he ever felt it necessary to assert his originality; his work itself proves him to be, like Picasso and Corbusier, among the greatest artistic inventors of all time. Nor was the miracle of Wright's response to these stimuli exclusively a matter of esthetics. Nontechnical problems always underlay them, and Wright's mastery of them is the evidence of the uniqueness of this contribution.

This process is very clear, for example, in the lovely Millard and Ennis houses in California, both of which belong to his so-called Mayan period of the early 1920's. They are clearly influenced by pre-Columbian architecture, whose acquaintance he had first made long ago at the Columbian Exposition. But these houses are not copies. The shining gravity of the Mayan temples sprang from their sculpture-encrusted limestone masonry. Wright could not, in fact, have copied these even if he had wanted to: the budget would not have permitted either carved sculpture or limestone, and the building codes of a California often shaken by earthquakes would have advised against rubble masonry walls. We can see instead the Wrightian process of transmutation; the special alchemy by which he extracted beauty from his cheapest building material, concrete, fabricated in its commonest form, cast block. Some of these blocks are plain, some are cast in geometric pattern. For all their basic simplicity, these create a rich and intricate fabric when woven into a wall. And this wall was simultaneously made as strong as it is handsome by an earthquake-resistant system of integral reinforcing ribs. The apparently effortless way in which Wright solved such problems lends an air of deceptive simplicity to his solutions. One needs almost to be an expert to understand the complexity beneath him.

Actually, as I have pointed out, he demonstrated this uncanny capacity to absorb technological advance and convert it into new esthetic discoveries very early in his career. And his career is marked continuously by such successive masteries of technological development. When all his colleagues were going to great lengths to conceal their electric lighting, steam heat, and steel frames in traditional forms, Wright was using them as a means of escape from the prison house of eclecticism. Out of technical progress, he made esthetic inventions. He is in this sense one of the few inventors of modern American architecture.

In the catalog for his 1954 exhibition house at the Guggenheim Museum, Wright said wryly that he would be accused of arrogance if he claimed that his early houses were the first "truly democratic expression of our democracy." Yet it is true that a distinguishing mark of his houses had, from the start, been their modesty.

Even large and expensive ones such as the Coonley or the Kaufmann houses lacked that browbeating pretentiousness which was always the trade mark of the homes of the wealthy.

Big or small, Wright's houses have always had the grace and urbanity of a mansion, but this is never the result of just shrinking the mansion down to cottage size, as the Amazon headhunter does his trophies. Many of his contemporaries tried that, but not Wright. Even his own house at Taliesin East, actually one of the largest country houses in America, is so demurely fitted into its terrain that its real size is never apparent. It is, on the contrary, deliberately concealed. There are impressive, even majestic vistas in these houses, but they are designed to delight the inhabitants, and not to overawe the passerby.

All elements of a house were to Wright equally important and hence equally beautiful. It had no front and consequently could have no back. Wright's houses were also, from the start, democratic in their choice of materials. The cost or rarity of a building material was never for him an argument either for or against it. He could create interiors of magnificent warmth, of stunning luxury, with the simplest materials -- wood, brick, plaster -- while his contemporaries were using imported marbles, cut velvets, and gold leaf with much less effect. How can one explain this? Wright said it was because these other architects had no real feeling for the nature of their materials. Because of this, they cut, carved, chiseled, clipped, painted, and stenciled. He, on the contrary, extracted from each material, no matter what it was, its peculiar properties, and then expressed them clearly in the way he used them. The result was a lack of bombast and pretension which had not been seen since Jefferson's day.

It is strange indeed that men who should have known better could have misunderstood Wright's principles, could have attacked them as "un-American" (as the American Legion did in the United States Air Force Academy case). A more typical American than Wright never lived. His strengths and his weaknesses are ours.

90

His artistic declaration of independence was at the esthetic level the precise equivalent of our noblest social and cultural perspectives. Both envisioned the fullest development of the individual in a new kind of society, free of the fetters of the past, the hierarchies of king and clergy, of hereditary power and privilege. Just as the Bill of Rights denies them power, so Wright's architecture rejects all of their iconography of caste, power, and privilege. His houses, like those of Jefferson, even the largest and most expensive, are democratic in spirit. The analogy, of course, is not accidental; Wright greatly admired Jefferson, and like him he was persuaded that democracy is the best forcing bed of ability, talent, and genius. Its function is to produce for each generation a cadre of true leaders, an aristocracy of intelligence and ability, not of inherited wealth and title.

Wright's youth had been spent in threadbare parsonage parlors, whose genteel, constricting poverty had provoked an allergic response of pride and arrogance from a thin-skinned and sensitive young man. Most of his adult life, on the other hand, was spent against a background of beauty and physical ease. But this never led to snobbery in Wright; he was entirely unlike the typical self-made man, that parvenu American who uses democracy merely to climb to the seats of power, and then, by denying his origin, dons the traditional accoutrements of power. It was precisely this American whom Wright detested as a climber, who in a desperate bid for a prefabricated background, bought geneology, coat-of-arms, period furniture, and an eclectic house.

The architectural expression of Wright's response to democracy and industrialism took the form of two of the loveliest houses in the world. To his Taliesins in Arizona and Wisconsin, he brought a real splendor, the excitement of a presence larger than life, a touch both passionate and gentle, and a composition at once both lyrical and strong. No one who ever had the privilege of visiting his Taliesins when Wright was in residence could fail to feel himself ensconced in a special kind of oasis, in which the raw and hostile forces of surrounding life had somehow or another been reorganized into a landscape of blessed peace and plenty. In these two wonderful houses, of all the wonderful buildings he designed, we can most clearly see the sort of world his genius would have built for us, had we but fully used it.

For a biography of Mr. Fitch, see page 23.

MIES van der ROHE, Ludwig, architect; b. Aachen, Germany, Mar. 27, 1886; D. Engring., Ill. Inst. Technology; LL.D., North Carolina State Colllege, 1956. Came to U.S., 1938, now naturalized Am. citizen. Began as apprentice to famous designers and architects of Europe; with Bruno Paul, furniture designer, Berlin 1905-07; apprentice, Peter Behrens, 1909; projected designs for steel and glass skyscrapers, 1919-21; for concrete office building, 1922; fgn. archtl. designs include, German bldg. Internat. Expn., Barcelona, Spain, 1920, Tugendhat house, Brno, Czechoslovakia, 1930, skyscraper on Friedrichstrasse, Berlin; also designed Seagram's bldg., N.Y.C. 20-story apt. building at 860 Lake Shore Drive, Chicago; formerly dir. Bauhaus School in Germany; dir. Sch. Architecture, Ill. Inst. Tech., ret. 1958, designer of Institute's campus, Chgo.; also designer of steel furniture. Served as 1st v.p. Deutscher Werkbund (orgn. to improve quality of indsl. design), 1926. Exhibited at Stuttgart, 1927; had one-man show of work Mus. Modern Art; N.Y.C. Recipient medal of honor Congress of Pan-Am. Architects, award of merit Ruskin Soc. of Am., Feltrinelli Internat. prize for architecture, Rome, Italy. Elected life mem. Order Pour la Merite (Germany). Fellow A.I.A., Am. Academy of Arts and Sciences; member of the Russian Acad. Art, Soc. Mex. Architects, Royal Inst. Brit. Architects, Internat. Congress Modern Architecture, Ill. Soc. Architects, Am. Assn. U. Profs., Am. Soc. Engring. Edn., Coll. Art Assn. of Am., Am. Inst. Arts and Letters. Home: 200 E. Pearson St. Office: 230 E. Ohio St., Chgo.

--from Who's Who in America, Volume 32, 1962-1963. Chicago: A.N. Marquis, 1962. (Used with permission of the publishers.)

emotional expressions. I don't trust them, and I don't think they will last for long.

BLAKE: Do you feel that you have come to your kind of architecture through construction and through knowing about how things are built, rather than through theory?

MIES: I think that goes together. I thought about architecture, and then I tried architecture to prove it. Often, experience showed that my thoughts were in no way right, but many times, experience proved my thoughts correct.

BLAKE: What have you learned from the old things in Europe? A lot of people, when describing your work, refer to Schinkel and even to the Renaissance.

MIES: When I came as a young man to Berlin and looked around, I was interested in Schinkel because Schinkel was the most important architect in Berlin. There were several others, but Schinkel was the most important man. His buildings were an excellent example of classicism -- the best I know. And certainly I became interested in that. I studied him carefully and came under his influence. That could have happened to anybody. I think Schinkel had wonderful constructions, excellent proportions, and good detailing.

BLAKE: What about the way Schinkel places his buildings on pedestals?

MIES: I think that is a good way of doing it, in spite of the fact that it is a classic way of doing it.

BLAKE: In your early work there was a tremendously sudden break. Whereas you had been working in the classical tradition up to the beginning of World War I, in 1919 you seem to have broken completely with everything you had done before.

MIES: I think the break started long before. The break started when I was in the Netherlands working on the problem of the Kröller museum. There I saw and studied carefully Berlage. I read his books and his theme that architecture should be construction, clear construction. His architecture was brick, and it may have looked medieval, but it was always clear.

BLAKE: You know, people who refer to your work now as being classical in spirit also say that the tradition of architecture in America, at least in the past one hundred years, has been romantic and anti-classical; organic in the case of Wright and quite romantic in the case of Richardson. Do you feel that your architecture is in any way in conflict with the basic motives of American architecture -- that it is a stationary kind of thing as opposed to a moving kind of thing, which seems to be the American theme?

MIES: I never think about it in these terms. And I think it is quite dangerous. You know, we had in Europe and in England, Morris, some, Arts and Crafts people, and we had them in Germany. We were quite romantic. I think that the main difference is that in the nineteenth century there was a great confusion. You could say that is a phase of democracy, but democracy does not have to be confused.

BLAKE: If you compare the Barcelona Pavilion with the first building at Illinois Tech, the Barcelona Pavilion had a very strong sweep. It was almost a building in motion, at least that is the way it looks in photographs. The buildings at Illinois Tech are very stable, very clear. They are objects that are standing there and are completely enclosed within themselves. Don't you feel there is quite a change between those two buildings?

MIES: No. If you remember, I made one design for the campus (it was not built) where I removed most of the streets, so that I could place the buildings freely there. I was told by Henry Heald, the president, that it could not be done at the moment. They would not permit me until much later to remove the streets. So

I was confronted with the past -- I had to develop a plan in the normal block pattern, and I did that. You cannot do much about it. And there is another question, too. To make things in motion, is that not a handicap to modern architecture and to building? We had to build school buildings, and we didn't know often for what they would be used. So we had to find a system that made it possible to use these buildings as classrooms, as workshops, or as laboratories.

BLAKE: One of the things that is sometimes suggested about your idea of a universal space, a building that might be used for one thing today and something entirely different ten or twenty years from now, is that the American economy depends upon rapid obsolescence of buildings, so that people can be kept at work. Do you think that the idea of a universal kind of architecture is a threat to the idea of some kind of accelerated obsolescence?

MIES: First, let me say that I think that the idea of rapid obsolescence is a very funny idea. I don't even think it is a good idea. I think that obsolescence is a kind of excuse. I don't think it is a real fact. There are things that don't have to last for a lifetime. This suit, for instance. In older times, we had one suit when we married, and we kept that all the time for good. Otherwise, we had only working clothes. That is no longer necessary -- that it will last forever. There are things that can be replaced and of necessity will be replaced, but I wonder if the buildings will be replaced. ... No, I think we should be reasonable. You don't have to build like the pyramids, to last thousands of years. But a building should live as long as it can live. There is no reason to make it just provisional. In that case, they should build a tent!

I come more and more to the conviction that architecture has a certain relation to civilization. If somebody says architecture is not related to civilization, there isn't any use talking about it. I personally believe that it does, and this seems to me the main task we have: to build an architecture which expresses this kind of civilization we are in. That is the only way I can see to overcome chaos.

96

Our civilization depends largely on science and technology.
That is a fact. Everybody should see that. The question is how
far we can express that. You know, we architects are in this
peculiar position. We should express the time and yet build in it.
But in the end, I really believe that architecture can only be
the expression of its civilization.

BLAKE: What would you say is the main problem of architecture
in America? What can architecture do to change the American
scene as it looks now, and how should architects go about it?

MIES: Yes, I think that is in fact the most important question.
You know, if somebody doesn't agree with me that there is a
relation, that architecture is only possible in relation to civilization, then there is no use in talking about it. But if somebody
accepts that, then we can ask ourselves: what kind of relation
is there, and what is our civilization like? Everybody talks a-
bout it, but it is really difficult to define. Civilization is a process partly of the past and partly of the present, and it is partly
open to the future. So it is really difficult to find in this moving
process the characteristic of civilization.

It is not enough that somebody has some ideas. It is not
enought to just say these things are architecture or just say, "That
is what I like to do." We had that when I was young. I listened
to these great people, around 1900. We were talented, we had
everything you could ask for to work in the field of architecture,
but we were just subjective, in my opinion, as most people are
subjective today. I think we can move on only if we really find
some ground to stand on. Architecture, in my opinion, is not a
subjective affair. The tendency should be in an objective direction.

BLAKE: To a great many artists (including some architects), the
natural reaction to our time is to revolt and be different. Do you
think that it is excusable for an architect to react to his time by
being different from his time?

MIES: No, I think it isn't. I believe he cannot, so that makes
it hopeless to try. But I don't believe that everything has to be
the same. But there must be, and I am sure there are, certain
fundamental principles that are given. We are, to a very small
degree, craftsmen. We build these machines. We use them.
More and more buildings become the product of machine production.

BLAKE: In the last few years Le Corbusier has been going in
the opposite direction -- making buildings more crude. There
are almost no details in his buildings any more. They are crudely
done and deliberately so. Do you think that that is the wrong
direction to take today?

MIES: I would not say the wrong direction. Le Corbusier, when
he made his postwar buildings, had to work with these primitive
craftsmen, and I think that is one of the reasons why he could
make them primitive. It was in France outside of Marseilles.
What would you think of such a rough building on Park Avenue?
Where the people that go into the building and out of the building
are well-dressed?

BLAKE: If you were building in India, as Le Corbusier is today,
how do you think you would build?

MIES: As simply as possible. If I could not use advanced technological means, then I would have to do what they did in former
times -- work with the hands.

BLAKE: If we are going to have these very complex mechanical
systems in buildings, doesn't it make some sort of sense to dramatize the mechanics of a building?

MIES: I think structural elements are very essential elements,
and I think that pipes are not. The structure can be integrated
into architecture, but I don't think that pipes can. We can bring
the pipes into our buildings, where they belong, you know.

BLAKE: Le Corbusier, in some of his buildings, has dramatized the mechanical parts, so maybe there are ways of elevating pipes into architecture too.

MIES: That is possible, and I think Le Corbusier did it well. But not everybody can do that, and I see no reason why everybody should do that.

BLAKE: When you talk about structure, I think most of the time you still talk about rectangular structures because they are the most reasonable, practical, and economical. But now that it is at least possible to have a very fluid structure, what do you think might happen to architecture if those very fluid structures take over from the simple rectangle?

MIES: I don't think that they will take over. I think fluid structures, like shells, have a very limited use. They are, in fact, open structures. You build a one-story building, and you can do about what you like with it; maybe in a two, even a three-story building, you are to a certain degree free. But then it ends. How can you use them in a tall building? For most things we do, we need space: living space, working space. If there is no reason for it, why make them fluid? A rectangular space is a good space, maybe much better than a fluid space. If you have some particular function or something that is fluid inside, I think it is a good idea to make it curved. But, it is not a good idea to make an office space an organic form just for esthetic reasons. You can do it if you have a theater, or a single building, or a site where you can be free-moving. But most of our buildings are quite patterned by the city.

BLAKE: People who are very much interested in these fluid structures think that if you were to do a whole city, it would be a rather dull place -- that the buildings would be very much alike, and that maybe there is some need for variation here and there.

MIES: But see the medieval cities -- there is a good example. All the houses are really the same. All the plans are really the same.

But who could afford it put in a fine entrance hall; you might buy and put on a fine door knocker; and if somebody could afford a bay window, he did that. But the plans are the same, and how rich is the medieval city!

BLAKE: Wright's buildings in the cities, at least his buildings in the last twenty years, seemed to have been very antagonistic towards the city.

MIES: Yes, certainly. I do not share his position, you know. I believe that you have to accept the reality. I don't think anybody can change it by a theoretical formula. I have seen that tried too often, and it has gone to pieces. I would accept it and then do something with it. That is the problem, you know. People often think I have a formula when I talk about structure. They think that I am talking about a steel beam. I'm not, you know. That has nothing to do with it. You can build in concrete. But if I had to build in concrete, I would not build like Wright. I see no reason for that, because I believe that these Wright things don't belong to our time.

BLAKE: Do you think that in a free enterprise democracy, where everyone is free to do just about what he wants within very slight limitations, that it is possible to create architectural order?

MIES: Yes, I think it would be an order in freedom.

BLAKE: But, do you think that it requires, perhaps, discipline on the part of the architects before it could work? Or how would you put it?

MIES: I certainly think that it requires discipline on the part of the architects. I think even Wright needed a lot of discipline in his work.

BLAKE: It seems to me that in some of your early buildings like the Barcelona Pavilion, there are traces of Wright's principles. To what extent has Wright impressed you and influenced your work?

MIES: For Philip Johnson's book, I wrote about Wright and the influence he had on us in Europe. Certainly, I was very much impressed by the Robie house and by the office building in Buffalo. Who wouldn't be impressed? He was certainly a great genius -- there is no question about that. You know, it is very difficult to go in his direction. You sense that his architecture is based on fantasy. You have to have fantasy in order to go in this direction, and if you have fantasy, you don't go in his direction, you go in your own! Wright had a great influence, but very late in his life. But his influence on the face of America is quite modest.

BLAKE: A lot of art critics claim that your work is very much influenced by De Stijl, by van Doesburg.

MIES: No, that is absolute nonsense, you know.

BLAKE: Why don't you explain why?

MIES: Van Doesburg saw these drawings of the office building. I explained it to him, and I said, "This is skin-and-bones architecture." After that he called me an anatomical architect. I liked van Doesburg, but not as though he knew very much about architecture. He designed houses or buildings together with van Eesteren, the city planner. But mostly he was interested in his particular kind of art. Like Mondrian. Once in Düsseldorf he proposed the dictum that everything should be square! But there is no influence. The same people claim that I was influenced by Mondrian in the first building for the I. I. T. campus, the Metals Building. This one has a wall that they say looks like Mondrian. But I remember very well how it came about. Everything was donated for this whole building. The site -- we had 64 feet from the railroad to the sidewalk. Somebody gave them a traveling crane -- it was 40 feet wide, so we needed 42 feet from center of column to center of column. The rest was laboratories, you know. Everything was there -- we needed steel bracing in the wall, the brick wall. It was a question of the building code. You can only make an eight-inch wall

101

so big, otherwise you have to reinforce it. So we did that.
Then when everything was finished, the people from the
Metals Building, the engineers, they came and said, "We
need here a door." So I put in a door. And the result was
the Mondrian!

BLAKE: What about the constructivists -- the Russian constructivists? Were you interested in their work?

MIES: No, I was never interested in formalistic ideas. I
was very strongly opposed even to Malevich, you know. Very
constructivistic. I was interested in construction, but not
in play with forms.

BLAKE: One of the things that is interesting about you, at
least to those of us who know you today, is that you seem rather conservative in many ways -- in your bearing, in your
work, in your preferences, and so on, and yet in the early twenties
and right after World War I you must have been a wild radical.
You were involved in very radical movements at the time. How
do you account for the change?

MIES: I don't think there is a change. I think there is a natural development. In the early twenties I tried to understand
architecture, and I tried to find positive solutions, and I am
still doing that now, you know. I don't construct sociological
systems. But I am very much interested in the question of
Civilization. What is it. What is going on. This is not the
system or the work of one man. It is the work of many. Civilization is given to us from the past, and all we can do is to
guide it. I don't think we can change it fundamentally. We can
do something with it in a good way or in a bad way.

BLAKE: Illinois Tech, which is the expression of your ideas on
education, is perhaps the most rigid and formal school in America today. What motivated you to make Illinois Tech what it is,
and what do you expect the students to get out of the school?

MIES: You know, when I came here to the school and
I had to change the curriculum, I was just thinking
to find a method which teaches the student how to
make a good building. Nothing else. First, we taught
them how to draw. The first year is spent on that.
And they learn how to draw. Then we taught them
construction in stone, in brick, in wood, and made
them learn something about engineering. We talked
about concrete and steel. Then we taught them something about functions of buildings, and in the junior
year we tried to teach them a sense of proportion and
a sense of space. And only in the last year we came to
a group of buildings. And there I see no rigidness in
the curriculum at all. Because we try to make them
aware about the problems involved. We don't teach
them solutions, we teach them a way to solve problems.

BLAKE: You read a great deal of philosophy. What
philosophers interest you most . . . and what historians?

MIES: I was interested in architecture all my life.
And I have tried to find out what was said about architecture. I have tried to find out what can influence
architecture. I feel that architecture belongs to certain epochs; it expresses the real essence of its times.
It was to us a question of truth. How can we find out,
know, and feel what is the truth?

What I say is the result of a lifetime of work. It is
not a special idea I have when I say that architecture
should be the expression of structure. But the interrelation of these things was not clear at the time. So
all my reading was about what influences architecture.
When I read about sociology, I wanted to know what
ideas were there that would be an influence really on our
time.

I didn't want to change the time; I wanted to express
the time. That was my whole object. I didn't want to
change anything. I really believe that all these ideas,

103

the sociological ideas and even the technological ideas
would have an influence on architecture. But they are
not architecture themselves. What we really need is to
know how to build with any material, and that is what
is missing today.

Mr. Blake is a practicing architect, author of The Master
Builders (1960), a study of Mies, Wright, and Le Corbusier.
He has been curator of architecture and design at the Museum
of Modern Art, and is now editor of the Architectural Forum.

MIES VAN DER ROHE AT I. I. T.

Henry T. Heald

In these days of new technology and the practice of architecture by huge firms on a world-wide basis, only a handful of people in our lifetime have exerted a profound influence on architecture and society. All of us hope that creative architecture will continue to be an individual endeavor, even though its translation into final structure may involve a great corps of specialists. Architecture, like art, will continue to be an individual accomplishment.

I had the privilege of inviting one of these creative individuals, Mies van der Rohe, to take a position in this country. I invited him largely on the recommendation of John Holabird, a leading Chicago architect, who said, "I don't know Mies van der Rohe, but the Barcelona Pavilion and one or two other things that he has done are outstanding. And," he continued, "after all, even if we don't know too much about this fellow, he's so much better than any of the people you could get to head a school of architecture, why not take a chance?"

So we invited Mies, and after some time he accepted the post. I still remember the first day he came to my office on the old campus at Illinois Tech. He couldn't speak English, and my German was far from adequate, so we sat and looked at each other until one of our professors who had a mastery of German came in to interpret for us. That was our introduction to each other.

In his characteristically thorough fashion, Mies soon went to work to rebuild the architectural curriculum at the Institute. He was joined by Ludwig Hilberseimer, Walter Peterhans, and

105

by two Americans who were former students of his in Germany, Rogers and Priestly. In a very short time, I. I. T. became the only American school of architecture where the teaching was in German. Mies, a perfectionist, was reluctant to use English in public. It was not until after Pearl Harbor that he began to use English. I remember having lunch with him shortly after the beginning of the war. Somehow the question of language came up, and I said, "Why don't you start using English in your teaching?" He said, "Very well, we start now." And he did. Never after that did he do his teaching in German, and, of course, he soon became quite articulate in English.

I recall the dinner held by the architects in Chicago to welcome Mies to the city. As it turned out, this was a nightmare. The then president of the Chicago Chapter of the American Institute of Architects was a man who prided himself on his German. He delegated to himself the responsibility for and the honor of translating Mies's remarks to the group that evening. But his German and Mies's German didn't come out of the same book, and it early became evident that he was getting bogged down. Fortunately, Mies's young friend Rogers leapt into the breach, but Mies was never very popular with that particular gentleman.

I don't remember exactly what Frank Lloyd Wright, who came down from Taliesin to be the main speaker, said that night. I remember only the end of his speech: "Now I give you Mies van der Rohe -- God knows you need him!" Then he walked off the platform, stomped through the great hall filled with people, and left. I thought at the time that he went off to catch a train, but after the dinner was over, I found him at the bar, where he'd been waiting out the rest of the program.

Mies made his first American speech that night, and he hasn't made any others. As president of Illinois Tech, I used to think it would be nice to parade this ornament on our faculty. Once or twice I got him to agree to make a speech. But usually, as the date approached, it became evident that one of his associates was going to take his place. When I questioned Mies, his answer was, "Well, we do a good job, and people will know about it. We don't need to tell them."

The life and career of Mies were the result of forces which were not of his own making. He lost a lot of time in his professional career in World War I, and the Nazis ruined his European career about the time it was beginning to come to fruition. The invitation to teach at Illinois Tech came to him, in a sense, as an accidental combination of circumstances. Yet that, too, had a great influence on what he did in later years. It's interesting to speculate on what his career might have been had he accepted an invitation to go to, well, let's say to Columbia. I venture to say that he wouldn't have had an opportunity to design a new campus, much as Columbia might have needed it. There's much that is accidental in the career of a great architect. Mies would have been great under any circumstance, and like the rest of us, he has been influenced by the circumstances in which he found himself.

Mies came to Illinois Tech not to design a campus but to teach architecture and did develop a completely new program in the teaching of architecture. About that same time, the Institute was trying to provide new physical facilities, and a very happy combination of circumstances took place -- not every dean of a school of architecture is called on for advice on architecture in his own university.

Maybe Mies wouldn't have had this opportunity at Illinois Tech, if it had not been for an act of God, so to speak. One of the members of the Board of Trustees who was an architect and who who was ready to design the campus was called to his Maker. Well, this gave the president of the Institute a clear field. This made it possible to select as the architect of the new campus a man of unquestioned distinction, a man in whom we had already placed our faith and trust, and yet one who would not have been selected by a committee of Trustees, and certainly not by a committee of the faculty. In fact, after we began to execute Mies's designs, I recall meeting with a committee of the faculty, who said in effect, "Are you sure you shouldn't have your head examined for being a party to this construction?" This was after the first building was built. The sun shone in on one side, and it didn't have any closets, and there were other points which bothered the professors. Nevertheless, Mies proceeded with the total design of the campus.

It was a difficult task indeed. But those of you who think Mies is a man who is hard to work with and inflexible are very much mistaken. There were many times, in fact, when I felt that he deserved a better client, or at least he deserved a wealthier one! The Institute had relatively little money. The site he was called upon to use was miserable for its purposes, restricted by railroads and the gridiron pattern of streets which, although many have since been closed, it was not possible to close at that time.

In spite of these limitations, Mies's design of the campus was one of the most, perhaps the most, significant thing that happened to Illinois Institute of Technology.

He showed a great ability to save money when the pressure was on. His meticulous attention to detail left nothing to chance. Many of the ways in which we were called upon to save money, I realized afterwards, were wrong. He pointed those out clearly, but the Institute had to make ends meet. I remember one very simple thing: the plans for the Chemical Engineering and Metallurgical Building called for a great granite slab at the entrance of the building. This cost several thousand dollars. In an effort to save money, a concrete slab was substituted for the granite. It's easy to see, if you look, that that was a mistake.

In the process of building, when we would discuss a particular problem, Mies's answer would be, "Well, we'll think about it," and he did think about it -- that's the difference between Mies and a good many other architects I know. He would think about it and come back with a solution. The relationship between Mies and the institution which was his client was a long and productive one, the importance of which some of those involved never fully realized.

Dr. Heald, as president of the Illinois Institute of Technology, was instrumental in appointing Mies van der Rohe to that institution. Since then he has been Chancellor of New York University and is now president of the Ford Foundation.

A PERSONAL TESTAMENT

Philip Johnson

I am proud to speak up for Mies van der Rohe of the four
men; I quite naturally am prejudiced. I'm prejudiced because of
working with him, and for a whole generation of writing about him
or getting exhibitions of his works together, and even of discovering
him. That sounds perhaps like a strange word to you -- discover.
Discover a man who has been honored for his designs more perhaps than any other architect in the world? Yet that's what happened. And it's a personal reason for my being extremely proud
to add my testimony tonight.

Try to think back to the climate of the twenties. No magazine,
no book on architecture in this country even mentioned his name.
In 1928-1929, it was almost as if the International Style, as if
modern architecture itself, simply did not exist in this country.
In some respects, Le Corbusier and Gropius suffered the same
fate as Mies, but Mies was even less known.

At that time I was an undergraduate at Harvard majoring in
philosophy, and I picked up an article in a foreign journal on
Dutch architecture, illustrating the work of J. J. P. Oud, one of
the leaders in the architecture of the twenties, and it was an immediate Saul-Paul-like conversion. I left the University; I left
philosophy. I went to Europe, and I discovered Mies, who, I felt
more than all the others was worthy of being called the greatest
architect in the world. Back here, no one, of course, would listen;
over there, however, I had one rather good backer and supporter
for my belief: the dean of all central European architects, Peter
Behrens, a teacher not only of Mies, but of Le Corbusier and
Gropius. He wrote, about the time the Barcelona Pavilion -- Mies's
greatest building -- was going up: "This building will someday be

109

hailed as the most beautiful building of the twentieth century."
Now, a whole generation later, I'm still inclined to agree with
him -- to me, Mies is the greatest living architect.

But in what way, we may ask, does he compare with the
others that we honor in this series? To answer this, we should
notice how very different Mies's contribution really is, so that
praising him in no way detracts from the honor and fame of the
other three.

Frank Lloyd Wright is surely beyond praise. Not only should
de mortuis still all criticism, but the plain truth is that he was
the towering and unique genius of his age: the one great American
artist of any art who, in a sense, put the United States on the cultural map of the world. He was better known, for instance, in
Germany, in his great period before the First War, than he was
here. He influenced both Gropius and Mies years before any notice of him was taken here. As late as 1923, he'd already had
several careers as an architect, and he was at the peak of his
fame in Japan, in Holland, in Germany. Here, he was hungry,
in the midst of our last boom, and he had no work until 1937 -- at
least no work of any size. He survived fifteen years of waiting
in the wings.

Walter Gropius, who is in his late seventies (and Mies and
Le Corbusier, don't forget, are in their middle seventies) is the
dean of the still-living three. His work started before the 1914
War -- his good work; we are indeed tardy in recognizing him today. His role is, however, so different, even opposite to that of
Mies. He is a school founder. He is an exciter -- the German
word Anreger is more apt. He is a genius at collecting genius.
It's uncanny, but at the Bauhaus were gathered around him the
greatest artists from all countries that could possibly have been
brought together in one institute. This was certainly due to a "feel"
that only he had. For a short time in the twenties, the Bauhaus
was perhaps the only school that carried the thread of what we now
call modern, not only in architecture, but in all the arts. Precisely at the moment in the history of modern architecture when
such a school was absolutely necessary, Gropius was there, and he
organized it.

110

In these years where was Mies? Mies was a lonely man, as he is still. Mies spent them alone, working alone. He had a small amount of work of a neoclassic type, but he was near to hunger. Once a year, he exhibited one building, and only a rendering of it, at that. But the work that he was doing, for example, in 1919, was on the glass skyscraper, which forty years later, he was more than able to build on Park Avenue. Gropius stressed teamwork, but Mies was alone. Gropius spread the gospel; Mies will never make a speech, and never write an article. While Gropius is interested in the social problems and the social welfare of his world, Mies is first and last a builder.

Le Corbusier is, of course, the cantankerous one of the four. He is the most individualist, the most purely an artist; very different from Mies, Le Corbusier is a sculptor and a painter, and a poet. He writes, "Architecture is the wise, correct and magnificent play of forms under the light." And that's all architecture is to Le Corbusier God bless him. To Mies, however, the work of architecture is to build. While Le Corbusier does not design unbuildable buildings (he designs almost unbuildable buildings), Mies starts from the normal. Le Corbusier invents magnificently, as at Ronchamp, where he made a new shape of monument for the world to admire. But Mies purifies, until, as at Seagram, he makes the paradigm of the American tall building.

Some critics go so far as to say that Le Corbusier is not an architect at all, but a painter and sculptor at large scale. No critic could possibly say that of Mies. The truth is, they're both geniuses and both architects, merely different kinds. Certainly Le Corbusier is the more flamboyant, the more original, the more pyrotechnical. But Mies may be the strongest, as he is surely the purest. And his answer to the pyrotechnicians is classic: "I don't want to be interesting, I want to be good." His aims have always been central to the problems of his time; he has always given himself the main task to solve, not caring, as unfortunately so many of us do, to think what fun it would be to build fantastic shapes. He tries to figure the role of steel as steel, of

111

glass as glass, to figure what it will do and how it will do it. He always figures the main point, always aims toward the technological, the sociological best that our culture can offer. And the results? The results you see around you. Ronchamp is amazing; the Guggenheim far more extraordinary; but Seagram may, perhaps, be good.

There is no question that if imitation is the sincerest form of flattery, Mies should be pleased these days. But he would not say that we are children or that his pupils were copying him. His highest word of praise to another's building is this: "This building is really built." And I've never heard him say any other word of praise. So firm is Mies's faith in the objectivity of his design that he is convinced that if you know enough about building, you too can be a great architect. This modesty, this belief that he is following a high, objective, truthful pursuit of the nature of things, makes him a serene and beautiful presence, as those of you who have ever seen him know.

To those of us who have worked long with him, he is also a sort of saint. We know that the world thinks him great, but those of us who are closer to him have no real way to communicate to you what his greatness has done to our lives.

Mr. Johnson has been curator of architecture at the Museum of Modern Art. With Henry-Russell Hitchcock he wrote The International Style (1932) and Mies van der Rohe (1947). As a practicing architect, he is perhaps best known for his collaboration with Mies van der Rohe on the design of the Seagram Building in New York.

112

MIES, THE EDUCATOR

Daniel Brenner

Le Corbusier, Gropius, and Mies van der Rohe spent a significant part of their youth in the office of Peter Behrens. They were there because of a man, an idea, and a way of work. Those of us who were students on this campus twenty-five years ago hardly had such compelling reasons for our presence. But none of us can have forgotten the visit of Le Corbusier, the colored chalks, wrapping paper, and verbal fireworks, or the pontifical session with Frank Lloyd Wright in the student lounge. The recollection of these potent extracurricular experiences inhibits a discussion of academic programs. After all, Wright told us to clear out of school post haste or our souls would be forever damned.

So, for a moment let us ignore the 1961 Illinois Institute of Technology catalogue and spell out such 1920 names as <u>November</u>-<u>bergruppe</u>, "<u>G</u>" magazine, <u>Werkbund</u>,and <u>Zehner Ring</u>. For these names are the locus of Mies van der Rohe's first efforts as an educator.

"<u>G</u>" magazine, titled with the first letter of the German word meaning "Creative Force" was published by Hans Richter, a painter and pioneer in abstract movies. Lissitsky, George Grosz,and Tristan Tzara wrote for it, as did Mies.

In an early issue Mies wrote: "We reject all esthetic speculation, all doctrine, all formalism. Architecture is the will of an epoch translated into space: living, changing, new Not yesterday, not tomorrow, only today can be given form. Only this kind of building will be creative. Create from out of the nature of our tasks with the methods of our time. This is our task."

The Novembergruppe was named after the month of the 1918
Revolution. In a series of yearly exhibitions, the group revealed
to the public the ferment that was taking place in all areas of art.
Mies headed the architectural section, and here he professed his
magnificent series of revolutionary projects: the Prismatic
Glass Skyscraper of 1919, the Curved Glass Skyscraper of 1920,
and the Concrete Office Building of 1922. You see, technology
works for Mies, so he could say of them: "The structural system...
is the basis of all artistic design. Maximum effect with minimum
means. This is skin-and-bone construction." In 1923 and 1924,
Mies exhibited the Brick Country House and Concrete Country
House.

These five projects were each a superb generalization of a
building problem. They were a statement of principles. They
were an education. None of these projects was ever built, and it
is highly probable, even though the first was ostensibly for a competition, that Mies had little expectation of their ever becoming
"skin and bones." But he had always remained a firm believer in
projects for the projects' sake and has told his students, "Make
a project a year," in the same way that his long-time associate
Ludwig Hilberseimer has wryly urged his students to make a new
revolution. Mies's admonition seems to fall on very few ears. A
project for a master's degree? Yes. A project for a tile competition? Yes. A project to salvage every possible piece of ornament from the Garrick Theatre? Yes. But a project which attempts to make a significant statement about architecture -- rare,
indeed.

Wright, Le Corbusier, Gropius, and Mies have always been
ready to do a project at the drop of a hat. Perhaps we could use
a few less conferences, symposia, and cycles and settle for a
few more projects motivated by nothing more than a desire to
say something about architecture.

At the risk of seeming contradictory, one must mention the
unique capacity our great architects have had for transcending
the specific requirements of a commission and producing a

solution that has nothing of the special or arbitrary about it.
The Tugendhat house did an excellent job for the clients, but,
in addition, represents a whole curriculum of architecture.
The same could be said for the Robie house or the Savoy house.

In 1928, when Gropius left the Bauhaus, Mies was offered
and refused the directorship. It was not until 1930 that Mies came
to Dessau to take over from Hannes Meyer who had succeeded
Gropius. Meyer was a man with strong social orientation. He
left behind him considerable unrest and an extremely vocal group
of adherents committed to his doctrine of rigid utilitarianism.
They called Mies a "bourgeois formalist" and sent a delegation
to him with a list of demands which included a demand that he prepare an exhibition of his work so they could pass on his qualifi-
cations. Mies countered by closing the school for three months
and personally interviewing each student.

When the Bauhaus reopened, the architectural course had a
completely new direction. Using atrium and row houses as a
medium of instruction, there was a stress on structure, space,
proportion,and use of materials. These basic principles of the
Miesian approach were studied in very much the same way and
with very much the same concentration and discipline that was to
prevail later at I.I.T. Hilberseimer, the planner, alternated
with Mies in working with the students, as he continues to do to
this day.

In 1932, the Nazi party in Anhalt gained a majority and
closed the Bauhaus at Dessau, which was a public school, as an
offense to their theories. A slight air of legitimacy was given to
this proceeding by having an ultraconservative architect pass
judgment on the work being done at Dessau. Mies moved his "de-
generate" institution to a factory in Berlin, but within a year Hitler was in power, and the school was closed. But Mies continued
to work privately with a few of his students.

Five years later, Mies came to Armour Institute in Chicago
and developed a Department of Architecture that continues to

impress, amaze, and puzzle our visitors. If it has been mentioned that a Mies building was like a curriculum, his curriculum is like a building. The course of studies has the simple, direct quality of necessity that characterizes his architecture. First, the school is guided by a clear philosophy which is applied with conviction. Then, the curriculum proceeds in a consequential manner to build one study upon another. It is a disciplined and rigorous training and has little to do with "education for design." The word "design" is not used at I.I.T. There is too much in it of the arbitrary, the self-conscious, and the superficial. We look for universal rather than special solutions and give problems that are general, not specific. We hope our students leave I.I.T. with a knowledge of fundamentals, clarity of purpose, and a sense of true responsible development.

In 1950, when the Institute of Design joined I.I.T., Mies said, "Technology is rooted in the past. It dominates the present and turns into the future. It is a real historical movement, one of the great movements which shape and represent their epoch. It can be compared to the classic discovery of a man as a person, the Roman road to power, and the religious movement of the Middle Ages. Technology is far more than a method. It is a world in itself. As a method, it is superior in almost every respect. But only when it is left to itself, as in the construction of machinery or in the gigantic structures of engineering, does technology reveal its true nature. There, it is evident that it is not only a useful means, but that it is something in itself: something that has a meaning and a powerful form -- so powerful in fact that it is not easy to name it. Is that still technology, or is it architecture?

"That may be the reason why some people are convinced that architecture will be outmoded and replaced by technology. Such a conviction is not based on clear thinking. The opposite happens. Wherever technology reaches its real fulfillment, it transcends into architecture. It is true that architecture depends on facts, but its real field of activity is in the realm of the significant.

116

hope you will understand that architecture has nothing to do with the invention of forms. It is not a playground for children, young or old. Architecture is a real battleground of the spirit. Architecture wrote the history of the epochs and gave them their names. Architecture depends on its time. It is the crystallization of its inner structure -- the slow unfolding of its form. That is the reason why technology and architecture are so closely related. Our real hope is that they grow together, that in some way the one will be the expression of the other. Only then will we have an architecture worthy of its name -- architecture as a true symbol of our time. "

Mr. Brenner, a graduate of the School of Architecture, Columbia University, has worked and taught with Mies van der Rohe for several years. He is associate professor of architecture at the Illinois Institute of Technology.

117

HAS "LESS IS MORE" BECOME "LESS IS NOTHING"?

Sybil Moholy-Nagy

The leitmotif of the Four Great Makers Program is that
Walter Gropius, Le Corbusier, Mies van der Rohe, and Frank
Lloyd Wright are the "great founders of modern architecture."

I must dissent. I do not believe in ascribing to four individuals the creation of a movement that took almost two centuries
from its first definable beginnings, even if their contributions
were uniformly great. This is not, however, my main concern.
The main source of my distress is the unrelatedness between
the declarations of the architects under consideration and the
visual evidence of their buildings. After the talks by and about
the Great Makers, I am more than ever convinced that the prime
condition for fame in architecture is to be a schizophrenic whose
pencil does not know what his typewriter does. A simple juxtaposition of these two unrelated forms of genius expressed could
keep a dozen Guggenheims in clover for years.

But it is not my assignment to indulge in my misgivings; it
is to investigate just one aspect of amply certified greatness, and
my theme is Modern Architecture -- the Doctrine of Less is More.
In discussing this theme I shall be critical. It is the privilege of
contemporaries to judge each other as peers because they participate in the actuality of the time in which their work has to serve.
The histories of the European Beaux Arts Academicians, and of
our own Gold Medal recipients, should remind us that time, and
time alone, takes care of immortality, regardless of what we
try to dictate to future generations.

Although Mies van der Rohe has written no books and few
articles or speeches, his aphoristic statements are as esoteric

118

and ambiguous as those of his fellow Makers.   One of these statements was made on the occasion of the Gold Medal ceremony at
the A. I. A. convention: "Truth is the significance of facts." In
simpler times, simpler minds expressed the same content as
"Facts speak for themselves," and if this is what Mies believes,
we shall look at the facts he has built and perhaps get a glimpse
of the truth.

When Mies was a young man, architecture as art was purely
symbolic, either in the building itself or as art added to symbolic
meaning. From the historical base of a cohesive culture with common images, this symbolic art had degenerated into such literary
images as the fancied Medicean palaces for the millionaire
collectors or murals like Klinger's "Christ and the Seven Christian
Virtues Invading Mount Olympus." If architecture as art was to
have any significance again, it had to discover fundamental relationships characteristic of itself.   Mondrian's neoplasticism and
Mies's floor plans were charts in search of these self-evident
characteristics.   In the 1920's all the arts fed from the same
source -- a passionate desire to create visual identities that were
not symbolic truths but true expressions of their own values.

The cautious hand that pushed these dreams of delicate contrasts and tenuous harmonies from the drafting board into the
third dimension was actually that of a constructivist painter.   The
impact through the eye on the senses was calculated within a fixed
framework and from a fixed viewpoint.   It mades no difference
whether the figure in the Barcelona pool is Kolbe's "Dancer" or the
"Kneeling Woman" by Lehmbruck as had been originally contemplated.
What matters is the compositional counterpoint, within an art work,
of highly abstracted visual relationships.

Here was a creative vision of architecture as self-expressive
art, a vista of designed environment in total harmony with the other
arts and in harmony with the highest aspirations of the day.   It was
the first evidence of a new phase in the history of man's desire
for the Gesamtkunstwerk (total design) following the two previous
phases of art as magic environment and art as a giant charade --
the symbolic phase.

119

If we accept "less is more" as a doctrine, then the "more" in Mies' architecture up to about 1930 derived from the purity of means which visualized a morphological harmony in architecture without losing the basic architectural condition of change and adaptation. The stamp of an idea on the material reality of building was strong enough to unite the diversity of form and function. Up to this time then, the architecture of Mies as art was the result of the architectural process. This gives to his European work its uniquely convincing quality.

Years ago I heard Mies speak at the Architectural League. He told his audience that, being without formal education himself, he had asked all the well-known, educated masters what actually was the essence of architecture. They all had furnished him evasive or highly abstract answers, and he had finally arrived at his own definition which he, very handsomely and not a bit uneducatedly, formulated as "Architektur ist formgefasster Zeitwille," which one can translate insufficiently as,"Architecture is self-realization of an epoch through form." And this Zeitwille (this epochal essence) said Mies, was technology. It was under this flag that he started working in the United States.

In an address to the Illinois Institute of Technology in 1950, Mies likened technology to the greatest historical movements in history -- such as Platonism, Scholasticism, Humanism. To him, technology was "something in itself that has a meaning and a powerful form" and which, wherever it reaches its highest fulfillment, transcends into architecture. In a slightly overstrained Aristotelian syllogism, Mies identified technology and architecture. Architecture he called "an activity in the realm of pure significance, arriving at the synthesis of "technological architecture, which is the significant crystallization of the times. "

As his designs for the Illinois Institute campus took shape, the meaning of this exercise in architectural logic became evident. In 1950 exposed steel framing, modular repetition, the refined detailing of machine-produced building materials created an art that was new in America. This was no longer the pure morphon of

120

Mies's European youth, but an industrial esthetic signifying the total acceptance of technology as a creative medium.

When Mies extended technology as formgefasster Zeitwille into domestic buildings, he found a new interpretation of "less is more" in the proclaimed anonymity of our time. "The individual is losing significance," he had written, "his destiny no longer interests us. The decisive achievements in all fields are impersonal, and their authors for the most part unknown...." This anonymity deprived the technological living cell of any means of personal identification. There is no space for paintings and barely room for a minimum of personal possessions.

This identity of technology and architectural design on the highest level was the second of Mies's contributions. It was not as original as his self-evident constructivism of 1920 -- Le Corbusier and others had plowed the ground simultaneously -- but totally unique for America and uniquely suited to the expanding economy after the second world war. It might be assumed that this country would have gone wildly and exuberantly "concrete brut" had chance given Le Corbusier and not Mies the professorship in Chicago in 1938. As it was, America accepted the message of technological architecture unreservedly, and with almost indecent haste started the time-hallowed tradition of imitation. It has been said that romanticism is an attitude and classicism a science. Mies's technological classicism was eminently reproducible, and it covered the land with modular glass curtain walls from sea to shining sea.

No matter how inadequate the copies were, there was the master himself -- the first of the architects who had created a new building art. He had applied the first principle of architecture -- selection with discrimination -- to an indifferent wealth of new materials and methods. For a decade we all believed that a life so dedicated to the contemporaneousness of architecture would create a whole new vocabulary of spatial and structural variations. Mies did take one more step: he refined the steel cage into a shaft of faultless technological modality. But already the concept had

121

cracked. The Seagram Tower is spaceless, and its formal elements lack the constructivist's composition of unequal equivalents.

From then, Mies van der Rohe's designs have been the strangest case of self-plagiarism the history of architecture has ever seen. The two principles that raised technology into architecture were discarded -- selectivity and the variety of spatial expression. The building technology of Mies was like a stuck record moving in the same groove with less and less sound. Between the rigid steel frame and the external truss, the most varied and unrelated architectural needs were solved, or rather, not solved. Is there really no difference in expedient and esthetic function between a National Theater in Germany and a bank in Des Moines, Iowa?

Architecture is essentially "the thoughtful making of spaces" (Louis Kahn) rather than the amorphous loft subdivided by plywood partitions which defeat every spatial and functional purpose. Of course, the physical requirements of apartment dwellers are the same in Detroit and Newark; but is there not more to a designed environment than a minimum protection against the elements? Must chapel and one-family house have the same module, the same transparency, and the same disregard for climatic realities? If the enthusiastic trade publications have their way, New York's Battery Park and Chicago's Civic Center will be as indistinguishable from housing projects and commercial towers as Mr. Biddle's Andalusia was from the Philadelphia Waterworks.

The doctrine of less is more has finally petered out into less is nothing: nothing but a standard frame without space, without form, and technically obsolete. No slogan can make these subtractive end results into architecture, and no gospel of technology transcending the realm of design by its contemporaneousness can conjure up the illusion of art.

If, as Mies has said, "truth is the significance of facts," then the facts prove that the doctrine of "less is more" is at best a fallacy, at worst a deception. Architecture is evidence of doing, of making, not of subtracting. It is the architect's fate to wrestle with the chaotic wealth of material and artistic possibilities until they submit to selection and creation. It has seemed tragically significant to me that Mies closed his Gold Medal speech with these words: "The art of building cannot live from inventions -- inventions are not ideologies." To which one could reply, "Possibly so, but ideologies coined into slogans are less than art and less than building; they are, quite plainly, architectural death."

Mrs. Moholy-Nagy is a teacher of history at Pratt Institute, and a critic of architecture and the arts. Among her books are Moholy Nagy: Experiment in Totality (1950; a biography of her late husband) and Native Genius in Anonymous Architecture (1957).

HABITATS FOR AMERICAN COSMOPOLITES

Charles Genther

The cosmopolitan American is one whose taste for communication has not been satiated by the transatlantic cable, radio,
and television and whose desire to conquer and consume space
is not satisfied by the DC-3 or the DC-8. He now probes outer
space. This is the bent of less than two generations

His annihilation of distance, his comprehension of space,
his desire for the long view, mark and define this difference of
two generations. But this difference is not so much a difference
in aspiration, perhaps as a difference in the capacity to realize.
He now actualizes the age-old desire to fly, to be where he wishes
in a short time, to communicate over vast distances.

Will this person be content with shelter as we have understood shelter in the past -- construction that enclosed, protected,
and warmed or cooled him? I think not. Our cosmopolite wants
to view the horizon, to comprehend what is beyond, and to know
that there is a beyond.

The glass towers Mies built with strips of glass in his garden in 1919 were part of a study of reflected light. Yet, the concept of the view from within such a space was latent in the form.
The seed of desire for the vast view was germinated in the garden, but it was 1937, in Chicago, before Mies van der Rohe's
related studies of the high rise building were rigorously pursued.

The postwar demand for buildings brought the opportunity.
At this time, a number of projects based on design concepts and
construction methods of the 1920's failed to develop because of
high construction costs. Chicago newspapers of the time carried

124

feature articles claiming that the day of the high rise building was over; that it was impossible to cope with the problems of construction costs. All future urban residential construction, these articles claimed, would be garden apartments of not more than seven stories.

Mies's proposal for the building now known as Promontory Apartments refuted this contention first in theory, then in actuality. Applications for the first mortgage were made by the developer, Mr. Herbert Greenwald, to almost every source known at the time. The adverse criticisms made then are still the classical comments of the uninformed or inexperienced man who has not had the view from within: "It looks like a Boston sugar warehouse." "We don't understand how people can live with so much glass." "There is a lack of privacy." There was, indeed, a flood of adverse publicity, and it was extremely difficult to convince anyone that they should seriously prepare proposals for the work. But Mies and his colleagues persisted and the mortgage was finally placed through a man who might be called a representative American cosmopolite, C. A. McCelvain, a man of action and interest in urban affairs, a believer in cooperative housing, and, significantly enough, a flying officer in both world wars.

As construction proceeded, it became apparent that Mies's principles defined the limits under which we could continue to build economically and well. In fact, the principles developed in the construction of this building were later utilized by the Chicago Housing Authority in several thousand housing units. The skin and bones principle established in the architecture extended through the engineering work. Better concrete control, radiant heating, modern electrical distribution systems set new standards of excellence for housing.

The straightforward and honest building, realized under difficult circumstances, prepared the way for the elegance and daring of 860 Lake Shore Drive and established the frame of reference which produced the Seagram Building and the Newark apartments, all realizations and extensions of the studies made in the garden in 1919.

Once a project is built, the market is one measure of its acceptance and livability. Despite uninformed criticism claiming excessive heat, intolerable glare, high operating costs, and lack of privacy, there are now completed fifteen similar buildings with a total of more than 2,500 apartment units. And the vacancy rate and turnover is substantially below average.

An esthetic principle must be realized within the limitations of the materials and methods at hand, but once the principle has been demonstrated, it is possible to interest others directly engaged in the development of new materials, equipment, and techniques. A movement is well begun in which a progressive refinement of the concept is possible.

In the meantime, let us hear from a few cosmopolites in their platonic palaces. A lively old lady who sheds no tears over an abandoned, understaffed house in Lake Forest, says of her apartment in 860 Lake Shore Drive, overlooking the tree-tops and the Drive: "Why, this is the front porch I've always wanted." Suzuki, the Zen scholar, looking over all Chicago from the twenty-sixth floor, states: "Only Americans can live without definition in the middle distance." Kate, aged four, riding her tricycle full speed to within a foot of the glass, laughs at her horrified elders and says: "Don't be afraid -- I know where the glass is."

John Cage, the composer, was seated with Mies in one of the glass houses during a storm. We were talking about the fact that this simple and elegant definition of space without the deification of the architect permitted other personalities to blossom and, in effect, let the whole world in. Just then a great flash of lightning tore open the city sky and lit up the Michigan Avenue towers that have been called the most hedonistic architecture in the world. Cage said, "See what I mean? Wasn't it clever of Mies to make the lightning?"

Philip Johnson, who enjoys working in the Seagram
Building, insists on returning to earth for rest and refreshment.
The architect's work is a discipline of projection. The down-
to-earth short view is its logical counterpart for leisure hours.
The average American, if there is an average one, spends
most of his days, visually speaking, in short-focus activities,
in enclosed spaces. For him, his glass wall means release
into a longer view, an orientation compatible with both his intellectual and visual needs.

There is a tendency to think of a Mies structure as an in-
flexibly transparent box. In reality, it permits the greatest
range of openness or closedness in the history of architecture.
The technological developments that have followed in the wake
of public acceptance have greatly augmented the flexibility of
this architecture.

Certainly Mies's credo "less is more" has brought out
the essential qualities of his materials and the volumes they
define or enclose. The precise edge of a marble wall keeps
its distance from imprecise plaster. A Barcelona chair in its
own free space is beyond doubt a classical and essential statement. In the eight years we lived in a Mies building, I became
convinced that other objects seen in this structure became
blessed with their own uniqueness, their particular individuality
or essence.

My wife, who was both disdainful and ignorant of the nature surrounding her childhood in western Nebraska, as a city
dweller at 860, became a regular Deerslayer. She could
tell you within seconds when the moon would emerge from those
scudding clouds, or when the storm, which had just reached the
river, would be pounding at the windows.

For my part, being in the middle of a storm, or surrounded
by an opalescent fog, with glass and steel not just protecting,
but defining, has given me an entirely new notion and feeling about
the meaning of shelter. I belong, perhaps sentimentally, to the

old-fashioned, untinted glass school, preferring my moonlight and sunlight straight, flooding the room, or, perhaps, simply filtered through light net. Otherwise, I want the windows completely curtained off. But this is an idiosyncracy and not an esthetic.

In the early stages of the development of the 860-880 Lake Shore Drive project, it was important to convince Mr. Robert Hall McCormick that the building would be a credit to him and to his family. Considerable time was devoted to the development of a precise model. The model was mounted in a table in Mies's office at the proper viewing height for Mr. McCormick, and he was brought in one evening and wheeled about the model. He said, "It is a fit monument for any man." And it is, indeed, a monument for all men.

Mr. Genther, a graduate of the Illinois Institute of Technology, has been associated with Mies van der Rohe on such noted Chicago projects as the 860 Lake Shore Drive apartment buildings.

MIESIAN SPACE CONCEPT IN DOMESTIC ARCHITECTURE

Howard Dearstyne

Architecture is a three-dimensional art, rooted in utility. The architect provides a physical environment for living and working, but if he is an artist, he also seeks to satisfy human spiritual needs.

Mies van der Rohe is from start to finish an artist. I am sure that he frequently grumbles inwardly over the fact that the character of his work compels him to satisfy certain functional requirements. He sometimes pinches these a little drastically in the interest of achieving a larger end, and a hue and cry is raised by those who fail to appreciate his objective. He made the nature of this objective clear to me almost twenty-five years ago when, walking with me on Fifth Avenue, he said, "I am no longer interested in anything but the spiritual in architecture."

According to Mies, several influences helped to shape his architecture. One should mention first, no doubt, his master, Peter Behrens, seeker after the large form. In his factory buildings for the German General Electric Company in Berlin, Behrens created some of the greatest structures of the first quarter of the twentieth century. He had the most distinguished architectural office in Europe before the first world war, and Le Corbusier, Gropius, and Mies once worked there simultaneously. From Behrens Mies learned that "less is more", an expression Behrens often used, and this has since become the motto on his shield.

After leaving Peter Behrens' office, Mies worked for a year in Holland on a great house for Madame Kröller, which was never built. It was during this time that he became acquainted with the

work of Hendrik Petrus Berlage, the Dutch pioneer of modern
architecture. From Berlage Mies learned, he often says, of
sound building and the honest expression of structure.

Thereon hangs a tale. When, in the early thirties, I went
to Brno , Czechoslovakia, to see his celebrated Tugendhat house,
I was received, as a student of the architect, very graciously by
the lady of the house. Standing in the great open living room, I
asked Mrs. Tugendhat how it had come about that she and her husband had chosen Mies van der Rohe as their architect. She replied
that it was because he had the reputation of being a sound and sub-
stantial builder. They had had no inkling, she said, of the kind
of house they were going to get since they were not good at reading
architectural drawings. They were surprised and somewhat taken
aback when the house actually stood there and they saw what they
had bargained for. They had had some trouble adjusting to it at
first, "But now, " she added, "we are beginning to enjoy this way
of living. "

Among the historic figures, Mies proudly acknowledges his
debt to Karl Friedrich Schinkel (1781-1840). The classic breadth
and serenity of Schinkel's buildings attracted him, for Mies is a
latter-day Greek himself, and his structures are Hellenic in
spirit. But he also learned from Schinkel the importance of fine
proportions and meticulous detailing.

There were, in addition, certain prophetic elements in Schinkel's architecture, and one of these influenced Mies's thinking in
a decisive way. Some thirty years ago, inspired by Mies's admiration for Schinkel, I sought out all of the Schinkel buildings I
could find in Berlin and its environs. I searched for any features
which might have influenced Mies's architecture, and the search
was not unrewarding. I found that Schinkel, in the façades of his
Theater, his Museum and others of his buildings, sought to distinguish between structure and enclosure by setting recesses between corner piers and adjacent enclosing walls. This device is
seen most clearly in the side and rear elevations of the Museum,
where the wall planes, separated from the piers by indentations,

130

resemble screens loosely inserted between structural elements.
Although these seeming screens must be bearing walls, Schinkel foreshadowed, by this detailing, the actual separation of
structure and enclosure, as we know it today. Some three years
ago, I asked Mies if he had derived from Schinkel his practice
of isolating, by means of recesses between them, structural
columns and beams from non-bearing wall members in the façades of many of his buildings. He replied, positively and une-
quivocally, that he had. In this practice of Schinkel's, indeed,
lay the seeds of an idea which Mies was later to develop: the
separation of the function of supporting from the functions of enclosing and dividing, by the use of isolated columnar supports
and independent wall planes.

When, in 1930, Mies took over the directorship of the Bauhaus,
he arrived in Dessau to find the institution in a state of chaos,
largely provoked by the resentful adherents of the dismissed former director, Hannes Meyer. In the course of weeding out refrac-
tory elements, Mies interviewed each student in his office. When
my turn came I was at a loss to find something to say to him.
Since, however, I had chafed under the sterile functionalism of
Hannes Meyer, I asked Mies if it were not still possible to strive
for beauty in architecture. I didn't know the man to whom I was
talking when I asked that question. "Of course," he said, "it is
still possible to seek beauty in architecture."

Then I asked Mies what he thought of our American architect,
Frank Lloyd Wright. Without hesitation he replied, "He is a very
great architect." He then went on to relate how, when he, Gropius,and Le Corbusier were working for Peter Behrens, the latter had brought to the office the first reproductions of Wright's
work which they had ever seen. (He referred, doubtless, to the magnificent Wasmuth portfolio, published in Germany in 1910.) Mies
said, "This came as a revelation (eine Offenbarung) to us."

It is not surprising that Wright's drawings struck Mies and
his associates with the force of a revelation, for they were harbingers of a great new architecture. Wright's singlehanded,

131

uniquely original achievement represents a significant development of the prophetic tendencies which Mies had already observed in the work of Schinkel.

Schinkel had, on occasion, arranged his windows in continuous bands, with, of necessity, supporting posts between them. Though Wright, no doubt, knew little or nothing of Schinkel, he did this too, and he also carried these windows up to the soffits of his wide-overhanging roofs. By running bands of windows to the plastered underside of his roofs, Wright contrived to separate and render distinct horizontal roof planes and vertical wall planes. This was an assault on the traditional architecture of mass, the solid house with holes punched in it for windows and doors.

If Wright's treatment of his exteriors suggests that he was seeking a spatial architecture, his handling of interiors leaves no doubt about this. He opened one living area to the next, so that the spaces flowed freely one into another. He completely swept aside the idea of a house as a collection of more or less rigidly separated, box-like rooms. Yet, like Schinkel, he was working with traditional materials and methods of construction.

As a young man, beginning his own architectural practice, Mies built several houses in a conventional manner, but these had, nevertheless, the simplicity and amplitude of all of Mies's work. The great house which he designed at this time for Madame Kröller had a measured stateliness and many reminiscences of Karl Friedrich Schinkel. A composition of more-solid-than-open blocks, it is still an architecture primarily of mass rather than of space.

But, in 1923, in a project for a brick country house, Mies discarded completely the traditional concept of a house as a box or series of boxes punctured with holes. In this famous design, a milestone in the progress of modern architecture, he resolved the house into a composition of planes -- vertical, freestanding wall planes of brick and glass, inserted between horizontal floor and roof planes. The vertical planes, placed now at right angles to each other and now parallel but staggered, served not only as

132

enclosing walls, but also as elements to divide the interior into a series of interlocking living spaces. Certain of the enclosing walls, extending outward beyond the limits of the house proper, formed a link between the exterior and the interior. Space seems to flow throughout the various parts of the interior and from the interior outward, only lightly impeded by the floor-to-ceiling window walls.

Here is the Wright open plan carried a large step forward in the direction of a house composed entirely of planes and freely flowing spaces. This was Mies's first announcement of an objective which he has ever since sought to attain: an architecture of space.

This was also the first time Mies had ever proposed the use of a freestanding wall. He once told a group of us at the Bauhaus that when the idea of a freestanding wall occurred to him he lay awake all night wondering whether or not it was a legitimate thing to use. He decided, of course, that it was.

The year after he made the brick country house project, Mies designed a very handsome house in concrete, but because of its predominantly boxlike character, this falls outside of the main line of his development. In 1926, he built the Wolf house in Guben and in 1928 the Lange and Esters houses in Krefeld. All three of these houses, though contemporary in detailing, were traditional in respect to their over-all form.

But Mies had not lost sight of the spatial concept he had enunciated in the brick country house, and in 1927 he tried out his space-dividing, freestanding walls for the first time.

It was in 1928 or 1929, while I was studying at Hannes Meyer's Bauhaus, that I came upon a photograph of this project, the first work of Mies van der Rohe that I had ever seen. The picture showed an exhibit made by Mies in 1927 for the German glass industry in the Werkbund Exposition in Stuttgart. Mies had seen fit to display the industry's product in the form of floor-to-ceiling-height

133

walls of glass (clear, etched, and green glass) so arranged that they formed a room giving out on a court. I well remember how impressed I was by the somber beauty of this space composition, and I wondered who Mies van der Rohe was.

Mies, luckily, was soon given the opportunity to demonstrate his space ideas in a major way. His government commissioned him in 1929 to design a reception pavilion for the German section of the international exposition to be held in Barcelona, and he responded by creating one of the great architectural masterpieces of this century. This brought to fulfillment the space concept of the brick country house, but in a rigorously disciplined and simplified form.

Though the brick walls of the country house were freestanding planes, they had continued to serve the time-honored function of bearing. In the Barcelona Pavilion, Mies relieved the walls of this bearing role by introducing eight cross-shaped steel columns to support the roof. The exterior walls of tinted glass and richly veined marble served only to enclose and help define the inner spaces. An interior wall of translucent onyx acted as a space divider. Two parallel walls of etched glass, with light sources between them, illuminated both the interior and the adjacent exterior space. A U-shaped wall of green Tinian marble contributed to the enclosure of the interior and, continuing outward, formed a court, embracing a pool. At the opposite end of the structure, a wall of Roman travertine linked the Pavilion with a small service building. One wall of this service building was extended to form a partially-enclosed entrance court, which was dominated by a pool, much larger than the first. The building with its related features was elevated upon a low platform, paved and faced with travertine.

The roof of the Pavilion was a simple rectangular slab covering the enclosed spaces of the building and the related adjacent exterior ones. The use of this rectangular roof slab is significant; Mies, having few functional restrictions to cope with in this project, felt the need of imposing a restraint upon his own otherwise nearly unlimited freedom. The flat slab defined the theatre of his operations, and he had to manipulate his forms and orchestrate his spaces beneath it.

The Barcelona Pavilion was dismantled, unfortunately, at the close of the exposition. I was living in Germany in 1929, and if I had known anything about Mies van der Rohe and the significance of this structure, I surely would have found a way of getting to see it. Mies's old teacher, Peter Behrens, went to Barcelona expressly to view the Pavilion. Mies used to like to tell of his reaction to it. "Mein Herz ging auf (my heart leaped up)," Behrens said, reporting on his student's masterpiece.

The Barcelona Pavilion was not a dwelling, but the space concept which Mies brought to realization in it formed the basis of most of his subsequent house designs. These are merely variations and elaborations on the Pavilion theme.

Mies proceeded, two years later, to apply the same principles to a house. This required only a rearrangement of the free-standing walls so that they formed the kinds of spaces needed in a dwelling, a house, in this case, for a married couple without children. In addition to the areas for living, dining, and sleeping, Mies provided a much-reduced service quarter, containing a kitchen and a maid's room.

Like the Barcelona Pavilion, this house was only a temporary structure, and it was erected, for demonstration purposes, within an exhibition hall of the Berlin Building Exposition of 1931. The functions of the building were more explicit than in the case of the Barcelona Pavilion, and the uses of its spaces were more clearly defined. But the exposition house closely resembled the Pavilion in its architectural treatment. It had the same steel columns (tubular here) supporting the same rectangular roof slab which coordinated all of the interlocking spaces of the house.

Once again there were freestanding walls of glass, and, in this case, walls of plastered masonry, with a centrally-placed screen of wood paneling. These were disposed as before, so as to provide for indirect movement from one space to the next. Such circuitous communication between spaces is characteristic of Mies's houses. He likes the suave, roundabout transition, a kind of slow

135

ceremonial progression from one space to an adjoining one.
This is a natural corollary of his space concept. Space will
not flow in a straight line through a doorway. It will seem
to flow only if it encounters some obstruction, such as a freestanding wall, around which it has to circulate.

I studied four years with Mies in Germany and, with one
exception, I designed only houses under him. He maintained that
if you could design a good house, you could design anything. The
second house I did for him in Dessau was a court house, that is,
a house situated in a walled-in garden. I hit upon a scheme for
a single-story one-bedroom dwelling with an elongated combined
living and dining room and, at right angles to this, a covered
porch extending from garden wall to garden wall. There were
some rough spots in the plan which needed ironing out, and Mies
worked very seriously on the house for days, making sketch after sketch over drawings which I presented to him. One of the
most troublesome problems was how to get from the entrance
hall to the living room in a manner less abrupt than I had provided. Mies finally solved the problem in a culminating sketch
in which he achieved an indirect passage not only from the entrance hall to the living room, but also from the kitchen to both
the entrance hall and the dining area.

The famed Tugendhat house in Brno , Czechoslovakia, was
erected in 1930, a year before the Berlin Exposition house. After
the Barcelona Pavilion, it was the most celebrated and influential
building of the German phase of Mies's career.

This house was built upon sloping terrain which determined,
to a large extent, the disposition of its spaces. The entrance, on
the street side, was at the higher level, and it is here that Mies
also placed the five bedrooms, the garage, and the chauffeur's
quarters. A circular staircase led from the entrance hall to the
living quarters below.

When one entered this living area, he found himself in a great,
open, irregular space divided by a straight wall of onyx and a

semicircular wall of Macassar ebony into areas for sitting, dining, and study. A kind of retreat for card playing or conversing, illuminated again by a double-glazed light wall, was provided next to the staircase. The room was enclosed by floor-to-ceiling walls of glass, equipped with curtains of Chinese silk which could be drawn to regulate the light.

The living areas of the Tugendhat house were an impressive demonstration of Mies's space conception, but, taken as a whole and judged in the light of his later projects, the house must be looked upon as a transitional building, half open and half closed. Structurally, also, it was mixed, being partially of bearing wall and partially of skeleton construction.

In 1932, Mies built the Lemcke house in Berlin, a small and pleasant L-shaped court house. This was the last structure of any kind which he erected in Germany before leaving for America in 1937. During this lean period, however, he designed a number of projects, among which were several court houses, four of them for clients. Because of restrictions imposed by the Hitler regime, he was unable to build any of these.

Let us examine the three-court house of 1934. The idea of a house having the living areas grouped around an open court was nothing new. Such houses were common in Roman times, and they have come right down to the present. Their aim has always been to provide privacy, and this has also been Mies's objective in designing them.

This court house is a T-shaped, one-story structure enclosed largely by floor-to-ceiling walls of glass and contained within a brick-walled rectangle which, with the glass house walls, forms three courts of different sizes. Except at the ends of the house, where the garden walls serve as bearing walls, the flat roof is supported by steel columns. One has the feeling that this is a house whose masonry walls, replaced by glass, have merely been pushed outward to become garden walls. There is a kind of design economy in this idea; the walls of the traditional house have not been discarded but only put to a different use.

137

It will be noted that the area of the walled-in enclosure is a multiple of the square of the paving blocks. The entire plot, in other words, has been brought under a modular system. The square module of the column spacing is six times the module of the floor paving so that each column stands at a point of intersection of the lines formed by the paving. The window mullions fall on the same transverse paving lines as the columns. The columns stand either so close to a window wall as to discourage any attempt to pass between them and the walls or at so considerable a distance as to invite movement between the two.

Mies preserves the planar character of his interior walls by carrying them beyond the point of juncture with walls meeting them at right angles. Walls running parallel with each other always overlap, so that one appears to slide by the other. When freestanding walls stand at right angles to each other, one always receives or intercepts the other. If Mies is obliged to put a door in one of his walls, he runs it from floor to ceiling, or, if the wall is a wood one, he makes it one unit of the paneling.

Mies's furniture is not architectonic like Wright's, but he relates it carefully to his architectural elements. He sometimes places a low cabinet at right angles to a screen wall at such a point that the furniture aids in directing the flow of traffic. Chairs, couches and tables almost always stand free in the room, and this, of course, accentuates its spatial character. Mies seldom, if ever, provides cozy corners to which one can retreat to experience the feeling of comfort which comes from sitting with one's back to a wall. He invariably, however, places a bed against a wall, possibly because he realizes that, in submitting to the helplessness of sleep, one needs to feel a sense of protection.

Mies came to America in 1937 to design the Resor house. The site chosen for it in Wyoming dictated a radically different type of house design from that of his then recent court house projects. The house was to span a stream and rest at either end on stone piers. So Mies designed a low, rectangular box to bridge the stream, a box, however, very different from the conventional ones. It was largely closed at both of its ends, which housed, respectively, the bedroom and service areas. The extended living-dining area was opened up completely by full height window walls which afforded a view, in both directions, of the magnificent mountain scenery. However rigidly delimited by the boxlike sheath, the living area within had all the spaciousness and freedom of Mies's earlier houses. The Resor house, unfortunately, was never built, but Mies presently found himself engaged in a much more extensive project, the design of a new campus for the Illinois Institute of Technology in Chicago.

Mies has built only two houses in this country, the McCormick house and the Fox River house, both on the outskirts of Chicago. The Fox River house, erected in 1950 in an area of potential flooding, like the Resor house, was treated as a box and elevated above the ground. In this instance, two rows of exterior steel columns support the floor and roof planes.

Roughly two thirds of the space contained between the roof and the floor slab is glazed, while the remainder is open and serves as a porch. The interior of this house is treated with more freedom than Mies had ever heretofore allowed himself. The only closed-off element is an H-shaped utility core, placed freely in the room space. This and a line of cabinets in the sleeping area are the only space-dividing elements. In front of the core is the sitting area and behind it an open kitchen. The dining space is toward the front left, and the sleeping area is at the right of the core. This house represents the full realization of Mies's space ideal, but it was planned for occupancy by a single person.

Mies did not hesitate, the following year, however, to apply the same freedom of design to a house scheme for four people, a married couple and two children. This house is a square glass-enclosed box, resting on the ground. Four columns, placed at the centers of the four sides, support the roof. Again, an H-shaped core encloses certain purely utilitarian features. This core and two cabinet walls define the interior areas of the house.

139

No doors impede the free flow of space, and the only possibility of separating the areas in the interest of privacy is by means of curtains. Whether the accustomed niceties of living could be maintained in a house such as this is a question, I suppose, which each individual would have to answer for himself in accordance with his own preferences and prejudices. Suffice it here to remark that this house represents the ultimate fulfillment of a space ideal toward which Mies has striven for many years and which he would like to realize not only in his houses, but in his other buildings as well.

There are few truly Miesian houses other than the handful built by Mies, himself, and his students. The reason for this is not hard to find. People cling to long-standing habits and ways of living, and they must be brought slowly to appreciate and enjoy the kind of breadth and freedom which a Mies house affords. Far from being an instrument for the fulfillment, merely, of human physical functions, a house by Mies van der Rohe is a work of art, and it is capable of bestowing spiritual satisfaction upon the dwellers within it.

Mr. Dearstyne teaches architecture at the Illinois Institute of Technology. A graduate of the Bauhaus -- the only American with that distinction -- he has done translations of books by Kandinsky and Malevich (and others) in the "Bauhaus-bücher" series.

THE URBAN SPACE CONCEPTS OF MIES VAN DER ROHE

Jacques Brownson

Mies van der Rohe's first executed venture in city building was in Stuttgart, where he was the director of the Werkbund Housing Exhibit of 1927. This exhibit brought together many of the leading architects of the day; they all did houses and apartment buildings which were somewhat in the same spirit. They were all painted white with the exception of one painted red, and were tied together by Mies's apartment building, which, seen from below, related the group to the horizon. To the Nazis, who were coming into power, this was not the things which the German people believed in, and they made a very interesting montage which shows this same group of buildings as an Arab village.

The apartment building which Mies developed in Stuttgart was based on the premise that the people living inside the space should have the ability to divide their space according to their needs and desires. This was possible because of a skeleton system, with the stairway, the kitchen, and the toilet being the only fixed elements in the space.

In the project for remodeling of the Alexanderplatz in Berlin in 1928, Mies, in competition with many others was one of the two people who placed the buildings freely in the space, rather than building them around the perimeter. In his buildings, he is concerned with the relationship of the building to the space and the relationship of the building to the other buildings on the site.

When Mies first came to Chicago in 1938, the area surrounding the Illinois Institute of Technology was one of the worst slums in the United States. He looked around and said to Dr. Henry Heald, then president of I. I. T. , that certainly it couldn't be worse; it was a great challenge, and he would like to work on such a group of buildings.

The plan for I. I. T. opened a small square to State Street, and buildings were grouped around this entrance square. Opening out of this smaller space through a narrow aperture was a large open space in the center.

Mies suggested that the interior streets be closed. The city did not think that this was possible then, but since have changed their minds and are now closing some of the streets in this area.

The buildings of the campus are based on a twelve foot high vertical module, which gives twenty-four feet in two stories, thirty-six feet in three. The campus itself is based on a grid of twenty-four feet center to center in both directions. This grid was arrived at through a consideration of the way classrooms were to be used and the amount of space required for various elements. Mies came to this conclusion simultaneously with some studies which were being made in Switzerland which concluded that twelve feet was the basic unit which should be used in developing the classroom. You could have one twelve-foot unit for an office or a small laboratory, a twenty-four foot unit for a classroom, and a thirty-six foot unit for a larger lecture hall.

When Mies began to work on 860 and 880 Lake Shore Drive in 1950, there was very little that had been done in this country using the advanced technology of glass and steel. The problem of erecting a large steel skeleton, then hanging a welded steel grid on the outside and placing glass between had not been tried. Much the same system is being used in his project for the new Federal Center for the city of Chicago. I think this shows the development of an idea, a foresight that Mies has carried throughout all of his work. But to him the idea is the important thing.

The ground floor plan of 860 and 880 Lake Shore Drive
demonstrates the principle, much used in Mies's late work, of
freeing the ground space for the pedestrian.

At Lafayette Park in Detroit, Michigan, both high- and low-rise
buildings are incorporated in the scheme. Mies worked on the
Lafayette Park Plan in association with Ludwig Hilberseimer
who has been associated since 1938 with the Illinois Institute of
Technology in the Department of City and Regional Planning.
By taking the public space which could be allocated for each individual building and combining it together in the center park
area, they were able to get enough land in one piece for schools,
churches, and playground areas. Children can reach these areas
without having to cross any streets, and as soon as they are out
in the open space, they have a large area for baseball and the
things so necessary and so missing in our present city living.
Shopping areas were proposed adjacent to the open space and
sidewalks and bicycle paths connected this center commercial
area with the housing.

This is one of the few areas in the United States (the other
one that I know of is Clarence Stein's Radburn, New Jersey)
planned for total separation of pedestrians moving inward to the
park and autos moving outward to the streets and highways. This
area in Detroit also includes a high-rise building for those people
who desire apartment living, with the lower dwelling units placed
among the trees, but still related to an overall geometric pattern. One difficulty in such a plan is the fact that the tall building
is too close to the lower building elements. There is opportunity
for people to look down from the high-rise unit into the lower
residences.

The location of this new group of buildings in the heart of
the city is within walking distance of the downtown area. Professor Hilberseimer has always stressed relating the city to the
pedestrian. The only thing that we know is not going to change
are the two legs we use for locomotion. A man who spends thirty
years of life going back and forth by rapid transportation from

a suburban home to his work in a downtown area would spend as much as five to nine years of that life riding the train. It would be much better to walk and contemplate than it would be to ride any kind of mass transportation.

When Chicago was considering the construction of a convention hall, Mies, at the request of the South Side Planning Board, made a project. He was interested in the political conventions which were held in Chicago, and in the great number of people using convention facilities. He decided to try to build a hall with a seven hundred foot span without any columns inside the space. Here would be a space where people could come and congregate in vast numbers, a large hall within the city. To do this, small outlying exhibition buildings were used, shaping a plaza much the same as San Marco in Venice. I think it is one of the greatest unbuilt buildings ever conceived. To see the model is an inspiration.

The building that was built instead is located along the lake front, blocking the lake from the city. And, as always, the amount of parking needed was underestimated, and now, slowly, the lake front is being further used up with asphalt parking lots.

The building was to be enclosed in marble, and the trussing of the building was defined through the shapes of the trusses and the marble inserted between.

The latest project that Mies is very actively involved in is the Federal Center for Chicago, located between Dearborn, Clark, Jackson, and Adams streets. The first building now under construction is the Courts Building and the Federal Office Building. It includes a very low Post Office Building element. At the present site there is a Courts Building which is being torn down, and a plaza will be made here. It is Mies's feeling that the street between these two sections will eventually be closed.

This is the same thing he proposed at Illinois Institute of Technology, and again the city is not agreeable to it now. But I

144

think, when they see this complex of buildings, the street will be closed. This will be one of the great centers within the heart of the city.

If you know Chicago, the one thing that Chicago needs more than anything else in its downtown area is open space. We have a fine lake front, but behind it is almost nothing. The Federal Center is a first step in providing that open space in the center of the city.

In all of these works we find the development of a concept of space. I think Mies has many lessons to offer in the opening up of our cities and in giving them again that scale which is now so lacking.

Mr. Brownson taught for several years at the Illinois Institute of Technology. He is a member of the architectural firm of C. F. Murphy and Associates in Chicago.

145

PEOPLE, MASS PRODUCTION, AND THE MIESIAN UNIVERSAL

Peter Blake

When I talked to Mies in Chicago in March 1961, the one subject he came back to, again and again, was the subject of civilization. He said that unless all of us were willing to agree that architecture must be an expression and a part of the civilization of its time, there could be no common basis for discussion. He suggested that it was perfectly all right for people to build anything that got into their pretty little heads -- snails and fish and ducks and what have you -- but that, unless what they were doing had some direct relation to the main issues of our time, they could not claim to be doing architecture.

I think this is the key to Mies's entire philosophy, and it is the reason why there is such a great schism between Mies, Le Corbusier, and Gropius, on the one hand, and Wright and some of the other dreamers on the other. It is not a matter of one group producing greater architecture than the other; it is -- at least in Mies's terms-- simply a matter of one group producing architecture, and the other group producing fantasies. The fantasies may be lovely -- and, indeed, in the case of Wright they frequently were -- but they have in Mies's view very little to do with the problems of contemporary civilization. Therefore, in the strictest sense, they are not architecture.

What are the paramount issues of our time, the things that make our civilization different from those that preceded it? One of them, perhaps the most important, is that we are living in an age of such intense crowding, of such vast population explosions, that every activity in which we are engaged is most profoundly affected, and the nature of our world is profoundly changed.

146

Let me just give you a few of the essential facts: in 1861, the population of the planet Earth was one billion; by 1931, only seventy years later -- a fraction of a second when measured against the life-span of our planet -- the figure had risen to two billion; and only thirty-one years later, in 1962, the population of the planet Earth is reaching three billion!

This may be a very boring statistic to those happy few of us who live on a spacious continent. It is not boring, however, to the rest of the world. But boring or not this population explosion is the one simple monstrous fact that makes our age entirely different from any other age before it. When Frank Lloyd Wright was born, in 1869, there were only 38 million people in the United States; when he died, in 1959, there were nearly five times as many -- and 75 percent of them were jammed into big urban centers. And yet, Wright continued to hope and dream and design for an agrarian America. What he produced, especially during those last years of looking backward to the days of his youth, was fantasy, and it was art; but if we agree with Mies that architecture is inseparable from its time, then what Wright produced in those last years was not architecture.

In what respect does the architecture of Mies van der Rohe relate more significantly to the paramount problems of our time?

When you have a planet Earth with three billion people, certain things become obvious and essential: first, it is clearly no longer possible to produce shelter by slow, old-fashioned handicraft methods. (Let me modify this: it is certainly no longer desirable to do so.) You must find methods that are faster, methods that do not use up too many natural resources, and methods that are reasonably flexible in being applicable to any number of different problems.

Clearly, this means industrialization. Only mass production of buildings or building parts can possibly hope to keep up with the mass production of human beings.

147

Mass production of any sort has certain characteristics: first, it is feasible (at present, anyway) only if the mass-produced units are identical; second, because the units have to be identical, it is necessary to find common denominators or universal solutions which will serve as many different purposes as possible. (For example, you have to produce interchangeable parts, and you have to produce parts that will serve interchangeable functions.)

All this is not esthetics. It is what Mies calls facts. When Mies talks about problems in contemporary architecture, he may often brush aside emotional or tendentious concepts and return to something very much like those characteristics I have just listed. "Now that is a fact!" he will say, and, of course, he is right. There is an absolutely unshakeable progression in logic which leads from the fact of a three billion population, to the fact of mass production, to the fact of universal application, to the fact of precision.

In the face of these facts, we may feel that it would have been lovely to have been born in the eighteenth century, and born rich, of course. But in soberer moments, we can recognize that our civilization can be an exhilarating time in which to be alive, and a time of great art as well. It is true that this art, in the area of architecture at any rate, cannot be very individualistic. But like it or not, this is the time in which we do live, so let's stop behaving like children and start acting like men. Let those architects among us who insist on playing with mud pies, big and small, go play in Disneyland.

"To do what Wright did, you have to have fantasy, but if you have fantasy, you don't want to copy Wright or anyone else! That's why Wright's influence will be limited," Mies has said. The first thing that we should realize about Mies's architecture is that he deliberately made it easy to copy. Now, what is wrong with that? If you have a staggering problem of mass shelter, isn't it essential for great architects to produce guidelines that can be copied by lesser men? After all, the beautiful houses in Salem

148

were largely copied from carpenter's pattern books, and that is one reason why the old streets of Salem have unity and serenity. Similarly, Mies has produced, in his buildings in America at least, a complete "pattern book" of details, of proportions, and of forms that can be copied by anyone, from architect to builder, to produce a townscape as unified and serene as that of Florence or Siena. That, I think, is responsible architecture -- architecture responsible and responsive to its age.

The next thing to realize about Mies's architecture is that he has tried to arrive at universal solutions to the greatest possible number of problems in our time. These universal spaces have often been misunderstood, in part because of the way Mies has presented them. It has been said that a single, great room with no real partitions and no privacy just doesn't work in a good many instances. This is quite true, but it is necessary to understand that Mies, like many other pioneers, often presents an idea in an entirely abstract, oversimplified form in order to dramatize it.

These abstractions of universal solutions are desperately needed in an age in which functional requirements of buildings change almost from day to day. Julius A. Stratton, the president of M.I.T., said recently: "The world into which we were born is gone; and yet we have little or no idea of the world into which our children may grow to maturity. It is this rate of change, even more than the change itself, that I see as the dominant fact of our time."

The old slogan "form follows function" has thus been made obsolete by the fantastic rate at which our functions change. It is no longer possible, in most cases, to give a form to a building that is not only valid today but will also be valid tomorrow.

The true test of universality in architecture is yet to come, for it will take a generation or two to test Mies's universal structures and to judge how easily they can be adjusted to tomorrow's requirements. But more and more buildings today by Mies and

149

others are based upon the same structural system, sheathed with the same enclosure of metal and glass, given the same basic mechanical layout -- and then adapted on the inside in an infinite variety of ways to the special problems at hand. Universality in form and space, like universality in external expression, is, of course, relatively easy to copy, and that, again, is precisely Mies's intention.

As I have described Mies's work so far, it may seem to have little to do with art. Nobody, of course, has succeeded in defining art to anybody else's satisfaction, but, obviously, art has not only to do with reason, it has something to do with the senses. What makes Mies's system of architecture art rather than, let us say, architectural logistics?

Mies's work is perfectionist in execution. His buildings look as if they had been put together by a jeweler. But this is a matter of technique and not art. There are a great many painters whose technique is superlatively good, but who are not very remarkable as artists. What makes Mies an artist?

Well, what is art, anyway? Is it beauty? I doubt it. In any case, beauty is simply another subjective term. I have talked a good deal about the terrifying population growth that will shape almost everything about us. One of the most frightening results of this explosion has been the total political, moral, and, incidentally, visual chaos in which we find ourselves. D. H. Lawrence once said something like this: "It is the function of an artist to stand outside his time and his society, and to throw rocks at it." (He didn't actually say "throw rocks at it," but this is what he meant.) In short, an artist functions as an artist when he re-examines his age and begins to attack its maladies.

If this is an accurate definition, then Mies sees his function as an artist as one of helping to put an end to the chaos of our time, and to replace it with order. This is not necessarily the way a painter would approach his problem but it is the way an architect

150

would and should.   To contribute more chaos to an already
chaotic time, as certain architects have done and continue to do,
is irresponsible.   It is certainly an impossible position for Mies --
or, for that matter, for Le Corbusier or Gropius..

So Mies acts as an artist when he stands outside his time,
examines its flaws, and proceeds to try and eradicate them.   He
is aware that all he can hope to bring to his time is order in
place of chaos.   But he is also aware that there can be no beauty
(whatever that means) and no civilization until there is order.
This is the first step -- and it is a step for the poets and the artists to take.   The politicians don't know how.

It has been said that it took the United States about 150
years to produce a workable political system, based upon the
rule of law, and that the time has now come to give the United
States a civilization based upon a rule of law.   The rule of law:
is that not the most moving achievement of man to date?   And is
it not the basis for all great periods of art and architecture?   I
believe that those who wish to give us a rule of chaos instead --
whether in painting, sculpture, architecture or politics -- have
no true interest in art.   They have interest only in themselves.

I could, I suppose, speak about Mies's attempt to find the
most perfect proportions for his surfaces and forms, to find the
most noble setting for his buildings; I could speak about Mies's
concept of color, about his ordering of related spaces.   But all
this has been said before, and more clearly than I could say it.

I want, instead, to rest my case on the proposition of Mies
as one of the great lawgivers of our time -- as a responsible
artist who saw his task not in leaving his own personal imprint
upon the face of the earth, but in creating a system of order upon
which future generations might build beautiful cities.

Mies has an essential modesty that is hard to grasp in this
age of the huckster.   People have said to Mies: "Would not your
city of anonymous buildings be a dull sort of place?"   Of course

it would be; but where within ourselves are the resources
to build an Orvieto or a Florence? You look at the skyline
of Florence, and you will find that only two structures rise
above the uniform pattern of houses and palazzi: the
Duomo and its Baptistry, and the Palazzo Vecchio, the
symbol of God and the symbol of Caesar.

What symbols have we produced to take their places?
Mies has said: "We will build no cathedrals." Whether we
like it or not, religion is no longer the focus of our lives.
And as for City Hall, the saying goes that you can't fight
it, but the fact is that popular democracy, to which we are
dedicated, means dilution of centralized power.

Well, should we raise the Chase Manhattan Bank to
the status of the Duomo? Indeed, we seem to be doing
just that: Chase Manhattan already dominates the New
York skyline (at least the downtown skyline; the uptown
skyline is still dominated by the uptown Rockefellers).
But I suspect that we don't really want to replace the
cathedral with a bank.

So what is the focus, the symbol of our time? We
don't know, and Mies knows that we don't . Paul Rudolph
has said that we should have background buildings and
foreground buildings, by which he means, I presume, that
Mies will do the background buildings, and Rudolph will
do the foreground buildings. But let's be frank: what
buildings do we want in the foreground? Not airline
ticketoffices, surely? Not ice hockey rinks? Not parking
garages?

The fact is, of course, that the foreground boys want
to put themselves into the foreground -- and Mies thinks
that civilization should be put into the foreground. He
has not given us all the answers, but he has created a
system of architecture that can bring order into a chaotic
mass-society -- and a system that will serve as a backdrop

for the great, symbolic structures that we will, undoubtedly, create when the time is right. "We will build no cathedrals," Mies has said. And we might add: "But we will build a new City of Man."

For a biography of Mr. Blake, see page 104.

MIES VAN VER ROHE AND THE PLATONIC VERITIES

James Marston Fitch

As disastrous as it was for Germany and the rest of the world, Hitlerism did America a great service when it gave us men like Albert Einstein, Walter Gropius, and Ludwig Mies van der Rohe. Each of these men brought us great talent, which our country was able to employ directly and immediately, with scarcely a dropped stitch in the changeover. There is a special kind of poetic justice in the spectacularly successful transplantation of Mies from Germany to Chicago. Who better than this poet of glass and steel could have carried on the skyscraper tradition of Chicago? Mies, in the years since he migrated to the Midwest, has raised the skyscraper to its highest level of elegance and refinement. The most talented and the most conscientious architect to work on this building type since Louis Sullivan finished the Schlesinger Building in 1899, Mies has brought to it a combination of monumentality and meticulous detailing which that bluff and pragmatic city had been in too much of a hurry to accomplish by herself and too insensitive really to miss.

When he came to this country in 1938, Ludwig Mies van der Rohe had to his credit a total of twenty-seven building projects, eleven of which had actually been executed. Even today, his immense prestige is based upon a far smaller corpus of work than that of Gropius or Le Corbusier, and, of course, only a fraction of that of Wright. Yet, thirty years ago, the fame of this man was already international. He had several honors to his credit, including the directorship of the Bauhaus after his friend Gropius had resigned. But Mies's fame was really founded on two buildings, both of them comparatively small, one of them so evanescent that it had come and gone before anyone had a chance fully to grasp its significance. These two buildings, the German

154

Pavilion at the Barcelona International Exposition of 1929, and the Tugendhat residence at Brno, Czechoslovakia, of 1930, proved to be two shots that would indeed be heard around the world.

Although both buildings played important roles in the battle for world-wide acceptance of the contemporary style, the Pavilion was perhaps the most influential. This elegant little building lasted only a few months and few people who saw it appreciated its significance. Fortunately it was photographed before it was dismantled, and through this medium it has survived to engrave its dazzling image on the modern retina. No other single building of the twentieth century was to do more in shaping the tastes of that era. It was one of those statements so rare in the world of art which established the artist at one stroke, imperishably. Mies could have died that summer, at the age of forty-three, and his position as a world historic figure in architecture would have been secure.

How was this possible? The building's success was certainly not due to its size, or to its cost or to its complexity. It was not due to any single innovation: both Wright and Corbusier had already employed the hovering roof, the nonstructural screen walls, the floor to ceiling glass. Nor was it because the building was especially advanced technically. Although it used chrome-sheathed columns, its marbles would have been familiar to the Romans.

The greatness of the Pavilion lay in something far more subtle. It lay in the fact that it managed to express, in the most exquisitely polished and exact terms, the highest aspiration of a Europe wracked by war and inflation. Here was that clarity, order, and peace that Europe longed for. Here were noble spaces, unpolluted by any connotation to a discredited, futile past. Here were fine materials, freed of decadent motifs and moldy symbolism, glowing with their own intrinsic beauties. Here was the catalytic image that was to clarify problems of design for whole generations of architects.

155

In this building Mies was able to dissolve the ordinary elements of enclosure -- floors, walls, and ceilings -- and magically to reconstitute them as abstract planes, divorced from structural function. Then, on a floor plan which might have well been a composition by his friend, the painter van Doesburg, he had reassembled these planes, not to form boxlike rooms, but to modulate a continuously flowing space. The elements are few and simple: an unbroken floor plane of creamy Roman travertine, a floating roof slab of immaculate plaster, and between these two, a series of vertical planes in green Tinian marble and gray and translucent glass which intersect or slide by one another as in a cubist painting.

Aside from his own thronelike chairs of chrome and blond pigskin and two pools, one with a sculpture (and with his usual consummate taste, Mies had wanted a sculpture by his friend Lehmbruck, recently dead, but could not get it), aside from this, there was nothing else in the building -- nothing else.

A statement of such shattering power and purity could have been possible only under the circumstances which surrounded its erection: a last-minute government decision to build a pavilion, a limited budget, no exhibit material, and no time to collect any.

"It is very curious how buildings come to pass, " Mies said many years later when recalling this incident. "I was told, 'We need a pavilion -- design it -- and not too much class.' I must say, " Mies said, "it was the most difficult work which ever confronted me, because I was my own client. I could do what I liked, but I did not know what a pavilion should be. " In retrospect it is easy to see that the greatness of the pavilion stems precisely from the lack of program. It gave free rein to his authentically platonic ideals of architectural perfection, without so much as a travel poster or receptionist to complicate his design.

In the Tugendhat house built the year after the pavilion, we can see another aspect of Mies's great talent. This is perhaps the least abstract and the most functionally satisfactory building of his entire career. Here he is faced with a concrete and complicated program, as well as a challenging site. The design is a marvel of domestic felicity. The way he explored the topography and exposure to win sunlight, view, and privacy for every room in the house; the beautiful fashion in which areas are zoned for efficient service and pleasant family life -- these make the Tugendhat house a mechanism which must have functioned beautifully. Nowhere does a formal preconception obtrude to mar the plan, even though the interiors have much the same splendor as the Barcelona Pavilion, the same pure forms and uncluttered, flowing spaces, the same severely restrained furnishings. It is for Mies an unusually humane and considerate design, giving all the appearances of having been carefully tailored to fit a family he knew and liked.

Yet, if we are to take at face value an account that Mies gave in later years, the Tugendhats got a distinguished house in spite of themselves. With a sardonic mixture of wit and (one can only say) genial contempt, Mies tells this story: "Mr. Tugendhat came to me. He was a very careful man. He did not believe in one doctor only -- he had three. He picked me out for a curious reason: he saw a house I built when I was very young. It was very well built, and he expected something similar. I went there and saw the situation. I designed the house. I remember it was Christmas Eve when he saw the design. He nearly died. But his wife was interested in art. She had some Van Gogh pictures; she said, 'Let us think it over.' On New Year's Eve he came to me and told me that I should go ahead. He said he did not like the open space; it would be too disturbing. People would be there when he was in the library with his great thoughts. He was a business man, I think. Later on he said to me, 'Now I give in on everything, but not about the furniture.' I said, 'This is too bad.' I decided to send furniture to Brno from Berlin. I said to my superintendent, 'You keep the furniture, and shortly before lunch, call him out and say you are at his house with the furniture. He will be furious, but you must expect that.' Tugendhat said, 'Take it out!' before he saw it. However, after lunch he liked it." Mies concludes, "I think we should treat our clients as children."

157

In over half a century of architectural practice -- he entered
Behrens's office in 1908 -- Mies van der Rohe has displayed an
imperturbable, almost glacial continuity in his work. The absolute consistency of his style is astonishing; so, for that matter,
is the constancy of his subject matter. In all his life, he has
been content to work in two forms only -- the single-story pavilion
and the multistory skeletal tower. This unchanging and unchange-
able path appears in retrospect both heroic and endearing. It
establishes the fact that he is incorruptible, absolutely impervious
to the dictates of fad and fashion, to the club and carrot techniques
which society employs to bring balky artists to heel.

Though his standards of craftsmanship are merciless, he is
actually a kind and gentle man. He is not conceited, merely secure, not taciturn, merely reserved. It has literally never much
mattered to Mies what the world thought of him, though it is
apparent from his work that he has thought long and hard about
the world. His unchanging style of expression is not the mark of
an isolated or insensitive man. The Barcelona Pavilion and the
Tugendhat house by themselves establish him as one of the most
sensitive designers of the century.

Unlike Wright, or Le Corbusier, he seems never to have
felt it necessary to convince people that they should follow him.
Hence the scarcity of Miesian polemics. Where those two wrote
dozens of books and manifestos, he has a total of fourteen short
articles to his credit. His attitude towards work is Germanic.
He describes one of his job superintendents as "terrible. He
wrote letters, " Mies said. "He should have worked instead of
writing letters." Indeed, this demanding statement reveals something else important about his architecture. All of his buildings
have a kind of glowing perfection which comes from flawless
detailing in the office and relentless supervision on the job. This
passion for fine workmanship is undoubtedly the legacy of his
youthful apprenticeship as a stonemason and a carpenter's helper
before he entered Behrens's office.

158

Two slogans are widely attributed to Mies. One is, "Less is more," and the other is, "God is in the details." Characteristically scrupulous, he disclaims inventing either. The first, he says, came from Peter Behrens, and the second, he thinks, comes from the art historian Erwin Panofsky. Whether or not he coined these dicta, it is perfectly apparent that Mies lives by them. He expresses himself in short, declarative sentences that often have the pungency of an early Hemingway. For example: "One little building," he says, "was painted blue on one side, red on one side, yellow on one side, and black on the other side. I said to the architect, "Paint it white! For heaven's sake, can you not do better than that?" He said, "You're afraid of color." I said, "No, you are color-blind." Or again, "I was once asked by an expert, "Why should everything be straight?" I asked that expert, "Why should it be curved?" Or finally, when asked if he was influenced by the Japanese, "I have never seen any Japanese architecture; I was never in Japan. We in our office do things by reason. Maybe the Japanese do it that way too."

The surprising fact is that Mies seems to design in exactly this pellucid, pragmatic, and disarmingly unpretentious fashion. He says, for example, that the module and hence the whole scale of the Barcelona Pavilion was established by nothing more abstruse than a block of magnificent marble that he was given for it. He had it sawn into as many thin slabs of veneer as possible; stacking two of these one on top of the other gave him his ceiling height. All proportions derived from this.

Another anecdote of the same sort concerns the design of the Metals Building at the Illinois Institute of Technology, whose end façade has been widely compared to a Mondrian painting. While observing that he had been an old friend and a longtime admirer of that Dutch painter, Mies says that the origin of this design was much simpler. The lot for the building, between a railroad and a parallel street, was so many feet deep. A company had donated a traveling overhead crane. It was so wide and so high, and required an outside door of a given size. The remaining space along the street was the only area left for classrooms, and they had to be stacked three high in order to get the required number. These volumes were all marked diagrammatically by the exposed steel skeleton, painted black. The gray brick panel infillings were standard for the campus. The only arbitrary act in the whole design process, Mies insists, was the decision to paint the crane door.

Of course, the real mystery of the creative process escapes from these anecdotes like water from a wicker basket. But they serve at least to demonstrate the directness and simplicity, at the conscious level, of Mies's approach to design. Nevertheless, behind this apparently casual method of design, there operates a philosophy that is absolutely Cartesian in its rigor and inflexibility. When Mies took command of the architectural department at Illinois Institute of Technology in 1938, he said that he had a single goal: to create order amid the desperate confusion of our time. "We must have order," he said, "allocating to each thing its proper place and giving to each thing its due, according to its nature." No one, amidst the squalid anarchy in which we live, today, can quarrel with this ambition. But every serious architect must ask himself what kind of order Mies has in mind.

The answer is, of course, visual order. However, this raises as many questions as it answers, because the creation of visible order in architecture is not, as in other visual arts, a separate, self-contained act, an end in itself. Architecture differs from painting and sculpture precisely in the fact that more intricate sensory impact on the spectator involves him in a more complex sensuous response. No one, least of all the architect, will deny that the visual response is important in architecture. It may well be the primary one. But it never, in real building, occurs in isolation.

The entire spectator, not just the spectator, not just the spectator's eyes, responds to the impact of architecture on his body. Truly great architecture therefore can never be based upon solely visual phenomena -- it can only be derived from the resolution of a whole nexus of forces which play upon man; forces

160

which, though equally important, are disparate, even contradictory, and very often not visible at all. To organize these forces rationally is to produce, inevitably, a visual order. But it is apt to yield forms less balanced and serene than those that Mies demands.

Mies therefore imposes upon reality a metaphysical order of his own. Even this dilemma might be soluble if only the ideal world for which Mies designs his buildings corresponded more closely to the real one. Unhappily, it does not. He has created an architectural order, imperturbable and implacable (the adjectives are those of his admirers) for an ideal landscape. Nothing ever happens here. It is airless, timeless, filled with light -- but not sunlight, since it has no heat, no direction, no fluctuation of color and intensity; no gales howl here, no dust blows, no insects fly. There are no excesses of summer humidity or drifting winter snows. There are no preferred orientations or exposures, since there is no weather in his compassless world. In sum, Mies designs for the golden climate of Plato's Republic -- but he builds in Mayor Daley's Chicago.

The consequence of Mies's metaphysics may be discovered in both the skyscraper and the pavilion, though they will vary in scale depending upon the programs given, the budget at his disposal, and the climate in which he builds. The theoretical and practical limitations of this approach in skyscraper design are equally apparent in his pavilion. This is what has been called -- that is, his pavilion has been called his universal space. Into this classic envelope he has been able to fit, with only minor adjustment in scale or structure, such varied operations as a museum, a rum manufacturer's office, a national theater, and an architectural school. And these are built in such diverse climates as Houston, Des Moines, Santiago de Cuba, Western Germany, and Chicago. As visual phenomena they are without exception handsome. But this does not tell us how, in multidimensional reality, they will actually perform.

In Barcelona the pavilion worked magnificently. Specific functional requirements were all but nonexistent; the building had only to meet the demands of one genial summer on the Costa Brava. But when, twenty years later, Mies repeated this design along the Illinois River as a house for a single woman, the contradiction between the real and the ideal could no longer be suppressed. This house achieved world-wide acclaim for its beauty, and, in purely visual terms (especially in terms of the photographs on which most critical judgment seems to have been based) it is indeed a little building of ravishing grace and elegance.

No one has ever denied that, including the owner. She merely claimed, in a lawsuit against the architect, that it was uninhabitable. The Fox River house is located in one of the most difficult climates on earth, with an average annual range from subpolar winters to summers of Congo-like heat and humidity. Comfort, indeed survival, under such extremes as these would seem to dictate an architecture of flexible response and accommodation to environmental change. Mies's design makes no such concessions. All the exterior walls are identical; all are of glass; and none of the glass is shaded. Hence (so ran the owner's testimony at least) glare was often severe inside the house, especially in winter, when the ground was covered with snow. Drawing the curtains won summer relief, but also, of course, cut out the view, which was the reason for the glass in the first place. In fact, control of light and heat in a glass house posed all sorts of related problems of comfort for the tenant. Direct sunlight penetrated the unshaded glare, sharply raising the temperature inside the house, even in winter. All the glass in the house was fixed. There were no openable windows, and only a single pair of doors. Natural ventilation was therefore limited, and the house had no air conditioning. To escape this hot weather dilemma one could move out onto that beautiful porch and famous floating terrace, except that, without insect screens, they too were uninhabitable at this time of year.

The controversy about this famous house, unfortunate as it was for all concerned, is now history. The owner has made certain modifications which presumably make it more comfortable to live in. But it cannot be held that they make it more pleasant to look at. In fact, in screening the porch, even with the care that was obviously exercised, Mies's beautiful creation has been not merely maimed, but destroyed. Where once pure space flowed between and around those

162

hovering planes, there is now a solid black tube, heavy and inert.

The necessary modification of his design constitutes an exquisitely painful demonstration of the dilemma which he confronts us with: his architecture is literally utopian. It is a dilemma of which Mies is not altogether unaware, and there is something at once admirable and ornery in his Olympian refusal to lift a finger to help us. The size of his talent is so immense that, from an esthetic point of view, it confers an air of classic nobility upon everything he does. But the shape of his talent is so platonically restricted that it exposes many of the same buildings to serious challenge from an operational point of view. To acclaim Mies for the monumental purity of his forms, and yet to deplore their malfunction in some pragmatic details, is rather like praising the sea for being blue, while chiding it for being salty, or admiring the tiger for the beauty of his coat while urging him to become a vegetarian.

The fact is that Mies accomplishes his ambition of an absolute purity of form only by doing what Plato did -- that is, by resolutely supressing many of the mundane details of everyday reality. The arbitrary limitations of material and palette in his buildings are self-imposed. He has found them essential to his integrity as an artist, to his peace of mind as a man.

For a biography of Mr. Fitch, see page 23.

163

La Maison des hommes, 1942; Entretien avec les Etudiants des Ecoles d'Architecture, 1943; La Charte d'Athènes, 1943; Les 3 Etablissments Humains, 1945; Manière de Penser l'Urbanisme, 1947; Propos d'Urbanisme, 1948; United Nations Headquarters, 1947; l'Espace Inédicible, 1947; Le Modulor, 1951; Les Plans Le Corbusier de Paris, 1922-55. Office: 35 rue de Sèvres, Paris 6e, France.

--from Who's Who in America, Volume 32, 1962-1963. Chicago: A. N. Marquis, 1962. (Used with permission of the publishers.)

today. In this remarkable milieu, in this quite remarkable place
where we are, in three strokes I am going to sketch the material
realization of this discovery.

This is the agricultural milieu, with the ox, the horse, the
much larger tractor, and the cooperative center.

Here at the crossroads of two roads, I am drawing the beginning of a radioconcentric center, the grocery store, the inn,
the hardware store, which go back as far as antiquity, even before the invention of nails; the center which has come to be the
source of all exchange. This is the radiocenter of exchange.

The logical consequence of this was the multiplication of
this phenomenon, the creation of a city with tentacles, the
sprawling city, which developed in a dramatic manner -- I am
writing "sprawling city." These must disappear, these must die,
must fall back into proportion and find the size best suited for
proper exchange.

Now we are witnessing the birth of the linear city of changes,
the linear industrial city which moves in around the waterways,
the road ways, and the railways, all of which bring in raw materials and which take away the manufactured goods. Along the
whole length of this linear industrial city, there shall be dwelling
places, building proportionate in size. These meet at the two
radioconcentric cities at the extremities, with a distance between
them of one or two hundred kilometers.

And these radioconcentric cities have their industrial units
and their means of habitation, of everyday leisure, the essential
joys of life, which are the gift of modern technology. They are
in the midst of nature, green growth surrounds them, and they
are joined by footpaths between the dwelling places and the places
of work.

They are linked to the radioconcentric cities where exchanges
of merchandise, of ideas, of government, take place. They are

165

linked to the manufacturing centers by means of transportation, covering the roads, the railway, and the waterway.

Thus, the world is divided by radioconcentric areas, by industrial establishments which are like this. Harmony is established between the works of exchange, with the peasant, the farmer who today is becoming a member of the mechanized society, and the industrial producer who is taking his place amidst conditions of life which are productive of joy and of harmony.

I shall finish this sketch with a picture which I shall draw here: the monument of the open hand, which is my only political intervention in fifty years; the open hand, open to receive and to give. With this gesture, which has no negative political quality, but only a positive human meaning, you open the doors to human sentiments of generosity, just as this evening, you have risked opening the doors of academism to me.

I shall end my slight intervention with geography. (I use the color orange in order to avoid the red -- because it is useless to try to make colors say the contrary of what one means). Here I am drawing a country -- I said I was becoming a geographer; here I shall place the linear industrial city, which aligns the three roads, land, water, and rail, going through the tunnels and linking them together.

You will find and follow those roads even if they lead far away -- what does it matter? Far away there are men like us; these roads follow the old roads of History, all the way to China. And at the end of these roads, I will take another color, blue, to show the context and continuity, and here I shall draw the building of Columbia University. I'm less good at drawing the United States -- I may make mistakes, but anyway, here are the lines of continuity and the sense of continuity which tie things together.

Mr. President, dear friends of New York and of Columbia, this is what I wish to say, this is what having a doctrine which is not totally concentrated in Vignola means. (Vignola was a man

166

of the Renaissance, you know. He has put architecture in formula; he created diverse orders of architecture with which I never agree.) In seeking the juncture of urbanism and city planning and architecture joined together in terms of human needs, one notices that the mechanical work opens an enormous and fantastic civilization, that it can be a brotherly civilization, and we might as well be brotherly as anything else. And the first manifestation of a realistic nature is for us to realize that we have to seek an alliance of constructors, builders. Here I'm sketching the engineers, here the architects, here physical laws, here man and his environment, nature, and the cosmos. And here I shall put in red the tasks of the engineer, and in blue that of the architect, the engineer in red because this symbolizes action and the power of natural forces, and in blue the architect because here we have a game of the mind.

I shall finish this talk and my sketch by this: two hands, one opposite the other; one is red, and no political aspersion is intended, and the other blue. They represent a friendly dialogue, a brotherly dialogue from beginning to end: and I sign, "Columbia, 28/4/61, a grateful Le Corbusier. "

167

A TALK TO STUDENTS

Le Corbusier
(Translated by Charles Rieger)

I shall not answer questions today, but I shall be only too glad to draw a few sketches evocative of problems of Architecture and Planning. I want to show you a few essential and binding points between architecture and planning and the treatment of land occupancy, which is part of the extension of architecture and planning as a whole.

You know that better than I do: I have seen your models; they are superb, full of hope and cut-paper, but nevertheless interesting. I shall ask you to forgive me, for my propositions will be much more modest.

I shall draw here a building that could house two thousand people. I state: if you want to live in solitude, in silence, with the delectation of essential joys: sun, space, and greenery, put together these two thousand people, enter from a single door, and go up through a group of harmonized elevators, for example, four elevators holding twenty people each. In New York office buildings, you notice when all goes well, when there are four elevators, one has the possibility of having one elevator very quickly; if there were only one elevator for the same height, one would never get a chance to have it ready for immediate use.

This is a building erected in Nantes. The entrance was there; here was a quarry filled with water. That pond was crossed with pipes for water, gas, electricity, and telephone, coming from a major road, and over these pipes was laid a footbridge six feet wide allowing the passage of two or three people walking abreast. The site was then cleared of building equipment, and a few years later, the tenants having been there for four years, one said: "But

where is the entrance road?" The access over the footbridge
had become the obvious one to them. That remained, and that
was enough. For once, this is a thing proved by human events
and not by theories. If the authorities had known, they would
have said that it had been impossible!

From this we may say that houses can be groups, with
roads about every four hundred meters, for example, on a grid
600 meters by 400 meters. Introducing a modulation of 400 meters by 400 meters into a grid 600 meters by 400 meters provides
varied views, never alike. That is to say that there are here
evident architectural possibilities.

What completes the sketch is the presence here of orientation; it should be on every architect's drawing, should it be a
bedroom, a house, an apartment house, or a whole city, because
this is the key: the sun with its two paths, winter and summer,
provides the mechanical possibilities to control it. As Socrates
said one day, "If you must build your house, put a portico in
front of it, for the summer sun will not be bothersome and will
cast a shadow beneath it, and in winter, the sun will penetrate
the house." These are fundamental elements.

I now leave architecture and pass on to land occupancy. I
draw a road -- and another road; here at the intersection is the
beginning of a radioconcentric group. The phenomenon develops
and multiplies into wider and wider belts, and an unquestionable
radioconcentric network is established.

I write: radioconcentric city of exchanges: goods, ideas, and
government, because there is another human establishment that
exists; its name is the unit of agricultural exploitation, which is
the first event of land occupancy by men. The third human establishment, the linear city of the industrial age, does not exist yet,
and if it were created, it would soon bring to the world conjunc-
tural solutions, among them the casting away of tentacular (from
tentacle) radioconcentric cities, and would bring about unity, union,
and fraternity among countries by creating contacts by economic
units of favorable sizes.

The evolution of this city in a machinist civilization must be geographical first. This is a radioconcentric unit that has been started, has evolved thus, and constitutes an unquestionable element of radioconcentric nature, absolutely the opposite of the parallel system of the linear city. Paris is an example of a city that has spread into suburbs, thus introducing the problem of distance. This city has become an absolute drama, similar to the drama that weighs upon New York, Berlin, Moscow, London: the drama of the tentacular city. Facing this dramatic situation means going somewhere into enormous spaces. These main roads will have to be created, or those, synthesized by this essential diagram: here you have the road to Spain, to Italy, Germany, to the North, to the West.

I have finished. As you see I go over those things with a lightning speed. How will this take place in New York or in Paris? It requires courage and self-control, and authorities must understand. But authorities are not informed; they are afraid, afraid to recognize the true nature of things; they are afraid to be forced to adopt solutions. They prefer to go to the moon, or they prefer to say that everything is all right, or to say that every man has only the idea to escape, to find a tree somewhere -- to put his house underneath with a happy man inside, the subway below, and cars at the front door! Multiply by eight million as in Paris, and it is a disaster.

I shall conclude with a drawing to tell you that if men were to be directed, it should be toward the occupancy of areas where waterways, highways, and railways should be located; to employ them to find on this earth that is so big, plains between mountains and between valleys, parts of zones of unoccupied land. We believe that there is no more land available on earth. Traveling by plane proves, on the contrary, the existence of immense free lands, provided that roads and water be made available.

I shall show you, for example, for Paris, what such decisions must bring: I draw the Seine with its bridges, its Cathedral, its St. John Tower, with Montmartre and its dome of the Sacred Heart.

here I put the Arch of Triumph, and there with the palaces of
the Louvre and the Concorde, I draw the junction of essential
roads coming from the north, and the new road east-west to
Paris, and then the roads toward Italy and Spain, and the Pan-
theon, and then the four office skyscrapers which will satisfy
the essentials of business life; here the new civic and business
centers of the center of Paris. Doing so, you have respected
the indispensable, fatally obligatory radioconcentric phenomenon.

LE CORBUSIER AND THE IMAGE OF MAN

José Luis Sert

In a world drifting towards dehumanized abstractions, Le Corbusier, like Picasso, remains obsessed with the human image. The human element, human scale, and the concern of providing for a better and happier life are at the roots of Le Corbusier's architecture. The image of man is ever-present in his works. This presence gives life to his architecture and adds visual interest to his buildings. This concern with man is to be found in everything that comes out of his mind and from his hands.

Le Corbusier visited a Carthusian monastery in the town of Ema in 1907 and wrote, "L'organisation harmonieuse du phénomène collectif et du phénomène individuel est résolu dans la sérénité, la joie, et l'éfficience. . ." He lists in order: first, serenity; then, joyfulness; and last, efficiency. I believe this statement is more representative of the man and his attitude towards life than his much-quoted and abused, "The house is a machine to live in."

It is interesting to observe the evolution of his work in painting, architecture, city planning, and writing. Man and the human image become increasingly important as his work de-develops. They are at the roots of his richer and more complete vocabulary.

In his early years, L'Eplattenier, who was his master in his study of nature, made him design natural forms and become aware of the structure of things alive. Le Corbusier remembers his teacher with gratitude, and he has never forgotten his lesson.

172

...ells, roots, plants, the way leaves grow, the skeletons ...ls, are patterns that stayed in his mind and have in ...ifferent ways influenced his designs.

His first paintings, in a style then called "purist," are still lifes, geometric in character, very carefully painted with the love of the craft of the primitive painter. Such things as bottles, glasses, and pipes predominate. By the standards of today we would call his first works the most abstract.

In architecture his early works show his awareness of the human presence and the need to re-establish a human scale, absent from the Beaux Arts school plans. He had rediscovered this human scale in the anonymous architecture of the people.

The plain white walls, the flat roofs, the simple, honest expression of volumes, and the bright accents of pure color in the Mediterranean towns impressed him in his early travels. His sketch books show his interest and preference for such simple buildings, and in his writings he states his aversion for the dishonest Renaissance "façadism." Peasant houses, seen as clusters in the Greek islands and in Turkey, and in towns like Ghardaïa in North Africa and Chioggia in the Venetian lagoon, raised many questions in his mind and provided many answers.

Le Corbusier, the man, has been given a rigid façade or front that does not correspond to reality. I know how many friends were surprised when they visited him in his old apartment at 20 Rue Jacob, near St. Germain des Près, to find him working in an old Louis XV house, surrounded by books, pictures, and cats. He is said to have told the well-known pioneer of modern architecture who visited him there in the twenties and registered surprise at the looks of his apartment, "Mon ami, l'architecture moderne c'est pour les clients. . ," which must have shocked his puritanical friend.

Nonetheless Le Corbusier has a great admiration for precision in general, and for machine precision in all its forms. When he

writes he makes it a point to be precise. He has a rare combination of the spirit of architecture and of plastic creativity.
His father worked for the watchmaking industry, and this side
of his ancestry may account for his more organized and precise likings. But his ancestors came up the Rhône River valley,
escaping from Provence because they were involved in the Albi-
gensian heresy. This would mean that he is originally of Mediterranean ancestry, which may explain the other side of his personality.

Le Corbusier is a man of strong principles and beliefs, and
it is only his faith in man and his conviction that there will be a
better future for humanity that has made him what he is. The
young people of today who are so much in need of leadership have
discovered these qualities in him, and this explains the appeal he
has for the younger generation.

Good architecture cannot be the product of compromise or
hesitation; architecture today is a statement, an act of faith in
humanity and its progress towards a better future. During the
last fifty years, his work in architecture and city planning is an
exponent of his faith in a better world of tomorrow. His "Civilization Machiniste" represents a world where the machine is put
at the service of man to allow him to live better and more happily.
He is aware at every moment that man's happiness is not only dependent on material values, but also on spiritual factors to which
he refers very frequently in his writings and with which he is increasingly concerned in his architecture. The great quality of Le
Corbusier's buildings is that they are an expression of what happens in them, and consequently, they are alive. He plans his buildings from the inside out. We could here quote the words of Maître
Pierre de Craon in Paul Claudel's L'Annonce Fait à Marie, "For
the heathen artist made everything from the outside, but we make
all from within, like the bees."

Having worked with him and become familiar with his methods
of approaching problems, I know how carefully he studies and con-

174

the changing effects of light ani-
his architecture. He is not a fast worker. He is a careful
thinker, and sometimes his forms take a long time to crystallize
because they develop from the very roots of things. Once his ideas
have crystallized into forms, they then develop in a natural and
easy way. His method is diametrically opposed to the quick sketch,
the brilliant but superficial Beaux Arts method.

This is why his buildings are so different; this is why his vocabulary has been developing through the years; this is why he is
always able to produce something new. But his novelty is not superficial and he does not believe in the new for the sake of the new.
His novelty has roots in the changing human needs and the high aspirations of man. Modern techniques are always a tool in his hands,
never an end in themselves. He generally leaves engineering to the
engineers and has always been content with assuming the role of the
architect in its fullest expression. His big work has never made
him forget the importance of the more modest things in life. After
publishing many books dealing with large-scale planning and the design of important public buildings, he can write a small essay, "Une
Petite Maison," describing the house he designed for his mother many
years ago.

The placing of a small window in a wall, a bench in a garden,
or a terrace in front of a lake are to him as much architecture as
the biggest and most monumental building. He has the modesty of
greatness in approaching his work: a good lesson for many of our
colleagues today.

Through his life, his greatest satisfaction has not come from
the praise of the art critics, but from the simple comments of the
people who understood his buildings and what he wants to do with
them. He is a man of simple customs who has developed a horror
of luxury as the majority of people understand it today. He believes
in the basic, simple values of life. Things need not be complicated

175

or rare to please him. He admires the work of primitive people or early cultures, such as African sculpture or Romanesque painting. The direct approach to form and line and the use of pure color please· him. Simple food and simple life are enough to make him happy.

This approach to life may explain some of his more recent buildings, such as Ronchamp and La Tourette, which have surprised many of Le Corbusier's admirers who had, perhaps, not followed his work in painting and sculpture too closely. He once told me, "People are going to say I contradict myself; that after building Ronchamp and having many exclaim, 'Thank God that. Le Corbusier got rid of his box architecture,' I am going back to building boxes in the Brazilian Pavilion in the University City in Paris. This is because they do not understand that I am mainly concerned with the different nature of the problems that I have to solve, and Ronchamp could not be a series of boxes, while by nature (biologically, as he puts it) other buildings are.

The people who understand him have often given him the approach to problems that they know he can develop. When asking him to design La Tourette, Père Couturier explained: "We walk in procession in two rows; we chant office in two rows; we prostrate ourselves full length on the ground. All these things determine the pattern and dimensions of the places where we pray, work, and eat. You see, it's something entirely up your street! It is simply an exercise in human scale."

In his small modulor work cell at 35 Rue de Sèvres there is a picture on the wall, a photograph of children in the wading pool on the roof of the Marseille Unité d'Habitation. He says he likes this picture because it proves that architecture can make people happier.

Mr. Sert, professor of architecture and dean of the Graduate School of Design, Harvard University, has practiced architecture and city planning in Spain, the United States, and several Latin American countries. Dean Sert had a year of training in the atelier of Le Corbusier. The first of his numerous books is Can Our Cities Survive? (1942

Ruskin wrote in the preface to The Seven Lamps of Architecture that the architect who was not a sculptor or a painter was
nothing better than a frame-maker on a large scale. We can
recall innumerable architectural masterworks of the past such
as small freestanding chapels or great cathedrals, in which the
sculptural relationships of the parts to the whole and the quality
of such relationships are immediately assertive. In our own
time, certain ambitious structures come to mind in which functional ends have been completely disregarded in the effort for
a sculptural effect. In many cases, that effect was doomed from
the outset to lifelessness because of a drawing-board approach in
contrast to the direct construction and free interrelation of parts
which gave the earlier examples their vitality.

But in approaching Le Corbusier as architect, painter, and
sculptor, I do not intend to consider his architecture as sculpture, although certain examples such as the chapel of Ronchamp
might justify it. Nor am I going to look at his architecture as
the product of an age dominated by painting, as contrasted, for
example, with the pre-Renaissance which might be regarded as
the period in which sculpture played the prime role in forming
the architect's eye.

As the English critic John Summerson points out, one of Le
Corbusier's characteristics throughout his work is a "passion for
opposites." For example, Summerson writes: "If we observe,
naively enough, that a house stands in a garden, Le Corbusier
can be imagined to reply, 'No, the garden stands in the house,'
proving his assertion by an executed design in which that is in
fact the case. If we suggest that a building is in principle four

walls with windows for light and air, he replies, 'On the contrary, a building may just as well be four windows, with walls for privacy and shade.' We put it to him as axiomatic that a park is a space for recreation in a town and he replies, 'Not at all; in the future the park will not be in the town, but the town in the park. Work, after all, is an incident in life; life is not an incident in work.'"

Granted a trinity such as Le Corbusier's, one might normally expect in a similar way that his architecture would lean heavily toward either painting or sculpture; actually, his interest in painting or sculpture serve basically as the means to realization of an assertively architectural form with concessions to neither. Perhaps the explanation lies in the statement he expressed in an article written in 1948: "But where does sculpture begin, or painting begin, or architecture? The substance of the built domain is the expression of these three acts conjointly answerable." And Le Corbusier is an essentially "visual man working with eyes and hands animated by plastic endeavour," as he himself has declared.

Painting and sculpture for Le Corbusier are basically tools toward a fuller domination of nature and of his materials. They are means to an end, and the end is his architectural form and his individual expression through it. But they are invaluable means. If he did not have them at hand, as he found himself through the years, much of the quintessential Le Corbusier would be lacking.

Beneath them both lies drawing, which is, perhaps, Le Corbusier's natural medium of expression. In any case, it is the language which he employs to speak to himself, to record his visual impressions, to communicate and preserve them. In a sense, his painting is merely a broadened interpretation of his drawing through color; his sculpture a translation of it into three dimensions.

The elegance of his personality, however, resides in the graphic work, which gives his notebooks their life. Through his drawings he explores nature and rifles it to his purposes. "Everyone," he once declared, "has the right to define drawing his own way. For me, drawing is the means by which an artist seeks to seize that part of nature, of creation, which he feels he would like to observe, to know, to understand, to translate, and to express. This knowledge and this expression, eminently personal, will be the motive power of his paintings and sculpture." Again: "To interrogate nature, the line, the blot, color, and shadow are the means at our disposal."

Drawing therefore is the most effective way for the artist to arrive at an apprehension of either an interior or an exterior event. For Le Corbusier, as for many other artists, it is not merely a "particular technique of expression, but the initial moment of creation, or, more exactly, that on which it can lean."

"When one travels and works with visual things -- architecture, painting, or sculpture," Le Corbusier states in Creation is a Patient Search: a Self Portrait, " one uses one's eyes and draws so as to fix deep down in one's experience what is seen. Once the impression has been recorded by the pencil, it stays for good, entered, registered, inscribed. The camera is a tool for idlers, who use a machine to do their seeing for them. To draw oneself, to trace the lines, handle the volumes, organize the surface; all this means first to look, and then to observe, and finally perhaps to discover; and it is then that inspiration may come. Inventing, creating, one's whole being is drawn into action, and it is this action which counts. Others stood indifferent -- but you saw!"

Between his thirteenth and seventeenth years, Le Corbusier was apprenticed to a watch-case engraver. And his first client, L'Eplattenier, introduced him to formal design through Owen Jones's A Grammar of Ornament. He began to paint only in 1918, after Auguste Perret had introduced him to Amedée Ozenfant. In the early twenties, he held closely to the purist line with Ozenfant,

179

but during the preparations of the Esprit Nouveau pavilion for the Paris World's Fair of 1925, and shortly after that the influence of Fernand Léger's work, he was drawn step by step into a warmer palette and towards a bolder suggestion of the third dimension. In the thirties reflections of Picasso's linearism began to relax the Légeresque solidity of forms. All this time, painting was, as he wrote in his sketch book in 1960, "a bitter struggle, terrifying, pitiless, unseen; a duel between the artist and himself. The struggle goes on inside, hidden on the surface. If the artist tells, he is betraying himself. . . !"

He saw this struggle as a part of a "patient search," as he described creative work. While he undoubtedly would have been happier had his painting received a more enthusiastic reception, the search went on. For Le Corbusier, the draftsman, it is the outline which explains the volume. His pictures represent objects seen from the front, but their depth is implied in the lines. Of this he writes: "In architecture, this trait is very significant, for it is the plan and section uncompromising and precise which provide the entire basis for architecttural inventions."

From 1940 onwards, his paintings were often potential sculptures. A Breton woodworker recognized this and asked if he might use certain of them as models for sculpture. Since 1946, Le Corbusier and this Breton admirer, Joseph Savina, have frequently collaborated in three-dimensional carved and colored work. Insofar as it led to an architectural end, to a sharpening of the eye and a variegation in his vocabulary of forms, there is no question of the intimate relationship between painting, sculpture, and architecture in Le Corbusier's expression.

It would be difficult to say, however, on other grounds, how much Le Corbusier's development as an architect owed to his association with modern painting. Many of his plans certainly have the quality of a geometrical, abstract painting. The plan of a building is, as every architect knows, the key to its success or failure as a work of art: the whole building as an organism

180

is implicit in its plan. Le Corbusier has underlined this in his
writings, where he speaks often of le plan générateur. And if
we take the plan of the Pavillon Suisse in the Cité Universitaire
in Paris, for example, we see a pattern which has a nervous,
delicate beauty of its own.

But the question of the influence of modern painting on
modern architecture, to quote Summerson again, "is not so important as the historical truth that Le Corbusier, the architect,
has shared the same vision as some of the cubist and abstract
painters." Just as they accomplished a revaluation of the picture and the materials that make it up, "Le Corbusier effected
nothing less than a revaluation of architecture itself." Just as
his purist friend Ozenfant and his "mechanist" friend Léger
gave humble shapes pictorial dignity, so he "found fragments
of real architecture lying around outside the unreal category
of which 'architecture' is the traditional label. He found architecture in the worlds of engineering, of shipbuilding, of industrial construction, of aircraft design. His painting and sculpture enabled him to bring these fragments together and fuse
them into buildings possessing style in his own personal vision."

Aside from a consideration of Le Corbusier's architecture
as sculptural or pictorial expression, there is another product
of this trinity: the individual sculptural and polychrome details
of his buildings. Thanks primarily to the vitality of these
interests, Le Corbusier's work never finds itself like an "anonymous box." The quality of Le Corbusier's contributions in these
fields are, to be sure, not always equally happy. As a matter of
fact, they are extremely uneven. Even in a brilliantly sensitive
composite such as the Ronchamp chapel, the polychrome decorations
of the doors are distressingly crude in comparison with the design
of the stained glass windows or with the sculptural integrity of the
total volume of the building. Again, one may be disturbed by many
of the chromatic decorative effects of the interior of l'Unité
d'Habitation at Marseille, compared, for example, to the
sculptural monumentality of the roof elements. But throughout
Le Corbusier's work, color is used as a painter uses it, as
structural color or destructive color; to build out a plane, or
to bore through a wall, as the case may be.

It is in the details of Le Corbusier's work that the painter and sculptor of the trinity most clearly show themselves. Every element of the total construction in a building by Le Corbusier is studied in its sculptural individuality as well as in its sculptural relationship to the elements of the whole, whether in the polychrome interior walls and mural of the Pavillon Suisse or the more expansive later realizations of Chandigarh; whether in a wind break on the roof of the Villa Savoie, or the profile of Ronchamp.

Today, as always, we hear discussions on all sides regarding the possibility of an effective collaboration between painters, sculptors, and architects. Such a collaboration did occur in the past. In fifteenth-century Italy the architects assisted the painters with their architectural settings; in the Baroque age, the painters and sculptors joined hands with the architects in creating illusory superstructures to their churches. But only in our own day has the art of painting (cubism and De Stijl in particular) opened the world of form which has subsequently been explored by architects to their own great advantage. Perhaps it is true that today architecture and other arts do not collaborate, that painters and sculptors no longer adorn the works of architects as they did in the past. That, in one sense, cannot be contested, but in another sense, collaboration among the arts has rarely been so richly productive as in the past three or four decades. Thanks particularly to the trinity in which the painter and sculptor have always worked sensitively and boldly to point and clear the way for the architect, we have, in the work of Le Corbusier, the most nearly complete satisfactory example of this collaboration among the arts.

Mr. Sweeney has assembled and directed exhibitions of art for the Museum of Modern Art and other institutions in the United States and overseas. He has been director of the Solomon R. Guggenheim Museum and now directs the Houston Museum of Fine Arts.

THE INFLUENCES OF LE CORBUSIER

Harry A. Anthony

At the age of nineteen, Le Corbusier pocketed the fees from his first house and set out to Italy, France, Germany, to Central Europe, to Greece, to Asia Minor, and to Spain. While on the Acropolis of Athens, where he spent six weeks, he felt the columns of the Parthenon with his hands, caressed them, and studied their proportions. For the first time, he came to the amazing conclusion that "reality has nothing to do with books of instruction." In his notebook he wrote a warning to himself: "Do not believe until you have seen and measured and touched with your fingers." From then on, this was his only schooling.

Le Corbusier benefited greatly from these tours, interrupted now and then with work periods in Berlin and in Paris. That he completely understood the esthetic lessons of architectural history is clearly evident in his first book, Vers Une Architecture, published in 1923, in which he berated his fellow architects for having "des yeux qui ne voient pas," eyes which do not see.

He made hundreds of sketches and drawings during his trips so as to fix deep down in his own experience what he saw. He wrote: "Once the impression has been recorded by the pencil, it stays for good, entered, registered, inscribed. The camera is a tool for idlers, who use a machine to do their seeing for them. To draw oneself, to trace the lines, handle the volumes, organize the surface... all this means first to look and then to observe and finally perhaps to discover... and it is then that inspiration may come."

In 1908-1909, he spent fifteen months with the Perret brothers in Paris, a time of great significance to his professional development and the formulation of his city-planning ideas. Having introduced reinforced concrete to architecture in 1903, when they built the famous nine-story apartment building in the Rue Franklin in Paris, the Perret brothers were trying to achieve complete mastery of reinforced concrete, both as a structural and facing material. While working in that office, full of admiration for the great Auguste Perret and full of enthusiasm for the possibilities offered by reinforced concrete, twenty-one-year-old Le Corbusier conceived the idea of freeing the ground of cities for the pedestrian by lifting all buildings and roads above ground level.

Esthetically, such a concept would make tall buildings look much lighter, held up in the air by recessed thin columns, cantilevered on all sides and liberating the space underneath. Instead of the pyramid-like stone construction, heavy at the bottom and light at the top, a reinforced concrete stilted building could be designed to stand light and gracious like a tree, rooted in wide foundations, with a slender and strong trunk projecting out of the ground and with its heavy mass high up in the air, like branches and foliage. The pedestrian would regain complete possession of the ground, both around and under the buildings, and the whole ground level could become a large uninterrupted park.

After seeing the world and working in many places, Le Corbusier returned to Paris in 1917, when he was thirty years old, and established permanent residence. By 1930, just a dozen years later, he had become recognized as the foremost protagonist of modern architecture and city planning.

He never separated these two fields in his mind; in his practice and in his writings they were always one and the same. It is interesting to observe that he gave this most beautiful and poetic definition of architecture: "L'architecture est le jeu savant, correct et magnifique des volumes assemblés

184

sous la lumière. " In the English translation his words lose
some of their passion: "Architecture is the masterly, correct,
and magnificent play of masses brought together in light. "
What is most significant to me is that in his definition of architecture, Le Corbusier glorifies the outside of the buildings:
the way they look from the open spaces between them, the way
they relate to open spaces, the way their volumes form a
unified whole and harmonize under the sun. This is a notion
that urban designers and city planners today have very close
to their hearts, as constituting the essence of city architecture.

Le Corbusier introduced more forcefully than anyone
else the tall building as the new instrument for building cities.
His first major city planning creation was the plan for La
Ville Contemporaine for three million people, exhibited
at the Salon d'Automne in 1922. Its most important features
were these: the city was to be a huge park, studded by tall
office skyscrapers in the middle, and apartment buildings all
around; elevated highways, never crossed by a pedestrian,
were to handle all automobile traffic. They crisscrossed the
city in directions of 90 and 45 degrees, thus making the center easily and quickly accessible, and were joined at the outskirts of the city by a peripheral highway system that bypassed
the built-up area altogether.

As all buildings were raised above ground level on stilts,
or pilotis, the entire ground level was given to the pedestrian
who was free to walk everywhere, anywhere, without interference
by cars, without the slightest danger. The ground was richly
landscaped and provided a setting for outdoor recreation of all
kinds , as well as for schools, restaurants, cafes, clubs, and
youth centers. The density of population proposed was 300
persons per acre, approximately equal to the density of
nineteenth-century Paris. (This, incidentally, is less than
one-half of what we have in most blocks around the Columbia
University campus on Morningside Heights.)

185

The center of La Ville Contemporaine was to be a group of twenty-four skyscrapers, fifty or sixty stories high, cruciform in plan, very widely spaced, housing administrative, business, and professional offices. A civic and cultural center was located nearby. The residential sectors contained apartment buildings, all having twelve stories, or six double stories, in height. They were to be built en redents, like long, continuous walls wandering in and out and changing direction on two main coordinates, thus creating spacious courts, which in turn were freely connected with the adjoining courts through and underneath the various buildings.

The whole city was to be surrounded by a green belt, several miles wide, isolating and protecting it forever. Industrial districts, farms, a sports arena or, perhaps, a port could be located beyond the green belt. The optimum population of three million inhabitants was not to be exceeded -- additional new cities should be built to take care of the excess urban growth.

This orderly, geometric city is the embodiment of French rationale and clear thinking. A few years after its introduction, La Ville Contemporaine was followed by La Ville Radieuse, the Radiant City, a more refined scheme along the same principles, completed in 1929. In 1925, Le Corbusier's famous Plan Voisin was the first urban renewal plan proposed for the center of Paris since the days of Haussmann, back in the 1860's.

With his elevated highways and stilted buildings, Le Corbusier was the first man fully to develop and defend the theme of complete separation of vehicular from pedestrian traffic, the first man to treat the pedestrian with the respect and honor we now accord only to the automobile. What is most important is that this, as well as all the other principles of the forty-year-old Ville Contemporaine, are today the essence and basis of every radical "new" city plan being proposed seriously anywhere in the world.

186

Le Corbusier followed these principles in his practice during all his life, even if the resulting forms are not exactly the same as in his theoretical city planning schemes. Today, his genius, the analytical and creative abilities of his mind, and the freshness of his approach are still staggering. His chapel at Ronchamps is the building -- or, should I say, the sculpture -- in which "visual acoustics" appeared and found formal expression. He wrote: "Forms make a noise and are silent; some speaking, others listening." His Saint Mary's Convent in La Tourette (like the Swiss Pavilion at the Cité Universitaire of Paris in its day) is completely new, and although his city of Chandigarh little resembles in form the Ville Contemporaine, it follows the principles established in 1922. Thus, although younger than ever in ideas, vigor, and enthusiasm, Le Corbusier, at seventy-four, is still faithfully using the principles he formulated so many years ago.

With his extraordinary capacity to observe, to use creatively the results of cool analysis, with his artistic talent and his sociological approach, with his books and his buildings, Le Corbusier has tremendously influenced both architecture and city planning throughout the world. In France, he designed the master plan for the city of St. Dié, destroyed during the war. In South America many applications of his city planning principles and ideas are in evidence, among them the famous Ministry of Education and Health Building in Rio de Janeiro; the plans for the cities of Lima, Bogota, and many others, the Citade dos Motores, and the most recent city of Brazilia, the new capital of Brazil.

In America, most redevelopment projects and all large-scale urban housing developments have followed his principles, but, alas, superficially only, without understanding them and without an iota of his sensitivity. Look what was done with the open spaces of the large housing developments of New York or of the Golden Triangle in Pittsburgh. We have nothing but leftovers instead of real open spaces.

His 1929 plan for Rio de Janeiro and his 1930 plan for
Algiers are by now classics. In both of these, he combined
buildings and roads in continuous miles-long serpentine-
shaped structures that follow the contours of the city and permitted major highways to run along on top of the roof. This
concept of a city which, instead of having isolated buildings
connected by roads, has a spiral road which is itself a
building, was formulated by Le Corbusier in 1929 and 1930.
Yet, it is shown in the 1961 edition of the Encyclopaedia
Britannica Book of the Year as the major contribution to the
"city of the future" by British architects who designed it in
1960 !

In the field of housing, his apartment block, the Unité
d'Habitation in Marseille, houses about 1600 persons in 337
apartments. To put so many people under one roof is not in
itself so remarkable. New York has some monstrous apartment blocks with many more people piled on top of one another.
But Le Corbusier's Unité has a singularly high degree of social
significance and functional efficiency. For one thing there is
an unusual amount of flexibility of living quarters for accommo-
dating families with children, young couples, bachelors, and
older people. There is a street of shops on the ninth floor of the
seventeen-story building. There is also a hotel for guests, a
post office, and, on the top floor, nurseries for 150 children.
On the terraces there are play areas, gymnasiums, a swimming
pool, game rooms,and gardens. The interior is functional
convenience and simplicity itself, requiring a minimum of
furniture. The building is designed to enable its inhabitants
to live a rich and varied community life and still retain individual freedom and privacy. These are Le Corbusier's ideas,
works, and influences.

Mr. Anthony is professor of urban planning at the School of
Architecture, Columbia University, and head of its program
in planning. As partner of the firm of Brown and Anthony, he
is author of a number of master plans.

188

POTENTIALS OF THE SKYSCRAPER-STUDDED PARK

Harry A. Anthony

It is very difficult to undertake a critical re-examination of the city-planning theory of the man in whose studio, fifteen years ago, I had my eyes opened! But it is one of the purposes of this program to do this, and hard as it may be, I cannot escape the task.

The one consideration that was most seriously neglected in Le Corbusier's ideal city schemes is the mass use of the automobile, the new conqueror of our cities. Although for the time being an American phenomenon only, the mass use of the automobile has reached such extravagant dimensions that the harm done to the livability of our cities is becoming disastrous.

Merely to criticize the automobile, however, is no different from criticizing human nature. Like it or not, the automobile will be with us for many years, if only because it offers convenience and an escape from the urban problem it has created. Moreover, I am convinced that for long distances through large rural spaces and in low-density human settlements the automobile is and will remain -- in the foreseeable future -- a most essential element of transportation. For short distances within high-density urban areas, the pedestrian should be treated with the respect he deserves, and mass rapid transit should connect the neighborhoods and suburbs of dense urban areas with the center.

But let us go back to Le Corbusier's city. To park all the cars of the city in the areas allocated to them in the plan would have been impossible. If we were to build his Contemporary City today exactly as designed, the cars would either have to

189

go underground (at great expense) or into landscaped parks which they would swamp! A look from an airplane over the Pentagon and its surroundings shows clearly the amount of space needed for the automobile when thousands of people move by car to and from a large building in which they are concentrated. And this is only half the story, because at the other end of the journey of each of these cars, an equivalent amount of storage space in or near the house is needed.

Certainly, the extraordinary growth in the number of automobiles and in car ownership happened after Le Corbusier's Ville Contemporaine was designed, and we can justly say that he could not have foreseen it (as we cannot foresee or imagine a similar growth in helicopters or in space travel). The fact remains, however, that Le Corbusier's ideal schemes will have to take this automobile population into account and be revised accordingly if they are to remain applicable in the years to come.

A second shortcoming is to be found at the implementation stage of Le Corbusier's schemes. Le Corbusier is an intellectual, a great artist with a deep understanding of people and societies. His designs are outstanding; his buildings and his paintings are a delight to the eye. But, once he had designed the new plans for his ideal cities, he did not follow through the implications of his designs. He did not even try to find workable means to put them on the ground, to change human inertia or to adjust the complicated legal framework of land ownership and development. He simply said that the legal and economic aspects of his city designs were for others to study.

Now, in democratic societies we all know that unless a city plan is understood by the people and supported by their elected officials, it remains a utopia. At best, if it is rendered with beautiful colors, it becomes only a mural in the Mayor's office. Devising the means of effectuation of a plan, taking into account the legal, economic, social, and political realities and potentialities are within the city planning process. They are an inseparable part of the city planner's job.

190

A third factor that Le Corbusier underemphasized was the parents' strong desire to have their little children living near the ground, not six or twelve stories up. We can justify this underemphasis if we consider that Le Corbusier married late in life, and he has never experienced the rich and enormous joy -- and frequent anguish -- of having little children about the home.

A fourth issue which I take with Le Corbusier's ideal city scheme is its relatively antiurban character. This may sound like a paradox, but if Le Corbusier's city, particularly its center, is a park, does it not, therefore, violate the urban concept itself, the idea of what a city is supposed to be? The beauty and comfort of open space in the central areas of cities is embodied in its treatment as a positive element of design, contained within buildings, not as a negative element, a leftover space between or outside buildings.

Le Corbusier's plans for the cores of his cities seem to show a casual disregard for the concept of "containment" of open space. Chandigarh's open spaces in the core are everywhere, so much so that the beautiful buildings seem almost lost in the huge emptiness surrounding them. And this is an area where the impressive landscaping shown on the drawings is actually almost nothing but a large expanse of reddish earth. Now, I want to make sure that I am not misunderstood. I do not say that Le Corbusier did not pay attention to the design of open space -- I merely want to say that the open spaces in the cores of his cities do not exhibit the urban characteristic of containment, the tightness that all people seem to like and expect to see in cities.

Fifteen years ago when I worked in Le Corbusier's studio in Paris, I recall that my first assignment was to draw a site plan with five slab apartment buildings, unités d'habitation, for the French city of La Rochelle-Palice. When I placed the buildings equidistant from one another in logical and orderly fashion following some of what I thought were his ideas, I remember Le Corbusier came and looked at my drawing and said

191

to me: "Mais non, mon vieux, ce n'est pas comme ça! Les espaces, il faut que ça joue de la musique!" Spaces should play music! And he proceeded to relocate the buildings in a more esthetic arrangement with harmonious proportions between open spaces.

Although this incident indicates the sincere concern for the beauty of open space, I am afraid there is a fallacy inherent in this approach to the design of open space which seems to disregard human scale. It is an esthetic of the airplane view alone. Can the human being standing on his own two feet with an eye level five feet from the ground perceive these proportions of the open elements of the plan when translated to life-size scale? With all due respect to my former teacher, the great master and maker, I conclude that the human being cannot. The street views and the containment of space seen from pedestrian level are what create the esthetic of the urban environment. Only contained urban space can become a work of art like the Place Vendôme, sometimes even a masterpiece of urban design, like the Piazza San Marco or Rockefeller Center. Merely open noncontained urban space, providing light and air, serves only a practical purpose and very rarely provokes any esthetic emotion.

These open spaces designed from the esthetic of the airplane point of view tend to run amorphously at the level of the human eye, five feet above the ground. From this point of view they are deprived of any intelligibility, unity, harmony, character, or emotion. The plazas of the cities of Italy, among the most enjoyable pedestrian places in the world, are far more than just so many square feet of open land. They are really a way of life, a concept of living, and people use these contained open spaces as living rooms and even as dining rooms.

What are the future potentials of the skyscraper-studded park idea? First of all, its validity has already been established, at least in part, with such existing cities as Chandigarh and Brazilia; or sections of cities such as Marseille and Nantes; and the wide use of the skyscraper which is spreading here, in

Europe and even in Russia. But where are the potentialities
with respect to specific requirements which must be met in order
to accommodate our tremendous urban growth?

It is reasonable to suggest that the housing needs of people
could be broken down by age group and by house and apartment
dwelling units. Between the years from birth to approximately
fifteen, a house with a private play yard would be the most
desirable place to live. From fifteen to about twenty-five years
old -- a ten year age span -- an apartment would provide an
agreeable and convenient living accommodation. This is the
period when Johnny lives at college (in an apartment-like dormi-
tory) and Susie who has gone to work in the big city is rooming
with a girl friend in an apartment. Then for twenty years, from
age twenty-five to forty-five, children are being raised, and
again a house with private play yard would be more ideal. Following this, for about twenty-five years from age forty-five to
seventy, most people whose children are by then grown and on
their own would find apartment living again most convenient
and desirable. This little bit of theory says in essence that, for
Americans at least, half of our life might be spent living in an
apartment and the other half in a house.

The skyscraper-studded park would have good potential, then,
in serving the housing needs for those percentages and age groups
in our population who prefer to live in apartments and do not want
to live in the suburbs. The twenty-five-to-forty-five year old
people and their children, and others by preference, would continue
to live in the suburbs.

Let us hope that these future suburbs will be designed differently from those we now have. The solution may lie in increasing
the distance between car and home, clustering the houses in
tighter groups (leaving adequate permanent open space between
the clusters), and favoring mass transit for most of the travel
within the urban area.

The separation of vehicle and pedestrian in Le Corbusier's skyscraper-studded park has a functional validity which needs to be carried out much more positively and completely in the years to come. This is the best concept in contemporary city planning, the only hope of taking the city back from the automobile and returning it to man. In addition, it will automatically result in the decongestion of our highly populated urban areas by allowing three-dimensional solutions to problems of land use and traffic. What really produces urban congestion (in addition to too many people) is the extraordinary demand and competition for ground floor space, including the movement of vehicles and pedestrians, loading and unloading of trucks, parking, entering stores and apartment buildings, viewing displays in show windows, pushing the baby carriage, walking the dog or sitting on a bench to rest. Many of these activities could be separated vertically, and the ground floor, where congestion is now manifested, would become livable again. Incorporated into the design of the skyscraper-studded park must be new modes of transportation such as high-speed monorail trains with stations for each cluster of apartment buildings, and possibly, vertical take-off aircraft pads or helicopter platforms to meet the needs of more direct and rapid transportation while carrying out the concept of separation of various types and speeds of transportation movement.

Economic considerations favor the Le Corbusier city as a means of offsetting the high cost and relative scarcity of urban land while still providing the amenities of light, air, openness, and recreation facilities. After all, the tall building in America started purely as an economic necessity, and its economic advantages have helped spread it all over the world.

Esthetically, Le Corbusier's skyscraper-studded park, particularly in its central area, needs to become more tight, more urban in design and intent -- if it is to provide the urban character that is so successful in attracting people to live and work and shop in the city and which makes them feel comfortable and pleased. This urban character is tied inseparably to the concept of   containment   -- purely a subjective feeling of the human being for his surroundings. If this idea of containment together with the reintroduction of the street for the pedestrian can be incorporated in the core of the Le Corbusier skyscraper-studded park, there is every reason to believe that esthetically it has a most promising future potential in our solution to the problem of urban growth.

And lastly, what are the future potentials of the skyscraper-studded park with reference to considerations of new trends in land use? First, larger land areas of specialized nature, designed as super blocks are supplanting smaller areas and individual parcels. This is a trend in the direction of skyscraper-studded parks. Second, super-highways, expressways, and freeways are beginning to pierce the hearts of our cities. What is needed is the same treatment proposed in Le Corbusier's 1922 Ville Contemporaine, in which highways reached the center of city on elevated structures, never crossed by pedestrians, and were looped on the periphery by a highway system which bypassed the city altogether. Not until after World War II did we begin extensively applying this concept and treatment in this country, and even today with the crisis of the automobile already here, many of our plans are still only on paper, as it is the national weakness of this country not to prepare for a crisis until it is actually upon us.

In conclusion, the skyscraper-studded park idea, properly updated, holds great potential in helping us solve America's urban growth problem.

For a biography of Mr. Anthony, see page 188.

LE CORBUSIER'S MODULOR

Rudolf Wittkower

At a recent meeting at the Royal Institute of British
Architects in London to which I was a party (June 18, 1957),
the motion was before the house "that Systems of Proportion
make good design easier and bad design more difficult."
The motion was defeated. But in the debate Le Corbusier's
Modulor was constantly referred to, and the distinguished
architect, Misha Black, even said apologetically that "it
must inevitably be in our minds as we discuss the motion."
Indeed, after the Modulor we must be for it or against it;
it would mean deluding ourselves if we tried to be escapist
or neutral.

In 1948 Le Corbusier surprised the architectural world
with his Modulor. The book was quickly sold out. Le
Corbusier himself, whom I may (perhaps not too charitably)
describe as a cross between a prophet and a salesman of
rare ability, brought the story up to date in 1954, with the
publication of his Modulor 2.

What was the reason for the world-wide response to the
Modulor? Was it due to Le Corbusier's prophesy or his
salesmanship? Each may have played a part, but many a
prophet has cried in the wilderness, unheard. In all fair-
ness, we must admit that the time was ripe for the Modulor.

The Beaux Arts tradition, according to which proportion
is something vague, indefinable, irrational -- a "something"
that must be left to the individual architect's sensibility -- that
tradition is as dead as a doornail. If it is not, it should be.

196

Be that as it may, I find it difficult or even impossible to give paternal advice to practitioners regarding the suitability of the Modulor for the design of, say, skyscrapers. As an historian I am concerned with the past rather than with the future, and I can only discuss the Modulor in its historical context. Such an investigation may at least help to assess the validity of Le Corbusier's basic assumptions.

So far as I can see, the belief in an order, divine and human, derived from numbers and relations of numbers was always tied to higher civilizations. All systems of proportion are implicitly intellectual, for they are based on mathematical logic. Without a grasp of geometry and the theory of numbers, no system of proportion is imaginable.

It must be regarded as one of the most extraordinary events in the early history of mankind when a bridge was created between abstract mathematical thought and the phenomenal world that surrounds us; when geometry and numbers were found to govern the skies as well as all creation on earth. The Bible reflects this remarkable alliance between life and mathematics, between endless variety and numerical limitation. In the Wisdom of Solomon (XI, 20), we read, "By measure and number and weight thou didst order all things."

The intellectualism of this daring hypothesis must not lead us astray, for in reality we are here faced with a biologically conditioned sublimation. The quest for symmetry, balance, and proportional relationships is deeply embedded in human nature. Modern antagonists always claim that systems of proportion interfere with, and even impede, the release of creative energies. In actual fact, however, such systems are no more, and no less, than intellectual directives given to an instinctive urge which regulates not only human behaviour but even the behaviour of higher species of animals.

Man's predisposition for ordering complex sensory stimuli can easily be tested. For instance, we interpret automatically irregular configurations as regular figures (see Arnheim, Art and Visual Perception, fig. 44). Such incontestable observations permit us to conclude that we seek ordered patterns; systems of proportion are the principal vehicles to satisfy this urge.

All systems of proportion in Western art and architecture, the only civilization we are concerned with, are ultimately derived from Greek thought. Pythagoras, living in the sixth century B. C. , is credited with the discovery that the Greek musical scale depends on the division of a string of the lyre in the ratios 1:2 (octave), 2:3 (fifth), 3:4 (fourth), and 1:4 (double octave). In other words, the ratios of the first four integers 1:2:3:4 express all the consonances of the Greek musical scale. This discovery of the close interrelationship of sound, space, and numbers had immense consequences, for it seemed to hold the key to the unexplored regions of universal harmony. Moreover, if the invariable of all octaves is the ratio 1:2, it must be this ratio, the Greeks argued, that is the cause of the musical consonance. Perfection and beauty were therefore ascribed to the ratio itself.

Plato, in his Timaeus, expounded a geometrical theory which was no less influential. He postulated that certain simple figures of plane geometry were the basic stuff of which the universe was composed. I have no doubt that it was mainly owing to Plato's never-forgotten cosmological theory that such figures as the equilateral triangle, the right-angled isosceles triangle,and the square were charged with a deep significance and played such an important part in the Western approach to proportion.

We have overwhelming evidence that many medieval churches were built ad quadratum or ad triangulum, reflecting a platonic pedigree. Milan Cathedral is a well-known example: discussions on whether the church should be erected according to triangulation or quadrature dragged on for years.

198

From the fifteenth century on, attention was focused on musical proportion. Although never entirely excluded from consideration, the Renaissance and post-Renaissance periods preferred an arithmetical theory of proportion derived from the harmonic intervals of the Greek musical scale, in contrast to the Middle Ages, which favoured platonic geometry. The Renaissance, in addition, fully embraced ancient anthropometry. Following Vitruvius (whose treatise reflects Greek ideas), Renaissance theory and practice pronounced axiomatically that the proportions of architecture must echo those of the human body. This ancient theory lent itself to being incorporated into a Christian conception of the world. The Bible tells us that Man was created in the image of God. It logically follows that Man's proportions are perfect. The next axiom appears unavoidable: man-made objects, such as architectural structures, can only be attuned to universal harmony if they follow man's proportions. You may approve or disapprove of these deductions; you may find Renaissance architects' demonstrations of the connection between man and architecture naive and even funny, but some of you may detect that we are moving close to the Modulor. Moreover, because of -- or in spite of -- such convictions, the world was enriched by most beautiful buildings.

To postulate such a relationship between human and architectural proportions is, perhaps, not so far-fetched. The human body lends itself to an investigation of metrical relationships between parts and between the parts and the whole. You can express the parts in terms of submultiples of the whole; or you can operate with a small unit of measurement such as the face or the hand as a module, the multiples and submultiples of which guarantee metrical coordination.

Precisely the same principles may be applied to architectural structures: all the parts may be metrically interrelated by making them submultiples of a grand unit or multiples of a small unit. For the Renaissance, the tertium comparationis between man and buildings consisted in this: just as the beauty

199

of the human body appears to be regulated by and derived from the correct metrical relation between all its members, so the beauty of a building depends on the correct metrical interrelation of all its parts.

In the eighteenth century the old approach to proportion broke down. Enlightenment and empiricism militated against the notion that mathematical ratios as such can be beautiful. Romantic artists had no use for intellectual number theories which would seem to endanger their individuality and freedom. In the nineteenth century it was mainly scholars who kept the interest in problems of proportion alive.

The mid-nineteenth century, however, saw two events which had a direct bearing on the modern approach to proportion -- and on Le Corbusier's Modulor. First, Joseph Paxton built the Crystal Palace in London, the first structure of colossal size erected of standardized units over a grid. The logic inherent in the industrial revolution enforced a dimensional order. Secondly, the German, Adolf Zeising, published a book, Neue Lehre von dem Proportionem des menschlichen Körpers, 1854, in which he persuasively argued that the Golden Section was the proportion pervading macrocosm and microcosm alike.

The wonderful properties of the Golden Section, of course, had been known to the Greeks. The Golden Section is the only true proportion consisting of two magnitudes (instead of 3 or 4), and in it as you know, the ratio of the whole to the larger part always equals that of the larger to the smaller part:

$$\frac{a}{b} = \frac{b}{a+b} = \frac{.618}{1} = \frac{1}{1.618}$$

In the early thirteenth century Leonardo da Pisa, called Fibonacci, discovered that on a ladder of numbers with each number on the right being the sum of the pair on the preceding rung, the arithmetical ratio between the two numbers on the same rung rapidly approaches the Golden Section. Thus, for practical

In contrast to an arbitrary module, it offers the possibility
of harmonious integration of standardized products. Such
considerations show Le Corbusier in line of descent from
Paxton and competing with the propagators of standardization
through modular coordination. Thirdly, in contrast to the
technologists among architects, who consider a module
esthetically neutral, for Le Corbusier esthetic satisfaction
overrides all other considerations. Harmony, regulating
everything around us, is his ultimate quest. His aesthetic
judgment is buttressed, thus, by a metaphysical belief in a
divine order of things. Fourthly, the Modulor is a precision
instrument, comparable to the keyboard of a piano; like the
keyboard, the Modulor does not interfere with the individual
freedom of the performer. Nor does it help to make bad
designs good.

Meanwhile, modular coordination is on the march. An
almost unbelievable amount of research has been devoted to it
in recent years. The main purpose of these enterprises is
to economize on all levels: in the architect's and the contractor's
office as well as in the factory. Designs consist of multiples
of the basic module, and since F. Bemis's Evolving House,
published in 1936, the four-inch grid has been given preference
in this country. The difference between the static -- sterile, one
is tempted to say -- quality of the normal modular grid and
the dynamic quality of Le Corbusier's grid is most striking.

What is the balance sheet? As I see it, Le Corbusier's
Modulor, the creation of one man, has to assert itself against
the combined efforts of hundreds or even thousands working
on modular coordination. The odds favour the advocates of
modular coordination: their work is scientific, sober, and
objective. It is to the point, easily intelligible, and eminently
practical. Le Corbusier's is the opposite in every respect:
it is amateurish, dynamic, personal, paradoxical, and often
obscure. When you think you have it all sorted out, you wonder
how practical the Modulor really is. Le Corbusier's own
buildings at Marseille, St. Dié, Algiers, Chandigarh, supply
the answer.

Nevertheless, all his claims have been challenged.
Against his faith in the immense variability of design offered
by the Modulor, it is said that its range enforces an unsatis-
factory limitation. Against his canon derived from the six-
foot man, it is claimed that in order to be universal, other
human heights should be taken into account. His assertion
of freedom of design guaranteed by the Modulor is dismissed
as "just another rigid academic system." His play with the
Golden Section and the Fibonacci series is criticized as school-
boy mathematics wrapped in a cloak of mystification.

I do not want to continue this list of censure, for when
all is said and done, it is only Le Corbusier whose instinct
guided him to the sources of our cultural heritage; who
transformed it imaginatively to suit modern requirements;
who attempted a new synthesis, and once again, intellectualized
man's intuitive urge with which I began. It is only Le Corbusier who brings to bear on the old problem of proportion a
prophetic, unceasingly searching,and, above all, poetic mind...
the poetic and illogical mind of a great artist.

Since the breakdown of the old systems of proportion,
no architect has been so deeply engaged and none has believed
so fervently that "architecture is proportion."

———————————

Dr. Wittkower, chairman of the Department of Art History and
Architecture, Columbia University, is well-known for his
historical writings on English and Italian art and architecture,
as well as on systems of proportion. He has written, among
many other books, Architectural Principles of Humanism (1949)
and Art and Architecture in Italy: 1600-1750 (1958).

VILLA, TOWNHOUSE, AND <u>UNITE</u>: THE UTOPIAN SPECTRUM

Ernesto Rogers

History is a perennially open evolutionary process. History is not a goal already reached, closed now in definitive perfection, but a problem raised again with each new experience and requiring creative responsibility on the part of each of us. This individual task cannot be carried out without plunging into the cultural data before us, refusing to accept ready-made forms, and applying an active criticism. And this criticism must penetrate to the soil from which individual forms sprang up so that we can work out new contents and new forms. From this interpretation of history, dogmatic beliefs are excluded, whether we turn to the achievements of the past, those of today, or to those of the future.

The conviction, by now widely recognized, that we cannot utilize traditional styles must become a part of our awareness even when we are faced with the great works of our contemporaries, and, of course, even when faced with the outstanding works of Le Corbusier himself. Our admiration is not limited as a result of this awareness, nor does it drive us into isolation. On the contrary, in this way, experience does not lie outside of us as an image of impossible imitations, but becomes a part of us -- nourishment for new and vital energy.

The idea of creating through architecture and town planning an environment suited to a more advanced and happier society (or an environment determining that society) lies at the base of the modern movement. The utopian force of this idea gave strength to its ethical aspect, which was itself necessary for giving form to intuitions of an esthetic character.

The Renaissance, so bitterly opposed and even despised by the great makers of modern architecture, developed from stimuli

205

similar to these. Of course, comparisons hold only generally
for the formulation of problems. Their substance depends on
the particular cultural conditions of each age. For while the artists of the fifteenth century inherited the idea of perfection from
neoplatonic principles, it is the more recent aspects of philosophy
(from pragmatism to phenomenology) which guide the theoretical
or practical works of the artists of this century.

Of the four makers of modern architecture, Le Corbusier
is certainly the one who can most directly be compared to the
masters of the Renaissance. He is the one who, through his
personality and practical activities, most nearly approaches them
in the vast course of his experience. But owing to the dialectical
contradictions of his personality, rising from his rich and fertile
artist's temperament, he differs from those masters by the way
in which he undermines his own principles and in his continuous
and still unexhausted capacity for further development.

The changes of his "maison de l'homme," in their succession
of appearances, represent a useful biographical fact in the whole of
his phenomenology, for this phenomenology is singular even in the
development of a coherent, personal, daring, and original adventure,
in itself a story as imaginary as a fairy tale and as real as today's
news.

Like Michelangelo, painter, sculptor, architect, and poet,
this peerless son of our age has contrived to express contemporary
life; its concrete possibilities; its hopes, fears, and limits (that
is to say, its omissions and impossibilities). The importance of
Le Corbusier's various activities is not due so much to the
extrinsic value of each of them considered apart, as it is to the
intrinsic character uniting them into consistent qualities of his
inner artistic structure.

As in the case of Michelangelo, certain critics have tried to
diminish all the nouns with qualifying adjectives by speaking of his
"sculptural" painting and his "pictorial" sculpture, and these terms
include, of course, his architecture. But although Le Corbusier

the painter-sculptor, Le Corbusier the architect-town planner,
or Le Corbusier the writer and polemicist may seem like different
persons competing within the same individual, actually, the
paintings and the works of architecture do not represent distinct
developments. Rather, they are only a few discrete moments in
the dramatic formation and expression of a single, indivisible
personality.

Because they are discrete moments, one might say that they
may be critically evaluated to establish a scale of preferential
values between one work and another, or one activity and another,
but the objection to this, without falling into a paradox, is that they
are part of the same historical process. Not a single element
can be arbitrarily removed without violating the central figure.

Some object that the experience of painting, like so many
other of his experiences, is purely instrumental to the real purpose of his life, which takes shape and achieves the greatest
height only in architecture.

Although I must agree to the greater merit of the architectural
results, one cannot appreciate the meaning of these other activities
except by admitting their value in themselves. One thinks of the
reciprocal warming of several small nearby fires and of the benefit which each gets from the other; one thinks of each growing as
a result of this mutual relationship.

Indeed, we must acknowledge the commitment and the perfection which Le Corbusier attempts to achieve with his full sense
of responsibility towards the particular techniques and inherent
limits of each activity. So indispensable are these various activities to the drama of his existence, that it would be incomplete were
he not able to find expression and make incarnate these many
phenomena.

When Le Corbusier speaks about the   synthèse des arts majeurs
he is not formulating an abstract theory; he is faithfully reflecting
what has happened in his own mind. Synthesis, towards which most

contemporary art is tending (Tantalus-like), has been operating throughout his achievements. Here the antithesis of pure art and applied art reaches a dialectical solution in the concrete experience of a single artist. The perfecting of his sensibility and expressive means through constant daily application to problems of beauty in his art studio makes his work more fertile, agile, and robust on the construction site; the dialogue between beauty and utility is translated into terms of an ever-higher harmony.

Thus, while Le Corbusier improves his painting, he enriches the possibilities of his architecture and infuses his town planning with all this accumulated spiritual wealth in order to offer it for the benefit of citizens. The circle of experience he has suffered directly widens to the vaster circle of society, to which he offers these visions of town planning so that it can better express itself, and even hope for its utopia.

This explains how the forms of Le Corbusier's architecture are the direct result of a <u>Weltanschauung</u> rich in immanent values, in which the beautiful and the good continually fuse, both aspiring to the realm of poetry.

In truth, the problem of the technique of beauty is never separate from that of the technique of utility. Utility, however, must never be taken in the mean sense, but as the indispensable nourishment required to give concrete vitality to acts of the imagination.

Intelligent as he is, Le Corbusier always considers reason as a means and never as an end in itself. We need only recall his own words: "Love what is right and what is sensitive, inventive, and varied. Reason is a guide and nothing more." However, in the Maison Domino of 1914, reason seems to have been both the promoter and the end of the architectonic act. This house shows a precise and technically sound geometrical measure, but immediately is transformed into the manifesto of an ideal way, which the imagination corroborates and immediately translates into poetic idiom. The Pavillon de l'Esprit Nouveau of 1922 was already conceived as a model to offer to the consumption of a more advanced society, a society which uses the technology of the machine age and couples it with the forms of purism.

How far from the truth are those biased critics who consider him a geometrician, a builder of abstract formulas, or at the other extreme, those who look on him as a capricious tightrope walker.

Yet this mistake in the interpretation of the master is fostered by the private and antithetical values within which his personality struggles. On the one hand, he continually tends to move to the extreme, driven by an inexhaustible plastic inventiveness; on the other hand, he follows in the wake of the French Cartesian tradition, trying to justify rationally each successive position of his esthetics and his constructions. But while these antipodal tensions at each moment resolve into a temporary synthesis in which feeling and reason achieve a kind of harmony, it is much more difficult to determine critically, at first sight, Le Corbusier's coherent continuity within the apparent contradiction of the whole of his creative process. A few of the postulates which were essential to Le Corbusier's figurative idiom were laid down like universal laws, like fixed and immutable canons. A number of these ideas have been modified, and some have even disappeared through the years, and with them their forms have changed.

Even more typical than the Maison Domino, or the Pavillon de l'Esprit Nouveau, or the Plan Voisin, is the declaration of the famous "Five Points of a New Architecture" made in 1925: "The pilotis; the roof gardens; the free plan; the long window; the free façade." With them, Le Corbusier, like a Renaissance writer of treatises, seems to be giving a perennially valid formula for the construction of the House of Man. But it is the House of Everyman and therefore outside the parameters of time and space and the individual character of the individual man, as Le Corbusier considered him in that particular period.

Slavish imitators took this lesson, rich with promise, as
a magical formula capable of solving all difficulties, as if it could
be used mechanically. But Le Corbusier, with his own houses
linked to the five-point doctrine, surpassed himself. La Maison
La Roche, la Maison à Garches, la Maison à Stuttgart, la Villa
Savoie, not to mention that jewel la Petite Maison built for his
mother, are crescendos of volumetrical and spatial invention and
of poetic interpretations of life. And the five points have not
been fully respected. At most, they were like the five lines of
a musician's staff, on which a cantata, a ballad, a symphony, or
any other kind of composition was written. In the Villa Savoie,
the most faithful in its observation of the five points, there is
such a density of fertile invention that all these schemes are
passed over. One who strolls along the promenade architecturale,
the pivot of the building, feels himself rising into a land of dreams.
Moreover, all these constructions are continually controlled by
a will to form which, like the works of the Renaissance, is reflected in the geometrical schemes and is everywhere suitable to
the idiom. The choice of proportions has the symbolic value of
an ideal paradigm and is more metaphysical than concretely physical

But at the opposite pole to these objective (if not exactly rational) experiments, there is the equal interest that Le Corbusier
has always shown for nature. His pocket carnet, which has followed
him in all his pilgrimages since his youth, testifies to his passionate love of direct observation and, like the notebooks of Leonardo da Vinci, it carries the acute notations of the naturalist
and the immediate talent for translating the given fact into the
symbol of artistic representation.

The Maison aux Mathes of 1935 will seem either an accident
or a contradiction to those who are used to considering Le Corbusier as interested only in the particular discoveries of science
and technology. But this house, on the contrary, shows a wide
angle from which the Master considers existence. Compelled by
a particularly tight budget, the architect did away with his pride
and designed a construction which could be raised without his
direct presence on the building site, contriving it so that the

210

modest village contractor could carry it out with his own means.
All the devices placed at his disposal by industry were ignored,
and the craftsman's work was reinforced. Thus, Le Corbusier
seems to side with his great friend, Walter Gropius, according to
Gropius's words many years later on the occasion of his seventieth
birthday:"My intention is not to introduce a cut and dried modern style,
but rather to introduce a method of approach which allows one
to tackle a problem according to its peculiar conditions. I
want a young architect to be able to find his way in any circumstances; I want him independently to create true, genuine forms
out of the technical, economic and social conditions in which he
finds himself, instead of imposing a learned formula on surroundings
which may call for an entirely different solution. It is not so much
a ready-made dogma that I want to teach, but an attitude toward
the problems of our generation which is unbiased, original and
elastic." This is a house of our day, then, because the <u>ends</u> are
up to date. Immediacy has been conferred upon old means. Here
Le Corbusier not only falls in with Gropius but also with their
common master Peter Behrens who had given them this fundamental precept: "In der Architektur kann man alles losen." This
maxim has been forgotten by formalists past and present, who
are bound by exterior words and incapable of penetrating to the
heart of the matter.

The weekend house in a Paris suburb, also of 1935, built
in a mixed structure with cement vaults and stone walls, exhibits
with an even greater ease the same talent for giving <u>means</u> their
purely instrumental value without losing sight of the end.

But these small houses, scaled to the reality of what is possible, do not contrast in the end with the plan for the Ville Radieuse,
that long and never-abandoned hope for a redeemed and redeeming
city. Apart from the dwellings on the outskirts of the garden city,
the large parameters of the city houses arranged in indented subdivisions only enhance the example of the glass façade dwelling
built in Geneva in 1932.

This constancy in the architect's ends is what unifies all these experiences and holds them together, so that utopia and reality are only two degrees of the same impulse. A part of this utopia makes its appearance in historical reality, but in actual construction one finds a tension towards something very far off, something better but unreachable -- in a word, utopia. Le Corbusier's works reveal his continuous criticism of the society in which he has to practice his profession, his refusal to accept compromises or narrow-minded utilitarianism, and his almost religious faith in the redeeming qualities of order and independence required for achieving these ends. At times there is (we might as well admit it) the ingenuous and touching defiance of Don Quixote; for art is his Dulcinea, at once his vision, utopia, and glory.

The idea of the world, which in his youthful work tended to be sublimated into purism, the mathematically absolute, and the abstract identification of individuals and generalized humanity, becomes in his mature work warmer and warmer, even becomes affectionate and sensual. Thus, acting not only in practice but also in theory, this exceptional artist seems more and more to be approaching his fellow man and interpreting his exact characteristics. Without losing his moralistic, cathartic, or missionary character, his most recent works belong not so much to the rarefied heavens from which they seemed to descend, as to the earth. They have not given up their complex structure or mathematical image. Nature is also composed of complex and mathematical structures. Instead of crystals we now have luxuriant flowers and strong fragrances.

The postwar villa, la Maison Jaoul at Neuilly-sur-Seine of 1954-1956, seems informed with the anxiety of mankind. Without seeming to idealize them as does the Villa Savoie, from the outside its syncopated rhythm, the very strong contrast of the various thicknesses of the structure, and the arrangement of empty spaces into varying sizes and forms propose a theme of our age, which is no longer only mechanical but electronic and atomic, with all the sociological consequences which this involves.

212

The Indian houses, the Maison Sarabhai at Ahmedabad of 1956, bring us another contribution from the most recent experiments of Le Corbusier. Comparing them with the French homes I have mentioned is particularly revealing. This is no Maison Domino created to solve the problems of every man, but the deepening and widening of premises which bring us to the roots of man characterized by his climate -- not only his natural climate which could be interpreted rationally, but also that of his specific cultural climate.

At more than seventy years of age, Le Corbusier, still recognizable and unmistakable in character despite his heavily wrinkled brow, is like a ploughed and sown land ready to offer its fruits to men who have not only feelings and intelligence but also stomachs to be fed. You will see the anguish and the excitement of these men in his most recent paintings.

The Marseille Unité d'Habitation, which matured before these constructions of 1947-1952, is the great monument raised by Le Corbusier to man as he is. The historical importance of this building is no less significant than its esthetic and technical merits; for, indeed, this is the first palace raised by men not to the prince, but to the ordinary man. Other splendid dwellings are to be found throughout the land meant for simple men: a few fishermen's houses, some mountain homes, a number of modest houses in the urban centers; but this is a monument; this is a deliberate act of solemn celebration.

As in the case of every monument, its representative and symbolic value may have overwhelmed the logical and schematically practical objective which was the given problem to solve, but like all valid monuments it is a document of high aspirations and the proof of their achievement. If we do not accept his thesis, we can refuse it in its entirety and substitute, if we are able, a different ideology. But we cannot ignore this phenomenal work of architecture, so magnificent as a whole, and so coherent in all its details.

The Unité d'Habitation is the ripening of a long period
of work, the evolution of a good part of a doctrine and
experience which had been consummated: like a stone
picked from a riverbed, a stone bearing the dramatic signs
of the countless currents which had flowed over it, leaving
it polished but throbbing with life.

Quite far from us is the suggestive sequence of curves
in the Algiers plan (1930-1934), curves which seem the
expressionistic symbols of a Kandinsky, with houses
nestled below the highway. Far away are the sunbreakers
of his 1933 apartment house at Algiers with their vertical
and somewhat obsessive texture. The same function has
now been assigned to soft horizontal projections before
the wide windows of the living rooms, and the windows frame
the landscape much more individualistically than the indefinite
glass façades of the Ville Radieuse (1935).

Although it refined the geometrical scheme of the Plan
Voisin, the 1938 Cartesian skyscraper remained the picture
of an idea. But here, even in their hugeness, the measure-
ments are scaled to human life. The Modulor is the
microcosm, the symbol of the Unite d'Habitation, and its
merits and limits may be considered similar to the merits
and limits of the building, the macrocosm. In short,
with its brilliant and sculptural roof garden, its gigantic
pilotis, and brutally expressionistic reinforced concrete,
Unité d'Habitation is an example valid and useful as an
original, fundamental experience in architecture, but one
which does not shut out the possibility of contrasting experiences. In fact, Le Corbusier, himself, was at that
time planning a village at Cap Martin, a sprawling project
camouflaged by the surroundings. In experimenting with this
completely different way, his success was no less complete,
while his coal continued to be hedonistic: that of making life
more beautiful and happy for men.

These contradictions in his work should be considered as multiple directions in a fertile mind animated by a feverish search for what we have called utopia.

Dr. Rogers is a leading architect in Europe, and the editor of Casabella magazine. The Torre Velasca in Milan is one of his many buildings. He is professor of architecture at the University of Milan.

UNITY IN DIVERSITY

Walter Gropius

The architect is in an ambiguous position in his relation to society and in his double role as a citizen and a professional. Armed to the teeth with technical intricacies, design theories, and philosophical arguments, he still so rarely succeeds in pulling his weight in the public domain where decisions are made which vitally affect his interests. Since popular opinion holds him responsible for the condition of our cities, towns, and countryside, I would like to examine where he stands in this respect and which avenues of action are open to him to broaden his influence.

There are now certain "rumbles" in the architectural profession which have interested me as much as they have baffled me. Since architects possess in general a sensitive, built-in thermometer which registers the crises and doubts, enthusiasms and fancies of their contemporaries, we should listen to the notes of misgiving and warning emerging from their ranks.

All reports made lately by architects and educators on the state of architecture in the sixties are dominated by two words: confusion and chaos. It seems to them that the inherent tendencies of an architecture of the twentieth century, born fifty years or so ago and, then, a deeply felt, indivisible entity, have been exploded into so many fractions that it becomes difficult to draw them together to coherence again. Technical innovations, first greeted as delightful new means to an end, are seized separately and set against each other as ends in themselves; personal methods of approach are hardened into hostile dogmas; a new awareness of our relationship to the past is distorted into a revivalist spirit; our financial affluence is mistaken for a free ticket into

216

GROPIUS, Walter Adolf (grō-pī-ŭs), architect, b. Berlin, Germany May 18, 1883; s. Walter and Manon (Scharnweber) G.; ed. Humanistisches Gymnasium, Berlin, 1903; Technische Hochschule, Munchen, 1903-04, archtl. office of Prof. Solf and Wichards, Berlin, 1904, Technische Hochschule, Berlin, 1905-07; hon. Dr. Engring., Technische Hochschule, Hanover, 1929; M. A. (hon.), Harvard, 1942; D. Sc., Western-Reserve U., 1951; Arts D. (hon.) Harvard, 1953; Dr. Architecture (honorary) North Carolina State College, 1953, D.Sc.(honorary) University Sydney (Australia), 1954; Doctor Honoris Causa, U. Brazil, 1955; L.H.D., Columbia, 1961; m. Alma (Schindler) Mahler, 1916; 1 dau., Alma Manon; m. 2nd, Ise Frank, 1923; 1 daughter, Beate Eveline. Came to U.S., 1937. Assistant to Professor Peter Behrens, Berlin, Germany, 1908-10, archtl. practice, own office, Berlin, 1910-14; united two art schools under name of Staatliches Bauhaus, Weimar, Germany, 1918 and served as dir.; moved Bauhaus to Dessau, 1925; Priv. practice, Berlin, 1928-34; partner with Maxwell Fry, architect, London, 1935-37; sr. prof. architecture, chmn. Sch. Architecture Harvard, 1938, now prof. emeritus. Formed The Architects' Collaborative, 1946. Cons. Container Corp. of Am., Michael Reese Hosp., Chicago. Vice pres. General Panel Corp., 1942-52; mem. Vis. Com. Sch. Architecture and Planning, Mass. Inst. Tech., 1953-55. Served in German Hussar Regt., No. 15, 1904-05, 1914-18. Decorated Iron Cross. Recipient Grand Prix Internat. d'Architecture, Matarazzo Found., Saõ Paolo, Brazil, 1953; Royal Gold Medal, The Royal Institute of British Architects, London, 1956; Hanseatic Goethe prize, U. Hamburg, Germany, 1956; Ernst Reuter medal, City of Berlin, 1957; Grand Cross of Merit with Star, Fed. Rep. Germany, 1958; Gold Medal, A.I.A., 1959; Grand State prize Architecture Germany, 1960.

cannot be sidestepped by brilliant and diverting oratory   It also creates too rosy an impression of the actual influence architects are permitted to take in the shaping of our larger living spaces.

Whether a conscientious and dedicated architect of today resolves his personal design problem in this way or that way is, unfortunately, less decisive for the general looks of our surroundings than we are fond of believing. His contribution is simply swallowed up in the featureless growth that covers the acres of our expanding cities. In the last twenty years the United States has seen the emergence of an unusual number of gifted architects, who have managed to spread interest and admiration among designers in other countries. But when the curious arrived at our shores to see the new creations for themselves they were overwhelmed by the increase in general ugliness that met their eyes before they had a chance to find the objects of their interest in the vast, amorphous display. It is here where chaos reigns supreme; it is the absence of organic coherence in the total picture which causes the disappointment, and not the dilemma between different individual approaches to design.

Having been in the crosscurrents of architectural development for over half a century, I find that an architect who wants to help mould the evolutionary forces of his time, instead of letting himself be overcome by them, must distinguish between two sets of components which are apt to influence and direct his work. The first one consists of the human trends which gradually move a society towards new patterns of living; the second consists of the contemporary technical means and the individual choices of expression which help these trends to take shape. It is imperative never to lose sight of the first while embroiled with the second, because the architect is thus in danger of losing himself in the design by way of technical stunts or personal mannerisms.

The potentialities of the new technical means fascinated my generation just as much as they do the architect of today, but at

218

the beginning of our movement stood an idea, not an obsession
with specific forms and techniques. The activities of life itself
were under scrutiny. How to dwell; how to work, move, relax;
how to create a life-giving environment for our changed society:
this was what occupied our minds. Of course we went about the
task of realizing such aims in very different ways, but I do not
see why this diversity should by itself cause confusion, except
to those who naively believe that there is always only one perfect answer to a problem. There are, of course, many technical and formal approaches to the same task, and any one of them
may be successful, if it is well suited to the purpose of the building and to the temperament of the architect; if it is used with
discrimination in its given environment.

The great technical inventions and social developments of
the last hundred years set off a stream of changes in our way of
living and producing. They gradually established new habits,
new standards, and new preferences which have come to represent the unifying trends in today's general picture. Beginning
with the discovery of the Bessemer steel process and of Monier's
reinforced concrete (which freed architecture of the supporting,
solid wall and presented it with virtually limitless possibilities
for flexible planning), there has been a steady movement toward
a less rigid, less encumbered style of living and of building. The
skeleton structures enabled us to introduce large window openings
and the marvel of glass curtain walls (today misused and therefore discredited) which transformed the rigid, compartmental
character of buildings into a transparent fluid one. This, in
turn, gave birth to a dynamic and totally new indoor-outdoor relationship which enriched and stimulated architectural design beyond
measure. Pressure for ever more mobility and flexibility encouraged the evolution of industrial prefabrication, which, by
now, has taken over a large part of our building production. It
promises ever-increasing precision and simplification of the building process for the future.

The common characteristics which clearly emerged from
all these innovations are: an increase in flexibility and mobility;

219

a new indoor-outdoor relationship; and a bolder and lighter, less earthbound architectural appearance. These are the constituent elements of today's architectural imagery. An architect can disregard them only at his peril. If related to a background of meaningful planning, they would reveal diversity, not chaos.

I cannot accept, therefore, the verdict of the critics that the architectural profession, as such, is to blame for the disjointed pattern of our cities and for the formless urban sprawl that creeps over our countryside. As we well know, the architect and planner has almost never received a mandate from the people to draw up the best possible framework for a desirable way of life. All he usually gets is an individual commission for a limited objective from a client who wants to make his bid for a place in the sun. It is the people as a whole who have stopped thinking of what would constitute a better frame of life and who have, instead, learned to sell themselves short to a system of rapid turnover and minor creature comforts. It is the lack of a distinct and compelling goal rather than bad intentions of individuals that so often ruins attempts to set a more comprehensive character for general planning.

And this, of course, is where we come in. In our role as citizens we all share in the general unwillingness to live up to our best potential, in the lack of dedication to our acknowledged principles, in our lack of discipline towards the lures of complacency and of material abundance.

Julian Huxley, the eminent biologist, warned recently: "Sooner rather than later we must get away from a system based on artificially increasing the number of human wants and set about constructing one aimed at the qualitative satisfaction of real human needs, spiritual as well as material and physiological. This means abandoning the pernicious habit of evaluating every human project solely in terms of its utility...."

Our cunning sales psychology, in its unscrupulous misuse of our language, has brought about such a distortion of truth, such a

220

dissolution of decency and morality, that it is high time for the citizen to take to the barricades against this massive onslaught against the unwary. Naturally, the all-pervading sales mentality has also had its detrimental effect on the architecture of our time. Relentless advertising pressure for ever-changing, sensational design has discouraged any tendency to create a visually integrated environment, because it tacitly expects the designer to be different at all cost for competition's sake. The effect is disruptive and quite contrary to the desirable diversity of design which would result naturally from the work of different personalities who are aware of their obligations to environmental integration. Here again, we see that the forces which cause confusion and chaos originate from the excessive infatuation with the rewards of salesmanship. These rewards dominate modern life. We can influence this dominant mode only as human beings and democratic citizens, not alone as professionals.

I was somewhat startled, therefore, by a sentence in the recent A. I. A. Report on the state of the profession: "The total environment produced by architecture in the next forty years can become greater than the Golden Age of Greece, surpass the glories of Rome, and outshine the magnificence of the Renaissance. This is possible provided the architect assumes again his historic role as Master Builder."

How does this vision compare to the realities of the situation? Don't we need to remember that such high points in history come about only when the skill and artistic inspiration of the architect and the artist were carried into action by the clear and unquestioned authority of those who felt themselves to be the rightful representatives of a whole people? The Greek pinnacle was reached by the courage and foresight of their leader Pericles, who pulled together all financial and artistic resources of the whole nation and its allies (including the military budget) to force the erection of the Parthenon. The Romans, spreading this Mediterranean heritage over the whole of the Roman empire, made their buildings monuments to the centralized power of their leaders. The Renaissance, after giving birth to fierce political rivalry, harnessed all secular and

221

clerical powers, all craftsmen and artists for the glorification
of the competing principalities. Wherever we look in history,
we find that the rulers took no chances with the individual tastes
and inclinations of the populace, but imposed strict patterns of
behavior as well as a hierarchy of religious, civic, and economic standards which dominated architectural and artistic expression. In Japan this even covered the proportionate size of all
domestic architecture, which was strictly regulated according
to birth, rank, and occupation of the owner.

All these systems have produced magnificent results in one
period or another, but they have no roots in our modern world.
Even if some authoritative remnants are still around in the form
of large corporations and institutions, this cannot conceal the
fact that the architect and artist of the twentieth century has to
face a completely new client and patron: the average citizen or
his representative whose stature, opinion, and influence is uncertain and difficult to define compared to the authoritarian lord of
the past. As we have seen, this citizen, as of now, is not at all
in the habit of extending his vision beyond immediate business concerns,because we have neglected to educate him for his role of
cultural arbiter. He repays this neglect by running loose, only
here and there restricted by social ambitions from recklessly
following his commercial interests. Though he is quite aware of
the restrictions the law puts on his building activities, he is almost totally unaware of his potentialities to contribute something
positive, socially and culturally, to the actual development,
change, and improvement of his environment. So far we are only
trying to prevent him by zoning laws from committing the worst
abuse, but I feel that unless we take the positive step of trying to
mold him into the man of responsibility he must become, there
will be little chance for the Master Builder ever to assume
his comprehensive historic role as creator of cities again.

Our modern society is still on trial where cultural integration is concerned. This certainly cannot be accomplished by
handing out authoritative formulas for beauty to an uncomprehen-
ding public, untrained to see, to perceive, to discriminate. A

society such as ours, which has conferred equal privileges on everybody, will have to acknowledge its duty to activate the general responsiveness to spiritual and esthetic value. We will have to intensify the development of everybody's imaginative faculties. Only thus can we create the basis from which eventually the creative act of the artist can rise, not as an isolated phenomenon, ignored and rejected by the crowd, but firmly embedded in a network of public response and understanding.

The only active influence which our society can take towards such a goal would be to see to it that our educational system for the next generation will develop in each child, from the beginning, a perceptive awareness which intensifies his sense of form. Seeing more, he will comprehend more of what he sees and will learn to understand the positive and negative factors which influence the environment he finds himself in. Our present methods of education which put a premium on accumulation of knowledge have rarely reached out to include training in creative habits of observing, seeing, and shaping our surroundings. The apathy we meet in the adult citizen, who entertains only vague notions of wishing to get away from it all, can certainly be traced to this early failure to arouse his active interest in the improvement of his living area. Children should be introduced right from the start to the potentialities of their environment, to the physical and psychological laws that govern the visual world, and to the supreme enjoyment that comes from participating in the creative process of giving form to one's living space. Such experience, if continued in depth throughout the whole of the educational cycle, will never be forgotten and will prepare the adult to continue taking an informed interest in what happens around him. Recent research at the University of Chicago has shown that "the high I. Q. children seek out the safety and security of the 'known,' while the high creative children seem to enjoy the risk and uncertainty of the 'unknown.'" We should strengthen this creative spirit, which is essentially one of nonconformist independent search. We must instill respect for it and create response to it on the broadest level; otherwise the common man stays below his potential, and the uncommon man burns his fire in isolation.

My concern with the problem of drawing out the potential artist and of providing him with a stimulating educational climate and a chance to acquire a perfect technique prompted me over forty years ago to create the Bauhaus School of Design. In opposition to the then prevailing trend of bringing up a student of design on the subjective recipes of his master, we tried to put him on a solid foundation by giving him objective principles of universal validity, derived from the laws of nature and the psychology of man. From this basis he was expected to develop his own individual design approach, independent of the personal approach of his teacher. This novel method of education in design has been widely misunderstood and misinterpreted. The present generation is inclined to think of it as a rigid stylistic dogma of yesterday whose usefulness has come to an end, because its ideological and technical premises are now outdated. This view confuses a method of approach with the practical results obtained by it at a particular period of its application.

The Bauhaus was not concerned with the formulation of time-bound, stylistic concepts; and its technical methods were not ends in themselves. It wanted to show how a multitude of individuals, willing to work concertedly but without losing their identity, could evolve a kinship of expression in their response to the challenges of the day. It wanted to give a basic demonstration of unity in diversity, and it did this with the materials, techniques, and form germane to its time. It was its method that was revolutionary, and I have not found yet any new system of education for design which puts the Bauhaus idea out of course. In fact, the present disenchantment with the doubtful results obtained from simply imitating the highly personal design methods of this or that master, without adding to their substance, should give renewed emphasis to its principles.

It would be most desirable if the initial work done by the Bauhaus were continued and expanded so that we would be able to draw on an ever increasing common fund of objective knowledge, teachable to all age groups, and furnishing the much-needed vocabulary with which individuals are free to compose their personal design

224

poetry. If the capacity to focus and crystallize the tendencies of a period dims, as it has in our time, the necessity of intensifying our efforts at coherence becomes ever more important. There are some vital centers in this country where such work is pursued with dedication, but their influence is still limited. And even in these centers it is hard to find creative architects and artists who want to take on teaching positions along with their other work, because public opinion regards teaching as a mere backwater compared to the excitement and rewards of practical work. The idea that the two must be combined, if a healthy climate for the growing generation is to evolve, remains an applauded theory rather than an actual accomplishment.

I remember an experience I had myself years ago when, on the occasion of my seventieth birthday, Time magazine commented on my career. After coming to this country, they said, I had been "content to teach only," as if this were, in itself, a minor occupation as compared to that of a practicing architect. Apart from the fact that the paper was misinformed (I had never given up my practice), it brought home to me again the realization that the profession of the teacher is looked upon in this country as a kind of refuge for those visionaries who cannot hold their own in the world of action and reality. Though, admittedly, there has been a shift in this view lately, it is still much too firmly established as to become uprooted overnight. It remains a tremendous handicap for those who realize the importance of combining practice and teaching and want to make their contribution in both fields.

What, now, can be done by the individual practicing architect to promote a greater measure of cooperation between those groups who contribute to the development of our visible world? In spite of our partiality to togetherness, this fashionable trend has accomplished little in our field since it lacks a distinct purpose, a discipline, a working method of its own. All these must be found before we get more and more lost to each other.

225

I think we all agree that a relatedness of expression and a consolidation of trends cannot be consciously organized in a democracy. This relatedness springs from spontaneous group consciousness and from collective intuition which brings our pragmatic requests and out spiritual desires into interplay. I have tried for a long time, therefore, to give more incentive to such a state of mind by developing a spirit of voluntary teamwork among groups of architects. But my idea has become almost suspect and too many of my colleagues are still wedded to the nineteenth century idea that individual genius can only work in splendid isolation.

Just as our profession closed its eyes fifty years ago to the fact that the machine had irrefutably entered the building process, so now is it trying to cling to the concept of the architect as a self-sufficient independent operator, who, with the help of a good staff and competent engineers, can solve any problem and keep his artistic integrity intact. This, in my view, is an isolationist attitude which will be unable to stem the tide of the uncontrolled disorder engulfing our living spaces. It runs counter to the concept of total architecture which is concerned with the whole of our environmental development and demands collaboration on the broadest basis. Our present casual way of collaboration on large projects is simply to throw a few prominent architects together in the hope that five people will automatically produce more beauty than one. The result, as often as not, becomes an unrelated assemblage of individual architectural ideas, not an integrated whole of new and enriched values. It is obvious that we have to learn new and better ways of cooperation.

In my personal experience these call first of all for an unprejudiced state of mind and for the firm belief that common thought and action is a precondition of cultural growth. Starting on this basis, we must strive to acquire the methods, the vocabulary, the habits of collaboration with which most architects are unfamiliar still. And this is not easy to accomplish. It is one thing to condition an individual for cooperation by making him conform; it is another altogether to make him keep his identity

226

within a group of equals while he is trying to find common ground
with them. It is imperative, though, that we develop such a technique of collaboration to a high degree of refinement, since it is
our best guarantee of the protection of the individual against be-.
coming a mere number and, at the same time, for the development of related expression rather than of pretentious individualism.

There can be no doubt, of course, that the creative spark
originates always with the individual, but while he works in close
collaboration with others and is exposed to their stimulating and
challenging critique, his own work matures more rapidly and
never loses touch with the broader aspects which unite a team in
a common effort.

Communication from person to person is at an all time low
today, in spite of (or because of) our tremendous technical means
of communication. Most individuals are driven into shallow super-
ficiality in all their relations with other people, including their
own friends. But just as the airplane is no substitute for our legs,
so personal contact between people of like interests cannot be replaced by the vast output of professional literature and information,
because individual interpretation and exchange is still essential
for our functioning as human beings.

Our overextended receptive faculties need a respite so that
greater concentration and intensification can take place, and I
feel that a well-balanced team can help achieve just that. As we
cannot inform ourselves simultaneously in all directions, a member of a team benefits from the different interests and attitudes
of the other members during their collaborative meetings. The
technical, social, and economic data, gathered individually and
then presented to the others, reaches them already humanized by
personal interpretation, and, since all members of a team are
apt to add their own different reactions, the new information is
more easily seen in its proper perspective and its potential value.

For the effectiveness of this kind of intimate teamwork, two
preconditions are paramount: voluntariness, based on mutual

227

respect and liking, and exercise of individual leadership and responsibility within the group. Without the first, collaboration is
mere expediency; without the last it loses artistic integrity. To
safeguard design coherence and impact, the right of making final
decisions must therefore be left to the one member who happens
to be in charge of a specific job, even though he has previously
received support and criticism from other members.

Such principles of teamwork are easier explained than
carried into practice, because we all still arrive on the scene
with our old habits of trying to beat the other fellow to it. But
I believe that a group of architects willing to give collaboration
a chance will be rewarded by seeing their effectiveness streng-
thened and their influence on public opinion broadened. All
teams so organized, I trust, will eventually act as ferments in
our drive for cultural integration.

Considering the reservoir of rich talent and the wealth of
technical and financial resources available today, it would seem
that this generation holds all the aces in the age-old game of
creating architectural form for the ideas by which society lives.
Only a magic catalyst seems to be needed to combine these forces
and free them from isolation. I personally see this catalyst in
the power of education; education to raise the expectations and
demands a people make on their own form of living; education to
waken and sharpen their latent capacities for creation and for
cooperation.

Creativity of the makers needs the response of all the users.
I am convinced that a surprising amount of individual whimsey--
yes, even aberration and downright ugliness -- could be tolerated
without causing serious harm, if only the grand design, the image
a society should have of itself, would emerge clearly and unequi-
vocally. What we admire in the achievements of city builders of
the past is the fact that their work reveals so clearly the ultimate
destination of each individual feature as an organic part of the
whole. This was what made the city perform its functions well
and gave the people a stimulating background for all their activities. How else can the marvel of the Piazza San Marco, this arch-

example of perfection, be explained? Not the work of a single
master, like the Piazza San Pietro, we find instead that, over
a long period of growth, a perfect balance was developed between
the contributions of a number of architects, using many different
materials and methods. They achieved this miracle because they
never violated the main purpose of the general plan, yet never
forced uniformity of design. San Marco is an ideal illustration
of my credo "unity in diversity," to the development of which,
in our time, I can only hope to have made my personal contribution during a long life of search and discovery.

THE BAUHAUS IN WEIMAR

Wolf von Eckardt

First of all, let me relieve you of what must be an unbearable suspense; I believe that what the Bauhaus taught is still, or perhaps again, eminently viable. I say this despite the answers I received from some deans of architecture schools whom I consulted on this subject. These deans all politely acknowledged the great contribution the Bauhaus has made, both to the development of architectural and industrial design and to art education. But they seemed a little perplexed by the question. They didn't quite know what to do with it.

One of them wrote: "It is difficult for those of my generation to be very clear about the Bauhaus. There is a kind of intellectual father relationship at work. My personal position is comparable to my relationship with my own father -- gratitude for the gifts and respect for the person. However, there is no longer any need for the gifts nor is the person a source of help. The old saying still goes: 'Each generation must solve the problems with which they are confronted with the resources available to them.'"

Quite likely this statement just about sums up what most American professionals feel about the validity of Bauhaus teaching today. I dare say, however, without trying to engage in sophistry, that these very words prove the tremendous and viable influence of Bauhaus teaching on the present generation of designers, architects, and architectural educators.

Solving the problem with which you are confronted with the resources available seems to me the essence of the Bauhaus philosophy. It is not an old saying. Before 1920, or thereabouts, designers thought differently. It is what the Bauhaus taught.

There is indeed a father relationship between the designers of today and the remarkable group of artists and teachers Walter Gropius assembled in Weimar and Dessau forty years ago...a very special father relationship.

These masters and their students had the sort of influence on the ideals, the character, the basic approach to life, the basic values, or, if you wish, Weltanschauung, every father hopes to have on his child, whether he is grateful and respectful for it or not. It is the kind of influence that makes for tradition, which, in turn, makes for culture.

We are at the beginning of a new visual culture which the Bauhaus set in motion, and we still have a long way to go in the direction it charted. Whether we remember the navigator or not is perhaps irrelevant -- except in times when we tend to deviate from the course. It may be high time, in fact, that we recall just what the Bauhaus stood for, as we again drift into a new baroque and whimsical romanticism.

Just what did the Bauhaus stand for?

It is not easy to strip the essence from still current personality conflicts, stylistic prejudices, and Teutonic abstractions which so often obfuscate the best thinking that happens to have originated in Germany. Ideas, like design, can be perceived only in their context, within their environment -- their space and their time.

Das Staatliche Bauhaus was founded by Walter Gropius in the spring of 1919 in the sleepy little town of Weimar. Weimar, as you know, fancied itself the German Athens, because Goethe had lived there and because its rulers traditionally conceived of themselves as great patrons of the arts and of culture.

In the spring of 1919, however, that art and that culture crashed in what the art historian Egon Friedell has called "the collapse of reality." Comprehensible reality was and is no more. The world of comfortable absolutes had already begun to wear thin

231

before we knew that the universe is infinite, that everything is relative, and that human behavior stems from far more than rational, conscious thought. We know, but we don't comprehend. It eludes our powers of imagination and therefore literal representation.

Under the impact of this new knowledge, the artist found it -- and still finds it -- well nigh impossible to depict a fancied reality which no longer exists. The architect, too, had to search beyond previously conventional representation of classic thought.

It was, you see, not just a question of coming to terms with a new technology. All ages had to do this.

The Bauhaus struggled to find new laws of design -- laws fundamental enough to withstand the recognition that, as Paul Klee wrote in 1921, "for the whole there is no right or wrong, since it lives and develops through the interplay of forces, and in the universe, too, good and evil finally act together productively." No one but an oriental Zen master could have written these words a decade or two earlier.

And no school of design could have stated earlier what the Bauhaus said in its first statement of its theories. It said in 1923: "The old dualistic world concept which envisaged the ego in opposition to the universe is rapidly losing ground. In its place is rising the idea of a universal unity in which all opposing forces exist in a state of absolute balance...." This awareness coincided with the very tangible collapse of the social, political, and economic order. The collapse was most drastic in Germany.

Walter Gropius had negotiated his contract for taking over the Grand Ducal Fine Arts Academy and combining it with the Weimar Arts and Crafts School with the office of the Court Marshal of his Highness the Grand Duke. He signed it on April 1, 1919, with the representative of the provisional socialist government of the new Republic of Sachsen-Weimar-Eisenach.

232

The Kaiser had just fled to chop wood in Holland, leaving his
stunned and still somewhat loyal socialist opposition to form
quarrelsome coalitions and a new regime. There was still shooting
on the streets of Berlin. In Munich, of all places, angry workers
and intellectuals proclaimed a Communist People's Republic. In
the marshes and woods of eastern Germany, homeless army
officers, deprived of the comforts of war and command, formed
bands of mercenaries and plotted assassination and revenge.
There was hardly anything to eat. It was a time of turnips and
turmoil.

Yet there was a tremendous stirring, a new, incredibly creative search, -- again, perhaps, most intense in Germany. Those
were the fabulous twenties we are suddenly so nostalgic about.

In the cafés and unheated studios of Berlin and Munich's
Schwabing dawned what Alfred Kerr has called "the Periclean
age of German arts and letters." Thomas Mann and Franz Wer-
fel, Emil Nolde and Oscar Kokoschka, Max Lehmbruch and
Ernst Barlach, Arnold Schönberg and Kurt Weill, Max Reinhard
and Erwin Piscator, Bert Brecht and Carl Zuckmayer, Ernst
Lubitsch and Josef von Sternberg are some of the names of that
period.

Even my young daughter, who asked me only a few years
ago in all seriousness whether Hitler was a Republican or a Demo-
crat, had heard of Marlene Dietrich and the Threepenny Opera.

Much, if not most of what emerged at that time -- including,
be it emphatically said, the ideas and approaches of the Bauhaus --
had simmered under the surface for decades. But the artillery
shells of World War I burst the crust of bourgeois solidity, and
it all erupted like an incredible volcano. Its ashes, if you like
metaphors, still fertilize the soil of our present creative endeavors.

But when Walter Gropius founded the Bauhaus, he did not
just ride this wave. For much if not most of it was, however
creative, negative. It was an art of protest and rebellion, of dada,

233

of social criticism, of satire, of most skillfully and artistically flailing the horse that had already been killed in the war.

Gropius did not say as did, for instance, Adolf Loos, "I revel in the chaos of the time; we must destroy the old academies and the Beaux Arts. " He said: "The chaos of the time insulted me. I asked myself, 'What can one individual do so something new could grow ?' "

He has been much criticized for not wishing to look back. Today we can afford to study history. We probably can't afford not to.

Yet, remember the letter I quoted? Only a week or so ago an architectural educator wrote me: "Each generation must solve the problems with which they are confronted. . . we are left with our own needs to make our own contribution. " Can we really blame the Bauhaus, which consciously strove for new and valid forms of expression, for considering Picasso more relevant than Breughel, and Perret more interesting than Sir Christopher Wren?

You don't dare look back when you seek a path in the wilderness. Gropius drew up his road map for a new visual culture as an army officer in the trenches of Namur. He drafted a proclamation which said in part: "The complete building is the final aim of the visual arts. . . Architects, painters, and sculptors must recognize anew the composite character of a building as an entity. . . Let us create a new guild of craftsmen, without the class distinction which raises an arrogant barrier between craftsman and artist. Together let us conceive and create the new building of the future, which will embrace architecture and sculpture and painting in one unity and which will rise one day toward heaven from the hands of a million workers like the crystal symbol of a new faith. " It was the Bauhaus proclamation. And on its cover was the famous woodcut by Lyonel Feininger showing a cathedral immersed in the rays of three stars --presumably symbols of the unison of architects, painters and sculptors.

234

The response was immediate. Just how this proclamation got around Germany so fast no one can explain. But they came, and they came in droves. They were boys as young as seventeen in the blue shirts and leather shorts of the youth movement. They were men pushing forty still in the battered uniforms of the Kaiser's defeated army. Herbert Bayer, who apprenticed as a house painter in faraway Darmstadt, dropped his brush when he saw that leaflet and rallied to the call. Xanti Schawinsky heard about it from his tennis teacher in Essen and brought along two girls he picked up on the way. There were other girls, too, from the arts and crafts shops and the art academies. And most of these beatniks of their time were barefoot and in rags, not by choice, but because it was, as I have said, a time of turnips and turmoil and Germany's last bitter World War I winter still lingered on.

You recall the teachers of this motley crowd: Johannes Itten, Lyonel Feininger, and Gerhard Marcks were at the Bauhaus right from the start. Adolf Meyer joined a little later. Georg Müche in 1920... Paul Klee and Oscar Schlemmer in 1921... Wassily Kandinsky in 1922... and Laszlo Moholy-Nagy in 1923.

Imagine Klee and Kandinsky, to mention just two of these great masters, not yet floating in the cold, fluorescent light and serpentine space of faddishly intellectual adoration, but shivering in their overcoats teaching a group of eager youngsters weaving and stained glass and metal work and, as one irreverent student said about Klee, "turning out spiritual samovars and intellectual doorknobs." Imagine the effervescent Schlemmer applying the rhythm and motion of his ballet experiments and stage design to the never-ending discussions of architecture. These were not teachers in the conventional sense. And there was no hero worship about them. The identification was with the work in hand, not the master.

Neither was the Bauhaus, at least in the early Weimar days, a school as we know schools of art, design, and architecture. It was a laboratory. Gropius, his staff, and his students groped, fumbled, experimented, and "took chances together," as Anni Albers has put it.

235

Her husband, Josef Albers, then an elementary school teacher, came to the Bauhaus to do stained glass work. He was sternly told to take up wall painting first. But he played hooky and with rucksack and hammer rummaged the garbage dumps and collected old bottles and such. When the time came for the obligatory exhibits, he expected to be expelled for his crude glass paintings. Instead, he was put in charge of the glass workshop.

A little later, without previous warning, Gropius announced that the student Albers was to teach "principles of craft." Still a little later, without warning Gropius, Albers changed this course to "principles of design."

The world can be grateful -- as Albers still is, despite his initial hesitance to teach again -- but you can see that the early Bauhaus was a rather haphazard affair.

The curriculum was constantly changing as new ideas turned up and special talents asserted themselves. From all accounts, the Weimar Bauhaus was in a state of perpetual crisis with sparks of creative genius emanating from sometimes rather bitter internal friction. There wasn't a style, a movement, an approach, an experiment, an idea, or a fad of the time that wasn't tried, debated, and quarrelled over.

For some at the Bauhaus, this included Mazdaznan, a weird, pseudo-Persian cult the essence of which seems to have been that lots of garlic is good for the soul. Assemblies, I am told, sometimes so reeked of garlic that people fainted. And it included an improvement on the masculine attire -- which, heaven knows, is in need of reform. This Bauhaus dress consisted of a corduroy cossack blouse and funnel-shaped trousers in a wide assortment of colors. It was worn, by some, with hand-carved wooden slippers and a completely shaven head. Gropius eventually put his foot down on that and stated that the artist must accept his time and the dress that goes with it.

He always asserted himself in the end.   But his approach
was not to impose his individual will on anything but to give every
new idea a chance and to strive for synthesis and collaboration.
It was, as he has said, never "either -- or." Always "and." He
sought unity and synthesis.

Incessant and bitter attacks by political reaction drove the
Bauhaus from Weimar.   In 1925, almost the entire faculty and the
entire student body moved to Gropius's magnificent new building
in Dessau.   Here things settled down, the somewhat chaotic
fermentation period was over.   The Dessau Bauhaus was more
orderly and businesslike but still incredibly creative.   And it was
still essentially a laboratory.

I can think of only one other great laboratory of ideas which
matches in creativity and probably surpasses in importance to
you and me what transpired in Weimar and Dessau.   That was the
Georgia Augusta University in Göttingen at about the same time.
At Göttingen, physics and mathematics departments were
assembled -- studying, arguing and frolicking, making love and
making history, conscious at once of an Olympian mission and
not at all of self -- as teachers and lecturers such people as Max
Planck, Niels Bohr, Maria von Smoluchowski, and James Franck;
and as students such now famous men as J. Robert Oppenheimer,
Karl Compton, Norbert Wiener, Werner Heisenberg, Enrico
Fermi, as well as a number of Russians who, for better or for worse,
carried their knowledge back to the Soviet Union.   You know what
happened.

And you know what had happened by the time the Nazis closed
the Bauhaus after fourteen short years.   It had, indeed, made good
on that rather naively bombastic phrase and created and conceived
the new building of the future.   It rises from the hands of a million
workers from Park Avenue to Timbuktu.

It has, indeed, broken down the arrogant barrier between
craftsman and artist and in so doing re-formed (what an apt phrase --
given new form!) everything,   in Mies van der Rohe's words,

"from the coffee cup to city planning." The Bauhaus has not done this alone. Nor is there such a thing as a Bauhaus style. That, as Gropius has said, "would have been a confession of failure and a return to that very stagnation and devitalizing inertia which he had called it into being to combat."

The Bauhaus contribution to the re-formation of our visual culture is that it taught us a philosophy, an approach to design which calls for the investigation of each problem and giving form to its own inherent solution. Some of the existing Bauhaus products -- Marcel Breuer's early chairs and other furniture, Herbert Bayer's experimental lettering, Oscar Schlemmer's ballet costumes -- may seem quaintly dated today. The Bauhaus approach to design is not. It is all the more valid as our present-day "stylists" -- and they are not confined to Detroit -- again apply totally unmotivated surface decoration on industrial products and even buildings.

This design philosophy, this approach to design evolved, as the art critic John Canaday has written, because: "The Bauhaus was probably the most effective coordinating factor in the chaotic picture of modern art, and it developed teaching methods in connection with this coordination that are now disseminated all over the world." These teaching concepts were the one constant factor in the chaos of the early Weimar days and stayed with the Bauhaus throughout. They comprised three phases of training.

First was the six-month basic, or preliminary course or Vorlehre. Its chief function, in the words of the prospectus, was to "liberate the individual by breaking down conventional patterns of thought in order to make way for personal experiences and discoveries which will enable him to see his own potentialities and limitations." Johannes Itten, a Swiss painter, had taught art that way in Vienna before Gropius brought him to Weimar. He called his method "the big house-cleaning of the mind" and his students called it "the purgatory." Moholy-Nagy and Josef Albers refined this approach to elementary art education which is essentially based on the ideas of Froebel and Montessori and which is today practiced in just about every art course from kindergarten to university in

238

the Western world. If the Bauhaus had made no other contribution than this course it would for this alone deserve an honored place in art history.

Next was workshop instruction in a craft of the student's choice. This was a three-year course. It required a formal apprenticeship contract with the local trades council, an official body still much alive in Germany as an outgrowth of the old crafts guilds. At Weimar two masters instructed the workshop -- a craftsman and an artist -- to train the hand and the eye simultaneously. Later in Dessau, these two masters were replaced by one. For by now Gropius had trained what he has called creatively ambidextrous teachers from among his students. Among them were Herbert Bayer, Marcel Breuer, and Josef Albers. There were workshops in nearly all the crafts -- weaving, carpentry, metal work, printing, ceramics, stage craft, stained glass, mural painting, and what have you.

It all was to lead up to architecture, however. It all strove for what the prospectus called "the collective work of art -- the building -- in which no barriers exist between the structural and the decorative arts. . . Training in a craft, " the prospectus went on, "is a prerequisite for collective work in architecture. This training purposely combats the dilettantism of previous generations in the applied arts. "

This three-year craft training resulted in an official Journeyman's diploma and, if real design ability merited it, an additional Bauhaus diploma. Only with such a diploma could the student enter the third and most important stage of Bauhaus education -- the course in architecture with practical experience in the so-called Research Department where architecture was both taught and practiced.

Due to lack of space, funds, and commissions this phase of Bauhaus teaching was only partly realized. Times were bad. In the Weimar days, most of Gropius's own work remained on paper. The only important architectural products of that time were a theater in the neighboring town of Jena, an experimental building in the

239

1923 Bauhaus exhibition, and a villa in Berlin.   Students and masters of all workshops participated in all of them.

In Dessau architecture was taught in a more definite and systematic fashion, in 1928 by an architect named Hannes Meyer (apparently a rare error in Gropius's judgment of people) and later by Mies van der Rohe, who took over in 1930.

But the Bauhaus never had the opportunity to be really and essentially an architecture school.   Engineering and technical training had to be obtained elsewhere.   It was purposely a school, or, as I have said, a laboratory, of design, the culminative effort of which was to, and did in many respects, lead up to architecture, to the building of the future.   And therein lies idea number one -- an idea I consider eminently viable today.

In the high counsels of the architects, there is now increasing talk and concern for the architect's responsibility for the total man-made environment.   The recently published report of the AIA Committee on the Profession quite unconsciously reflects shades of the "crystal symbol" of the first Bauhaus proclamation.   It believes a new environment greater than the Golden Age of Greece, and outshining the magnificence of the Renaissance, is possible -- "provided the architect assumes again his historic role as the master builder.   In such a role he must retain the basic control of design, not only of individual buildings but of all design involved with man-made environment. "

The Bauhaus aim was quite directly to prepare its students for this role as master builder, as the design coordinator who could bring order and beauty into the chaos of the conflicting demands of our technological civilization.   This new environment of order and beauty cannot be created by individual geniuses -- even if, heaven forbid, we could produce enough of them.   Both technically and creatively it will require the humility and discipline of teamwork.

Gropius said: "I see in the systematic development of voluntary teamwork a two-fold guarantee: Protection of the individual and his specific qualities in his struggle against becoming a mere number and, at the same time, the development of a common expression rather than one of pretentious individualism. "

If you believe that our cities need order and uniform cornice lines and harmonious common expression, you have here viable Bauhaus idea number two.

Bauhaus idea number three seems equally obvious, equally viable, and in its idealistic aspects equally far from actual attainment. It is expressed in the simple and ancient thought of learning by doing.

There is of course much practical and experimental work being done in our design and architecture schools today. But most of this is in the nature of class problems. Gropius sent his industrial design students into the factories, and the Bauhaus made a handsome income from doing actual design work for industry in its workshops. His advanced architecture students worked with him on his commissions and, most important of all, were sent out on the building site to work on construction jobs. The term master builder seems to imply this approach. As we think and talk of broadening architectural education and architectural competence, this phase of the Bauhaus idea may be well worth reflective consideration.

My next point -- Bauhaus viability number four -- is this: Is not the real integration of art and architecture a still most valid goal? Should we still not be striving for the complete building as "the final aim of the visual arts" which architects, painters, and sculptors create from its inception? This is a far cry from the usual practice of designing a building and then, when it is all but completed, calling in a painter and telling him: "Here, paint something on that wall!"

We have heard this discussion and we all rejoice over such truly integrated works of art and architecture as Philip Johnson's roofless church in New Harmony, Indiana, which just won an AIA Honor Award. But the teamwork Gropius has preached for a life-

241

time is rarely practiced, and our architecture is the worse for it. Nor will we find many architecture schools which would invite the Feiningers, Klees, and Kandinskys of our time to teach, grope, fumble, experiment, and take chances alongside the craft teachers with their students.

You may say that all this is ideas and ideals rather than specific methods. They stand alongside the historic Bauhaus accomplishment of having brought art and industry together -- as was, probably, inevitable anyway. But in all this, as Lux Feininger has pointed out to me, Bauhaus teaching, and particularly that of Josef Albers, in its stress on art in craftsmanship and craftsmanship in art, has always emphasized thought. The German word for art, Kunst, derives from können, which means ability, power, faculty, knowledge, or, in the vernacular, know-how. This, as the Bauhaus knew and taught, implies thought and discipline in approaching any design problem.

I agree with Lux Feininger that while all else the Bauhaus did and taught may be contemporaneous to its unique period in history, this particular contribution absolutely lives on. If you look around in our art galleries today, you find that we are again, as I have said before, in a period of whim and utter romaticism. Thought is unpopular and is replaced by more or less phony spontaneity more or less falsely rationalized.

But you don't have to go as far as an art gallery. The sins of ingratiating surface decoration which the Bauhaus fought with thought and integrity are celebrating a gaudy and gleeful revival. If you are sick of berating superfluous fins on cars, we might, for a change, berate lacy and unfunctional skins on buildings. Surface decoration, novelty stunts, and gift wrapping are just that, whether they are eclectic or modern.

One of the deans I consulted wrote me: "In general, I feel that the Bauhaus was a needed strong medicine at the time." As I look around, I think we can stand another injection of this medicine; not, by any means, to stunt the development of bare and

242

square glass box architecture towards freer, more imaginative forms, but to discipline untrammeled self-expression in favor of thoughtful form. Herbert Bayer has almost poetically expressed this thought in a "Homage to Gropius" which he has asked me to read on this occasion: "For the future, the Bauhaus gave us assurance in facing the perplexities of work; it gave us the know-how to work, a foundation in the crafts, an invaluable heritage of timeless principles as applied to the creative process. It expressed again that we are not to impose esthetics on the things we use, or the structures we live in; but that purpose and form must be seen as one, that they seldom can stand alone, that direction emerges when one begins to consider concrete demands, special conditions, inherent character, but never losing perspective that one is after all an artist. Whereas, the painter can only be guided from within.

"The Bauhaus existed for a short span of time, but the potentials intrinsic in its principles have only begun to be realized. Its sources of design remain forever full of changing possibilities. The Bauhaus is dead. Long live the Bauhaus.

"I pay homage to Gropius for his creative intuition, for his relentless perseverance in the advancement of life, for his strength of mind and character in standing firm against opposition and slander, for his inspired leadership, for his deep concern with man and his community, for his search for a common basis of all understanding beyond the mastery of material and physical things, for his belief in personality as the ultimate decisive value."

Mr. von Eckardt's most recent book is Eric Mendelsohn in the "Masters of World Architecture" series. He is a free lance writer and is art director of the Journal of the American Institute of Architects.

THE INFLUENCE OF THE BAUHAUS

Esmond Shaw

In the 1930's, where else but in the Bauhaus of Walter
Gropius could training in the visual arts find a model for its
guidance? At Cooper Union in the years 1931-1937, the entire
Art School admitted its debt to the principles laid down at
Weimar and Dessau. To the extent of the ability of its students and its teachers, it tried never to copy end results, but
to abide by the basic tenets of Gropius, who wrote, "The Bauhaus was inaugurated with the specific object of realizing a
modern architectonic art, which, like human nature, should
be all-embracing in its scope. Within that sovereign federa-
tive union, all the different arts (with the various manifestations and tendencies of each) -- every branch of design, every
form of technique -- could be co-ordinated and find their
appointed place. "

There were, of course, other implementing reasons for
the form which the curriculum took at Weimar and Dessau.
Modern architecture should reflect the machine age and make
use of the machine and its mass-produced materials. Buildings
should be logical and direct statements of their structure and
function. Students were to receive "objective tuition in the
basic laws of form and color, " which would enable them "to
acquire the necessary mental equipment to give tangible shape
to their own creative instincts. " And "artistic design is neither
an intellectual nor a material affair, but simply an integral part
of the stuff of life. " Finally the Bauhaus laid great stress on
the need for designers to be familiar with both business proce-
dures and production methods. "Our ambition was to raise the
creative artist from his otherworldliness and reintegrate him
into the workaday world of realities; and at the same time to

244

broaden and humanize the rigid, almost exclusively material mind of the business man. Thus our informing conception of the basic unity of all design in relation to life was in diametrical opposition to that of art for art's sake, and the even more dangerous philosophy it sprang from: business as an end in itself.

All of these aims constitute at the same time the loftiest set of ideals and the most practical set of methods for training in the visual arts. They are just as applicable today as when they were first enunciated. Of course the obvious question arises. Did the Cooper Union School of Art and Architecture succeed in applying them? Equally of course the answer is: no, not entirely. But we had a lot of fun and excitement in trying to do so. It was much easier to find students who were willing to subject themselves to the new disciplines than to find instructors to teach them, but since everyone was trying his best to learn and to experiment, the end results were not too disappointing.

Geoffrey Scott, in the opening paragraph of his book, The Architecture of Humanism, quotes Sir Henry Wotton's paraphrase of Vitruvius on the requirements of architecture. Whether we call these essentials utility, strength, and beauty, or Commodity, Firmness, and Delight, Scott's thesis that architecture is a focus where three separate purposes have converged is essentially correct as his book attempts to prove.

Just as there are three disparate conditions to good architecture, so there are three separate branches of study in a good curriculum in architecture. And these three areas are the academic, the technical, and the vocational. Further, unless we succeed in making of our whole program a focus where "these three separate purposes have converged, " we will still have a long way to go before we produce ideal training for architecture. This is the new synthesis toward which all our energies should be directed. If we can evolve a curriculum which is a vital, living organism, and in which its three separate stems are joined and interrelated, we will have produced a good design.

But no matter how much we may want to achieve this new synthesis, it will be beyond our reach if we do not base it on an underlying philosophy at least as strong and uniform as that of the Bauhaus. Such an operative philosophy of education cannot be developed, on demand, as a good cook can prepare a stew. It is invariably the product of the thinking of men of deep conviction. Equally invariably it always reflects the temper of the times.

About fifteen years before Cooper Union was founded, Ralph Waldo Emerson wrote in his essay on art: "Beauty must come back to the useful arts, and the distinction between the fine and useful arts be forgotten. If history were truly told, if life were nobly spent, it would be no longer easy nor possible to distinguish the one from the other. In nature, all is useful; all is beautiful. It is therefore beautiful because it is alive, moving, reproductive; it is therefore useful because it is symmetrical and fair. Beauty will not come at the call of a legislature, nor will it repeat in England or America its history in Greece. It will come, as always, unannounced, and spring up between the feet of brave and earnest men. It is in vain that we look for genius to reiterate its miracles in the old arts; it is its instinct to find beauty and holiness in new and necessary facts, in the fields and roadside, in the shop and mill."

Mr. Shaw, a noted speaker and writer in the field of architectural education, is professor of architecture and head of the Department of Architecture at Cooper Union, New York City.

246

WALTER GROPIUS AND THE ARTS

Thomas H. Creighton

Walter Gropius is a difficult person to evaluate except in certain direct and physical ways. One can evaluate his personality, because it is a positive one: he is a charming, gentle, modest man, yet with tremendous conviction, drive, and purpose. One can evaluate his work, because its impact has been so great that it has been quite thoroughly documented, from the unheralded fresh breeze across the architectural landscape that the Fagus factory provided, to the most recent commissions of the Architects' Collaborative. One can evaluate his qualities as a teacher, from the Bauhaus and its continuing influence on architectural education, through the Harvard period and its measurable success in producing architects of unusual ability.

For the rest, for an estimate of Gropius's attitudes and philosophies, beliefs and standards, one must, of course, rely on what he has said and what he has written; and here is where the difficulty lies. In contrast to Mies, whose intervals between articulations are more conspicuous than the words themselves, Gropius writes and speaks a great deal, and with no hesitation. But in contrast to Wright, who wrote polemics, and Le Corbusier, who still writes tracts, Gropius expresses himself in measured, carefully phrased, fully considered aphorisms. He has, throughout his life, believed in the right and eschewed the wrong. That is not a deprecatory statement, because Gropius has believed in the right in an architectural sense when very few others did, and when it was an act of great courage to make the "right" statements.

But the fact remains that a review of his recorded expressions on any given subject, or even an interview or a conversation with him on a specific topic, is likely to turn up many handsome generalities and few controversial or even highly original opinions. Even in formulating the philosophy of education on which the Bauhaus operated -- and which became subject to various interpretations -- Gropius wrote in such terms as: " The Bauhaus felt it had a double moral responsibility: to make its pupils fully conscious of the age they were living in, and to train them to turn their native intelligence and the knowledge they received to practical account in the design of type-forms which would be the direct expression of that consciousness." That would not be an important statement were it not for the fact that no one had said those things for a long time; and the fact that Gropius and his staff were able to develop a curriculum from them. I suspect that this generality of statement, combined with the important truths contained in the generalities, may also account for the fact that much of the writing about Gropius has been almost embarrassingly generalized and complimentary. After all, what can one do but compliment a great architect and a great teacher who believes in the need to relate design in the twentieth century to machine production, who believes in the need to ameliorate unhealthy physical-social conditions, who believes in a unity within diversity, and who believes in collaboration among creative people?

It is the belief of Walter Gropius in collaboration which is of most concern to us this evening, because, to him, this includes collaboration with the other arts and the practitioners of those arts. His statements to this effect go back to the first Bauhaus proclamation: "The final product of all artistic endeavors is the building. The visual arts once found their highest task in contributing to its beauty and were inseparable constituents of all great works of architecture. Today each stands apart in independent isolation, and this situation can only be changed through conscious cooperative work."

Gropius is not himself a painter or sculptor. He has designed objects in addition to buildings, but his point of view in industrial design has always been that of an architect -- that is, of one concerned with programmed, objective, usable form and space -- rather than that of an artist, depending on emotional, subjective arrangement of form, light, color, texture, composition. In fact the thesis of the Bauhaus program was that there should not be instruction which "condemned its pupils to the lifelong practice of a purely sterile art." Even the interest which Gropius has always had in the use of color and texture in architecture has been a functional one, developed around the immediate physiological and psychological effect of these tactile and visual characteristics of materials and space.

If Gropius differs from Le Corbusier in this respect of not being himself an artist in any of the other visual fields, he differs from both Mies and Wright in desiring very ardently the integrated use of those arts in relation to architecture. We can begin an evaluation of the contribution of Gropius to the "greatness" of a "common esthetic," then, from certain premises which differentiate him from the others we are discussing: a belief in collaboration, many times stated, and a certain history of collaborative activity.

When we speak of the relationship of architecture to the allied visual arts fields, it seems to me that we must consider two kinds of connection. The "common esthetic" can be a cultural affinity, or it can be a physical intertwining: a kinship or a marriage.

Through most of the history of the arts, the cultural relationship has been a close one. That is to say, whether or not sculpture and painting were used on buildings, the plastic arts, the visual arts, and the mother of the arts moved together, in the same direction, at the same rate of speed, toward the same ends. Content, purpose, techniques, even materials were usually similar. The methods of expression and the things expressed were often the same. Certainly in the peaks of artistic development that we academically consider the "great" times, there was this sort of relationship. The high points of Assyrian, Egyptian, Greek, Gothic, and Renaissance art saw the artists and the architects -- and, it must be emphasized, the clients and society in general -- speaking the same cultural language, working toward the same artistic ends.

At other times, and it would seem they were often periods of early growth or late development, there was not this same relationship: the sculpture of classic Rome is tame compared to its structural innovation; the ceramic work of Byzantium seems naive in relation to the sophistication of the construction; Baroque sculpture and painting is often sweet alongside the violence of the architecture. All of this could make a fascinating historical study, but let's just accept the fact that at times artists and architects, art and architecture develop together; at other times they don't.

The lack of a relationship of any kind -- if not a kinship or a marriage, at least a decent love affair -- has been very uncommon through history. In general, the closeness has been such that history and criticism of the arts has lumped art and architecture together in a single package, so that the discipline of architecture today is suffering from the fact that it has never engendered a methodology of historic understanding nor a system of criticism of its own. The usable- space qualities of architecture and the emotional-space definition of sculpture are usually considered under the same set of criteria.

In the twentieth century this relationship has sometimes existed, sometimes not. Trends, styles, and movements have been rapid. There was certainly a close style kinship in the architecture, painting, and sculpture of art nouveau. The cubists were both painters and architects; so were the futurists, and the neoplasticists. De Stijl included van Doesburg and Mondrian as well as Mies and Kiesler. But what in architecture is comparable at this moment to abstract expressionist painting and the work of the New York school of action painters? It takes a great stretch of the imagination and much rationalizing to relate the sculpture of David Smith or Reg Butler to new brutalist architecture, or the painting of Rothko or de Kooning to the plastic forms that architects are now concerning themselves with.

It is characteristic of our time that today we find no closeness, almost no common understanding between modern-minded architects

250

and other contemporary artists. It seems to be true that today's
architectural profession is, by and large, artistically illiterate.
Not only is there no common esthetic, there appear to be very
few architects -- and I include the most respected and well-known
of our middle-aged group -- who truly know the currents and the
tendencies, the styles and the mannerisms, the hopes and the
fears even, of the painters and the sculptors of the time.

What is the history and what is the attitude of Walter Gropius
in this respect? What has been his personal relationship with the
artists of his time? And what has been the place of his architecture
in a common esthetic of his time? Here again, one must distinguish
between facts and opinions.

With regard to persons, Gropius has been close to many artists; how close he has been to their work is another question.
His brilliant gathering of the group of outstanding people around
him in Weimar and Dessau seems to have come from careful study
and intelligent appraisal, but little prior knowledge of their work.
When one askes him what artists he knew before the call to Weimar,
he searches for names and remembers Gerhardt Marcks and Hin-
nert Schaper, both of whom he took with him to the Bauhaus. Most
of the others apparently came from the group centering around the
gallery and magazine Der Sturm, from mutual friends in the musical world, and through the activities of Alma Mahler, his first
wife, who, as Giedion puts it, "had an extraordinary instinct for
the recognition of unknown talent in all fields of art, " and who
brought to his attention, for instance, Johannes Itten.

He was au courant then; he was vitally interested in the arts
and in artists; and he had strong enough convictions to build a school
around these people. However, it is very difficult, either through
reading the printed record or by talking to those who were there,
to visualize just what the relationship of Gropius to those people
was, except as an administrator. And it would seem, as one reviews his history, that this interest did not continue with the same
conviction. There is no record of close association with artists in
the period when he was in England. During the time at Harvard,

251

there was no strong attempt to continue the artist-architect relationship begun in the Bauhaus. "The time was not right for bringing artists to the Graduate School, as Sert has brought Mirko," Gropius comments today.

Gropius himself recalls no art-style relationship or associations at that early time. Certainly there was little in the theories of the Deutsche Werkbund group or among the people in Peter Behrens's atelier, in that first decade of the century, that would have accounted for the pure style he suddenly developed -- the "outright leap," as Giedion calls it. The purely architectural influences that Gropius wrote about--"the even greater structural importance" of glass, the "unconscious majesty" of the grain elevators, coal conveyors, and industrial plants in America -- these were technological-esthetic trends that also influenced other people who reacted, stylistically, in very different ways from his. As far as one can determine by what he wrote at the time -- or even what he has written later -- Gropius was not closely connected with the cubist movement further west; with the De Stijl group, although Van Doesburg visited and lectured at the Bauhaus later; with the expressionist trend, although he brought Feininger and others identified with the movement to the school; nor with the futurists, although he must have been familiar with the work of Boccioni and Duchamp. In any event, none of these movements took concrete form until several years after the Fagus works were completed.

Reyner Banham speculates on the possibility of Gropius's familiarity with a book called Glasarchitektur, by Paul Scheerbart, a writer of novels of the fantastic, which apparently also affected Mies van der Rohe, and which was acknowledged as a strong influence by Bruno and Max Taut, whom Gropius also knew. However, Glasarchitektur was published in 1914 -- three years after the completion of Fagus, and the architectural concepts were very different.

One has to come to the conclusion that Gropius is completely frank when he searches his mind for art-styles relationships in

252

his early work, that he was one of those whom Giedion describes as "not fighters in the futurist sense, more purely research men in their work, keeping to their ateliers, preparing quietly and without fanfare the symbols of our artistic language."

If Gropius did not conceive his early architecture as part of a movement, neither did he form a "school" or a "style" of architecture and the arts. He has always objected to the term "the Bauhaus style." Whether or not one agrees that there was -- and is -- no Bauhaus style in architecture (and many of us are very sure that we can identify one), it does seem to be true that no movement which included painting, sculpture, and the other arts grew from the Bauhaus, or the International Style concept. It seems impossible to see any plastic, or compositional, or manifesto-inspiring relationship between the architecture of Walter Gropius and the creative output of Klee, Kandinsky, even Schlemmer; certainly not in that of Feininger, and only in highly intellectual terms does the work of Moholy-Nagy relate.

As one goes on through Gropius's career searching for a link with art trends of his time, either as cause or result, another difficulty enters -- that is his history of collaboration with other architects. Although a Gropius touch unquestionably runs through all the work, there is a distinct style in the work with Meyer; there is a distinct style in the work with Fry; there is a distinct style in the work with Breuer; the product of TAC is in accord with, if better than, much of the other progressive design of the last decade in the United States; one could be cruel and say there is a Roth-Gropius style in the Grand Central Pan Am Building. But the point is that in none of these periods does the work -- brilliant as it was during each collaboration, influential as it was in each country -- seem to have been related to or to have influenced similar moves in the other arts. I am forced to conclude that the work of Gropius, undeniably "great" in the field of architecture, denies the need of a "common esthetic" -- a simultaneous esthetic development in other arts -- as an ingredient of greatness.

There is a second possible relationship between architecture and the other visual arts -- the one of direct physical contact; the use, in, on, and around buildings of the work of artists; the cliché term which is the <u>raison d'être</u> of such organizations as the Architectural League of New York: integration of the arts.

Gropius has stated his desire for such collaboration many times over. However, aside from work by Bayer, Albers, and a mural by Oscar Schlemmer (now destroyed) at the Bauhaus, there is apparently no use of commissioned, related art work in his buildings until the truly extravagant instance of the Harvard Graduate Center, where Bayer, Albers, Lippold, Arp, and Miro are represented. Since then, the work of the Architects' Collaborative has shown very little of that sort of collaborative enterprise. There have been sculptured block walls, as in the Littleton School, and there have been colored tile panels, as in the Needham School, but these have been a part of the architectural design of the architectural office, and it would be stretching the meaning of the words to consider them fine art. One turns in vain through the pages of his published work, including the important new project for Baghdad University, searching for examples of the visual arts.

We have here a situation which is of prime interest in architecture and the plastic arts today: an architect, one of the world's greatest, who is sincerely devoted to the principle of collaboration, who has been associated with some of the greatest artists of our century, who almost with one building initiated one of the great style movements of our time -- and who at this point apparently finds it impossible to integrate other arts with his architecture. It seems worthwhile to examine the reasons why.

The Harvard Graduate Center was the one big splurge. Gropius was not very happy with that experience. Giedion extravagantly speaks of Gropius's "daring in demanding that the works of creative artists should become the daily companions of student life." Gropius himself more drily says, "I asked the Harvard Corporation that any money left within the appropriation after the bids came in be used for art work. After this was approved, I immediately

254

got in touch with the potential artists." The potentialities of
the artists apparently did not include a great amount of interest
in what they were commissioned to do. Gropius has complained
in private conversation of the lack of true collaborative concern.
When Miro finally saw the wall he had done, he was so dissatis-
fied that he is substituting another work.

Another big disappointment was the UNESCO Headquarters
building in Paris, for which Gropius was chairman of the Architectural Advisory Committee. In a letter to Jean Gorin, he
describes the inception of the art program thus: "I can assure
you that we did everything in our power to make it clear to the
client that collaborating artists should be nominated early enough
to work with the architect right from the start. We did not succeed. Endless political drawbacks and financial difficulties,
which were very real indeed, caused one frustrating postpone-
ment after the other. Finally, the special committee to nomi-
nate the collaborating artists was not elected before all the working
drawings for the building had been already finished; so the architects had to make the best of it."

I would not so willingly absolve the architects -- or the artists. Granted the impossibility of early collaboration, there
apparently was little attempt at fusion into the architectural
scheme of the works which were finally commissioned. Breuer
is perfectly willing to defend the situation as it exists. Zehrfuss
is unhappy only over the quality of some of the individual works.
Picasso never even visited the building; he simply sent a canvas.
Afro, in response to sympathy expressed over the poor placement
of his painting -- on a comparatively narrow corridor wall -- is
completely unconcerned.

We seem to come to a conclusion that is not likely to warm
the hearts of those who believe in integration of the arts. It is
that even when architecture is a potential receptive container or
a potential collaborative partner of the other arts, the collaboration
in our time is not likely to be very successful. There are apparently several reasons for this.

255

First, the interest of the client and the budget that the client must supply normally do not exist, or appear too late for full collaborative effort. Gropius has written pessimistically: "Anybody who has undertaken to steer a client towards architectural solutions which would transcend the merely practical and economical approach knows that he will have his hands full without trying to add proposals for collaboration with painters and sculptors." This purely practical consideration might seem possible to overcome by proper argument on the architect's part. Indeed it has been surmounted in many instances: it has become almost a cliché that a major shopping center should have an "art program"; many of the corporate office buildings where prestige is as important as square footage have individual works of fine artists; some of the speculative imitations of the better buildings have imitations of the art also. But client interest and client budget remain problems, as Gropius has testified.

Secondly, the artist, in our age, is an independent artist, pursuing his own creative aims, and is not a good collaborator. Thirty-five years after the Bauhaus experiments in collaborative design, Gropius says, "The artist today does not know how to collaborate." Calder's work is in many buildings, but Calder has never designed for a building. One uses Rivera's sinuous metal or not, but its use is no more directly related to the architecture of a building where it is used than it is to a museum gallery where it may be displayed. The common juxtaposition today is typified by the Breuer-Gabo partnership at the Beehive store in Rotterdam: a strong work of art dwarfing the scale of a strong building; the too-adjacent building in turn destroying the impact of the sculpture. And when this does not happen, the architect is likely to play too strong a role in dictating not only the location and scale, but also color, materials, and even content. "Slow and painful are the attempts at seeking points of contact again after the long alienation between the different branches of the arts," writes Gropius.

256

Finally, an obvious, strong reason for the difficulty in collaborative effort is the fact that we do not have a common social goal, as other ages had when a common esthetic inspired the artists and the architects. There is no driving, dominating religious, political, or even social idea. Gropius writes: "I believe that, if we as a people cannot evolve a clearer picture of our common objectives and unite our moral forces behind their realization, the desire of the architect and artist to create unity will remain thwarted, and individual contributions toward beauty and order will remain isolated."

Because of these difficulties, then, not even Walter Gropius, with all his belief in collaboration, has succeeded in fusing art and architecture in our time. Certainly there is not any easy, comfortable, natural relationship as there was in other periods. Our architects are not providing pediments and friezes, niches and parapets, wall panels and squinch arches for the obvious placement of sculpture and painting and ceramics. Our architecture, whether it is an architecture deriving from Mies, industrially sufficient in itself; or influenced by Wright, organically complete in itself; or the architecture of Gropius, unified within its own diversity -- our architecture does not seem to need or allow for a fusion with the arts.

The relationship which implies subservience of the artist's contribution to a common design goal seems impossible; the architects are not even agreed among themselves about a common aim in design. I cannot imagine an artist finding an esthetic which would be "consistent" with an environment which juxtaposes concrete plasticity with steel modularity, which equally welcomes pierced screens, medieval masonry, curtain walls, and hyperbolic paraboloids. The relationship which simply permits coexistence and complementary position seems meaningless and vapid, and certainly contributes nothing great. The relationship of tension and creative independence, if not opposition, has been tried too seldom and requires a peculiar kind of understanding and cooperation, of the sort that Gropius initiated and apparently finished with at the Bauhaus.

257

It does not seem likely in the present climate that we will attain the ideal integration of the arts and collaboration among architects and artists that Gropius has so long described and advocated, but never has been able to achieve himself in practice.

I hope that one day he does succeed. I hope he has the ideal client who permits, even urges, an artistic collaboration from the beginning of the project, and provides sufficient budget for it. I hope he finds the right artists who will sympathetically and yet imaginatively and creatively work with him to provide a strong counterpoint -- the unity within variety he has so long advocated. And I hope that he himself will direct and coordinate the collaboration as subtly and as well as he did at the Bauhaus. It would be nice to have one good instance of a common esthetic in these current decades before we give over to chaoticism.

Mr. Creighton graduated from the Beaux Arts Institute of Design. An architect and critic, he is editorial director of Progressive Architecture and partner in the office of John Lyon Reid. He is the author of Building for Modern Man (1949; with Katherine Morrow Ford) and The Architecture of Monuments (1962).

LET US NOT MAKE SHAPES: LET US SOLVE PROBLEMS

Serge Chermayeff

In the thirties, Le Corbusier and Gropius shared the distinction of dominating a programmatic world of architecture.
Indeed, they led the International Congress of Modern Architects which was then turning, after years of war and frustration, to fundamental programs of action for architects and planners. On top of this international pyramid was their representative body, which had declared that its purpose was not to make
shapes, but to resolve problems.

This is very interesting historically because in those days,
the protagonists whose works we now see all over were relatively idle. They had, in fact, time to think, and they applied
themselves to that very necessary and basic task with a discipline and devotion which hasn't been equalled since. The social
disciplines as then laid down -- the human basis for architecture
and the creation of a human habitat -- were, in the towns of both
Le Corbusier and Gropius, the idea of the future. This idea
entailed the utilization of industrialization as a new tool for architecture and a restatement of the problems of humanity in relation to that industrialization.

It seemed to them that they were working at the beginning
of a new era, but I'm going to dare say that they were mistaken.
What they really did was to close an old era and establish principles which might be used by a new era, as yet unreached.

When Nikolaus Pevsner wrote The Masters of the Modern
Movement , he gave it a sub-title: From William Morris to
Walter Gropius . And, indeed, Morris closed the old period
with a revolt against industrialism which almost drove him to a

259

pre-Raphaelite romantic austerity denying the machine; while Gropius started the notion of properly employing the new means of production.

Gropius was particularly Teutonic, shall we say, in his logic and application, and very different in his method from the heretic Le Corbusier. He was also very different in his attitudes, which were much more quantitative and analytical than those of the philosophic Mies. And certainly, he was miles away from the romantic Wright, although he admired beyond measure the purely sculptural achievements of that great genius.

In February, 1929, there was a report published by CIAM which was characteristically in the German manner. It was titled The Social Basis for Minimal Dwelling: Flat, Middle, or High? We would translate it today, I suppose, "houses on the ground, walk-ups, or high rise." This report indicated typically the questions then on Gropius's mind. These questions were not formal at all. On the contrary, he went to endless trouble to analyze problems of land coverage in relation to the types of dwellings, of distances between dwellings, of land release and light penetration -- all physical aspects of dwellings -- simply because these were very largely neglected. In his analysis he didn't go so far as Le Corbusier, who at the CIAM Congress in Brussels in 1930 went so far as to say, "I only want twelve per cent of residential area covered with building, and I want eighty per cent of open space devoted to play and park and pleasure." Neither did he, and he admitted it, go so far as Richard Neutra in his analysis of the need for separation of the problems of rising traffic and shrinking pedestrians. But he did say, "Rationality only counts when it is life-enriching," and then he went on to spell this out by saying that the rational includes the psychological and social values. It is a magnificent statement of principle.

He also talked, then, of a healthy politic for living as though life itself could be measured and given form. Like an ultimate faith, he mentioned the economic limit. Economic limits were, in those postwar years, very much the limits of that which could be afforded rather than that which was desired, and there was still a lingering abstraction of the nineteenth-century economic man as a social entity, God help us. He said, "The economic limits are reached only when the balance between building cost and street and land cost can no longer be maintained." As we look upon our growing traffic, we can understand, and understand very well, how easily that balance was lost. Our houses are being built more cheaply, if possible, simply because our streets are costing more.

Also, he said, "If by-laws were replaced by notions of the cubic content of living space, that is to say the volume in which one may live, instead of the floor area of a dwelling (density figures of a meaningless kind), we could probably achieve greater health more economically." Remember, this was 1929, and a statement like that was practically an apostasy in those days. And he said, echoing Patrick Geddes, "For every grown-up person a room of his own, however small," a recognition of the need for privacy in a rising communality. But recognizing that communality had to be given shape and a heart, he also said in that time, "The essential provision of large, communal scale for community facilities such as playgrounds, community kitchens, play spaces, nursery schools, shops, mechanical equipment must not only be assured, but the building of the community center must come first before any houses are built or any dwellings are built," an extremely important contribution to the whole subsequent housing philosophy.

Some years later (to be exact, the year before Moholy-Nagy, who as his colleague and collaborator in the Bauhaus and Dessau had come to America and had started the New Bauhaus in Chicago, died), he said in a lecture at the Institute of Design in Chicago that there was a need to establish a human scale. I think this was a reflection of his concern with the changing postures of man. Man was becoming not only the little pedestrian, but he was leaping all over the place in seven hundred league boots. At the same time, he said that we must resolve the dilemma in land use between public purpose and private ownership. This is a dilemma which still haunts us most dramatically on the highways -- where the private automobile plays uncontrolled mayhem. At that point, he very nicely drew the ironic conclusion that there must have been something very wrong with our concern for life, if in the past fifteen years building costs had doubled, whereas automobile costs had been neatly halved. He couldn't see the logic of that, and I think we must honor him for that prophetic view.

These, then, were the questions Gropius was concerned with. Because it is our purpose to discuss the social base of housing, we can see from them that he is obviously very concerned with them in a rational way, that is to say, programmatically. Why build at all? What do we build for? For whom and how? Then he is very concerned with community, in the sense that our new community in large scale produces physical and environmental consequences of an entirely new kind. He is deeply concerned about the retention of privacy, but in juxtaposition to this; and, of course, he is very concerned with using industrialization as a tool to achieve our rational ends.

If we think of this now, almost fifty years after the original formulation of such thoughts, we must see that the theoretical base for action still rings true as a principle, but the action itself must be radically different. There has been a certain turning of the whole culture. None of our prophets, even those of recent years, could possibly have foreseen to what extent science, technology, and industrialization would have jumped forward. They could never have foreseen the explosive force of population to an almost cancerous dimension. They couldn't possibly have foreseen the exaggerated preoccupation with mobility for its own sake. They couldn't possibly have foreseen, as a result of endless road building in an autocentric civilization, the carving up of natural resources at a rate yet unprecendented, and they could not possibly have foreseen that man was going to continue to urbanize and to become technologically industrialized at a rate so fast that, if we do not take stock of our purpose at this moment, we shall soon have absolutely no purpose to discuss.

262

Yet, with these ominous thoughts, we must note that the pendulum has swung again. Architects still voice piously their belief in the esthetic principles which have been very eloquently propounded tonight and then parody these principles miserably in acts utterly contemptible. The kind of fashionable millinery which distinguishes our present architectural era surely calls again for the formulation of principles as serious as those which originally moved the men honored at these exercises.

The crisis in housing really lies in the larger environment, where, indeed, our human ecology is at stake. For Gropius -- and for us -- there was an untouched spot on the planet to which man, driven to discomfort, might sometimes escape. There is no such escape being promised to the immediate generation a-head of us. Our grandchildren will have very little natural space to escape to. In fact, the whole of the human environment, the whole of the human habitat, is very likely to be man-made in its entirety. This inability to escape from ourselves, therefore, poses an extremely important problem in which the architect and planner, providing this environment, have a great stake. Can we make the necessary leap forward in human terms and in concepts of the good life, commensurate with the leaps which technology and population are making? Currently, we are obviously prepa-ring to go popping off into space, but we are equally apparently prepared to let the inner sanctum go hang. This is not an en-tirely laudable program for survival.

One of the dilemmas with which we are faced is purely one of quantity: more and more people require more and more accom-modation. Our present preoccupation with the large, the specta-cular, the loud, and the conspicuous has all but eradicated our appetites for the small, the inconspicuous, the thoughtful, the ten-der, the private. Under these conditions the house begins to as-sume an extraordinary importance. For within the total hierarchy of reconstruction which we must undertake (and very boldly), this little segment, the dwelling, must be complete in itself. It also must, within the hierarchy, contain all the necessary ingredients of equilibrium between community and privacy, between the family and the individual, between the family unit and the neighborhood. This is not at all easy to manage in our time Because technology, at a tremendous rate and with such seductive manners that we have failed to perceive the dangers of the newly-acquired comfort, has done two things: it has made us much more mobile, and it has made us the victims of the noise it makes.

In the accidental historic development of the American technology, we have become almost entirely dependent on the automobile for transportation. It is quite obvious that we shall have to cope with the automobile very rapidly -- it will be a compelling need, and I'm sure it will be achieved. The car is not only a nuisance -- it is already obsolete. In general terms, we have to somehow restore the dignity, safety, and speed of the pedestrian.

Much more important, however, is the problem of the noise that came to dinner. Only a few years ago, there was just a telephone; then there was this charming little gramophone; then the miracle of radio; now we have television. It is appalling to know that the average American listens to television -- presumably he doesn't look at it for that amount of time, but he certainly listens to it -- six hours per day! This is a statistic that is monstrous and terrifying. It means that a house with this immense communication system has a vast range of available choice at the turn of a knob. Since this involves a family, three or four different sets of interest and different sets of noises compete, often at once. On these terms it is quite impossible for me to conceive of a family house with an open plan. I think the beautiful open space of the family house is obsolete for no other reason than that the noise came in. It is no good kidding ourselves: we are in fact building neuroses much faster than esthetic pleasure.

We have, therefore, to provide at this moment for action socially based, not only in terms of generalized and abstract good will, but in greatly particularized items. As Gropius insisted at the start, it is absolutely essential for us to recognize the new pressures which bear upon us. Our humanity is at stake, and the architects, in perhaps a dim way, are partially responsible for its survival.

264

I saw a full page advertisement in the **New York Times** last week, in which Webb and Knapp, probably the greatest providers of building from a single bank roll in the United States, announced the latest and plushest of El Dorados. Indeed, the ad implied that it was carefully designed by the American Institute of Decorators! I looked, after that staggering announcement, through the whole page to see whether there was mention of an architect's name. There was not. This is a matter one cannot be flippant about; it reflects, in a sense, the futility of people who are hiding their artistic, ostrich-like necks in the sand, when decision and power lie elsewhere.

In this matter, the best thing I can do is to quote again from Dr. Gropius. He said, in speaking at the Urban Design Conference at Harvard, in 1957: "An architect cannot disassociate himself from the struggles and aspirations of those who try to direct the future developments of our towns and cities into more promising channels, and it demands that he put this responsibility above all his other obligations." I cannot add anything more eloquent than that.

Mr. Chermayeff has been director of the Institute of Design in Chicago and professor of architecture in the Graduate School of Design, Harvard University; he is now professor of architecture at Yale. He is a Fellow of the Royal Institute of British Architects and of the Royal Society of Arts.

LESSONS OF THE BAUHAUS FOR THE SECOND MACHINE AGE

Gerhardt M. Kallmann

One day in the spring of 1960 an artist named Tinguely gave a demonstration in the gardens of the Museum of Modern Art of so-called auto-destructive art. It consisted of an elaborate apparatus made up of four hundred parts which contained bits of sewing machines, bath tubs, baby carriages, and an assortment of gears and wheels. After performing feats of trumpeting, panting, and spewing fire, the contraption proceeded to pull itself apart and within thirty minutes reduced itself to rubble. The work was entitled "Homage to New York." The performance was not flawless. Firemen had to put out the conflagration.

By and large this was not an altogether inaccurate image of a city and its cycle of life and decay, though it was reminiscent in its wry presentation of dadaist or surrealist demonstrations.

In one form or another, it represents an attitude which many of the inhabitants of the second machine age share. That is to say, a refusal to accept, comprehend, or participate in a very important aspect of contemporary reality, the reality of the machine age. This attitude differs greatly from that of, say, the futurists, who, at the beginning of the century, in the first machine age, regarded the machine as a life force, a poetic phenomenon for which they invented a kind of demonology or mythos. It is different also from that of the Bauhaus group for which the machine played a stimulating and moral role, or of Mondrian who saw in it a spiritual force.

266